Dear Bill,

Hope you enjoy reading my Dad's autobiography. Some great stories from an interesting span of history.

Richard

12/18/08

My Life

by Edward du Moulin

Herreshoff Marine Museum Press   Bristol, Rhode Island   2008

Printed in Canada

First Edition

ISBN 0-9710678-5-6

Library of Congress Control Number: 2008936982

CONTENTS

INTRODUCTION

By Richard du Moulin

In Dad's final 24 months he was encouraged by friends and family to write a book covering his non-America's Cup life. One month before Dad's passing, family friend Gary Jobson in his column in *Sailing World* commented:

"Ed du Moulin, age 91, is working on a new book that will cover 80 years of sailing, 47 years on Wall Street, 4 years of service during World War II, and a lot of 'crazy' incidents in his life. In 2001 du Moulin's recollections of seven America's Cup campaigns were published by the Herreshoff Marine Museum in *The America's Cup and Me*. Ed has always had a winning diplomatic manner and has often brought adversaries together. I recall being on an America's Cup team that was eliminated, and even though Ed was part of another team, he and Fritz Jewett had the courage and good sportsmanship to thank our crew for pushing their team so hard. His extraordinary class has served many as a good example."

Among Dad's many attributes were an incredible memory for names and events, and great typing skill that he learned at night school during the Great Depression. Dad's final entries in the book were made a few weeks before he passed away on March 29, 2006. As was his habit, he left a list of suggestions for publishing the book and having friends and family proofread certain chapters. His memory for detail was simply incredible, such as the name of a chief petty officer who assisted him with training Coast Guard SPARs (women) how to row in 1943 during a break from the convoys.

Dad reveled in other people's experiences, as will you when reading about "Cousin Norman's War" on the Murmansk run to Russia, or the voyage of brother Babe's troop transport *Randall* filled with war orphans from Europe in 1944. Some of these stories seem like movie plots, such as Dad's boss A.C. Schwartz's attempt to win the Grand National horse race in England in the 1930s.

Dad had a moral compass and genuine interest in people that showed up in all phases of his life — his youth, career at Bache, service in World War II, family life, and sailing activities. With amazing patience, natural grace, and good humor, Dad (and Mom) helped many others, as so many stories in this book illustrate.

When we lost my mother Eleanor, Dad's wife of 58 years, and my sister Cathy, both in the year 2000, it was Dad's fundamental optimism, strength, and love of family and friends that allowed him to carry on and still enjoy life.

Dad left me his draft on a CD with his typical "check list" to help me transform it into book form. Other than making a few grammatical corrections, the words are all Dad's. The period prior to the end of World War II is virtually untouched in terms of sequence. Post-

War, I took the liberty of grouping some stories in a more orderly manner. In his last few months, I believe Dad was busy recording interesting stories without paying much attention to chronology. He knew he had little time, but his perfect memory and typing skills just kept the stories flowing. Throughout this process, longtime family friends Kippy Requardt and her husband Roger Vaughan were of incredible help to Dad, and later to me. Their frequent collaborator, Austin Metze of Metze Publication Design, is responsible for the design and production of this lovely book.

Neither Dad nor I expect this book to be a best seller. It is aimed at Dad's family and many friends around the world. In that spirit, I believe it would be of interest to the reader for me to insert notes wherever they might add value to Dad's stories. I have also made liberal use of photographs from 1914 through modern times. Finally, in the Postscript I have quoted from friends and family. Many of the people impacted by Dad contacted us; some knew him many years ago and had not seen him since, but remembered him for his help and friendship.

Dad had a great life, interacting with so many fine people, through undeniably interesting times. This book is his gift to us all. Please enjoy reading it.

DEDICATION

From Charles Simon in a 1952 Letter of Recommendation

To Whom it May Concern: I remember once reading that a man applied for a high office, and he bore only one recommendation and that was a brief note which follows:

"The bearer of this note is a man of gentle breeding. He is a fine competitor and honorable in all his dealings with his fellow man. He is the type of man I would hope my son might be."

There is no more fitting description for my friend Edward du Moulin.

King Edward I.

1916

PART I
Childhood and
The Great Depression

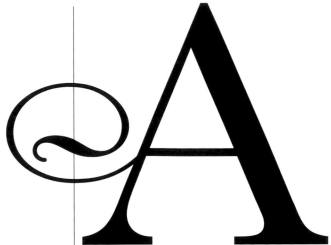

dele Carolyn Isarr, in 1912 at the age of 21, married my father, Theodore du Moulin. At the time he was a young lawyer, having passed the New York State Bar in 1908. He did legal work for Carl Fisher who developed Miami, the Indianapolis Motor Speedway, and Montauk Manor, still a popular resort on Long Island. Father was retained by Presto-O-Lite in a patent infringement suit which took him to Indianapolis. My parents married on the strength of this retainer, spending most of their honeymoon there.

Both of my parents were sports lovers, and they attended the first Indianapolis 500 car race. They rooted for the Giants and watched them play the Reds in Cincinnati. In later years, Mom became an ardent Mets fan after the Dodgers left Brooklyn. She took her grandson Richard to the 1956 World Series during which Don Larsen pitched a perfect game against the Brooklyn Dodgers.

Dad was a strong admirer of Theodore Roosevelt and worked with T.R.'s Bull Moose Party. He and his law partner George Thoms, a wonderful Scotsman, were located at 37 Wall Street in Manhattan. When Dad died, my mother gave Mr. Thoms his law library. Until George Thoms died in the 1940s, he handled family legal matters *pro bono*.

My nephew Gary du Moulin developed the du Moulin-Isarr genealogy in 1992. The Centraal Bureau Voor Genealogie in the Netherlands listed Zacharias du Moulin as being born in Amsterdam in 1794. From Amsterdam his son Tobias, my grandfather, moved to Paris in 1859. He left for America in 1882, where my father, Theodore du Moulin, was born (in New York) in 1885.

My mother's family came from Baden, Wurttenberg, Bavaria. My great-grandfather August Isarr was born in 1828 and came to America in the 1840s. During the Civil War, he served as a sergeant in the New York Fifth Regiment for a short time until he received his discharge.

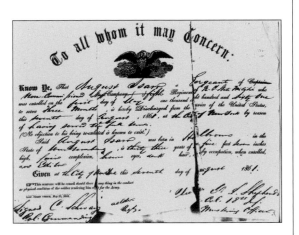

The Civil War discharge papers of Ed du Moulin's grandfather, August Isarr, born 1828.

BIRTHS AND TRAGEDIES

My sister Julia was born in 1913, and I followed in 1914 (the first year of the Income Tax), on December 31. My brother, Charles Theodore, came four years later on my fourth birthday. Sixty-nine years later my grandson Mark du Moulin was also born on December 31, the three of us now sharing the same birthday.

Sis and I were born in New York City; brother Charles, later known as Ted or Babe, was born in Jamaica, Queens. We all lived in Jamaica (just outside of Manhattan) and had a summer home, built in 1908, at 435 Beach 135th Street in Belle Harbor. It is still there with its unusual overhanging roof. In Belle Harbor, my sister and I, and later our baby brother, had a great time at Rockaway Beach in our early years, before the terrible influenza pandemic of 1918-19 swept through the world — and our lives.

Ed's sister Julia (left) with father Theodore and Ed on Rockaway Beach in 1917. Ed's mother, Adele (top). Julia holds her brother at the family's Belle Harbor summer home.

Ed's mother, Adele (top), and Eleanor
du Moulin on the front steps at Belle Harbor.

Influenza killed between 20 and 50 million people worldwide - 500,000 in the U.S. (The New York Times 11/7/04). In the recently published book The Great Influenza, John M. Barry proposes that it could have been l00 million worldwide – the deadliest plague in history. The pandemic touched tragically close to home: my grandfather Charles Isarr passed away on February 21, 1919. My father caught the flu at the funeral, and less than two weeks later, on March 3, 1919, died at the age of 34. Sis was six, I was four, and Babe was three months old. Mom and Grandma Carrie, who had lived next door, moved together to 96th Street in New York.

MOVE TO BELLE HARBOR

In the early 1920s, Mom and Grandma moved permanently to Belle Harbor, between the Atlantic Ocean and Jamaica Bay. Grandma had built two similar houses next to each other which were a couple of houses down from 435 Beach 135th. One was rented to the famous boxing referee, Lou Magnolia. A final move was made to 254 Beach l39th Street where I lived until l950, except during the war years (l94l to l945). All of these homes were wooden shingled with wrap-around porches.

Grandma Carrie, who lived upstairs, passed away in 1934. When I entered military service, we converted the house into a two-family home so Mom would have rental income while I was serving. I married Eleanor Lewis, in a very simple service, on August 30, 1942, in my "bell bottom trousers, shirt of navy blue." My brother could not attend as he was on duty in the North Atlantic. After the war, Eleanor and I moved into Mom's upstairs apartment. While there, we had Richard (11/9/46) and Cathy (3/21/49). The relationship between Eleanor and my mother was close, to the point where some thought I was the son-in-law. They were both attractive women, good conversationalists, avid readers, and of calm manner. My absence and my brother's helped them develop a very close relationship that lasted through the years.

GROCERY STORE JOB

Mom was a graduate of Wadleigh High School and held a substitute teacher's license. After my father's death, this became the family's main source of income. The fact that our home was mortgage-free helped make ends meet during the Depression days. As a boy, I worked afternoons and Saturdays at H.C. Bohack, our local food market, located on 145th Street in Neponsit. I received $2.50 a week for delivering groceries. My fondest memory of that job was a weekly bicycle delivery to the Sisters of St. Francis de Sales Church on 130th Street on the ocean, for which I received a lordly tip of 10 cents – my biggest tip. St. Francis de Sales produced great athletes like the McGuire brothers and Joe Sullivan. More about Joe later.

St. Francis was recently in the news when, on November 21, 2001, American Airlines Flight 567, a few minutes after takeoff from JFK, crashed nearby with a loss of life of all 260 passengers, crew and 5 civilians on the ground. The flight was heading for the Dominican Republic. At first, it was generally considered another terrorist incident, a sign of our times, but later it was determined to have been a rudder problem.

MR. TOUGH GUY

Brother Babe was Mr. Tough Guy. His main supporter was Grandma Carrie who always protected the "baby" of the family – hence the nickname. This, often enough, led to some family arguments. When I sneaked some ginger ale from Grandma's bottle, I did not have the sense to replace it with water. Babe did. "Who has been drinking my ginger ale?" I was the one to admit it, and I was the one to be punished.

The first day Babe attended kindergarten at PS 43, my mother received a call from the school to come and pick him up. It was a rainy day. Even at that young age, he didn't like to take orders. At home, our ever-watchful Grandma would put his rubbers on. When the kindergarten teacher told him to put his rubbers on himself, he promptly told her to "go to hell."

At PS 114, I would be called to come to Babe's classroom to take him home. An example: the time he nailed the shop teacher's record book to his desk. Babe was always was very popular, and a good athlete. He played quarterback for the CYO, for Far Rockaway High School, and the New York Aggies, where his jersey number was 29. Sixty-nine years later my grandson Chris Morea wore the same number when he played football for Schreiber High and, later, lacrosse for Cornell.

Babe squeaked through school. I was a serious student, and proudly received 100 in an American history Regents exam, and made the Arista

When the kindergarten teacher told him to put his rubbers on, he told her to "go to hell."

Far Rockaway High School
Report of Du Moulin, E section X-3
Term ending Jan. June, 19   S. J. Ellsworth, Principal

Subject	1st Mark	2nd Mark	Final Mark
English 7	75	76	78
History, Civics 8	90	95	100R
Ph. Training	90	90	85
Hygiene			
Drawing			
Music, Economics	75	85	88R
Latin, French, German			
Spanish, Latin, French			
Mathematics			
Science 6	90	88	92R
Bookkeeping			
Stenography			
Typewriting			
Domestic Art			
Oral English			
Arithmetic			
Office Pract.			
Com'l Geography			
Com'l Law			
English 8	72	72	80R
Math 7	85	90	100
Absent / Late			

J. WERDE   Official Teacher

Passing Mark is 65%.

Ed du Moulin with his diploma at graduation from Far Rockaway High School.

Honor Society. Babe was always good with machinery, but was not much for books. Edward Ellsberg's book On The Bottom, which told of submarine disasters, was Babe's perennial high school book report – the same for all four years. Babe had a steady girl friend when he was 15. I relied on the theory "safety in numbers."

One summer Sunday, cousin Sam Lauterbach's older brother, kind of eccentric, was to visit Mom. He got off the bus, walked down 139th Street. Babe was watering the lawn. When the "old man," dressed in full suit and tie, arrived at our house he yelled to Babe to put the hose on him. Babe was tempted but hesitated until he was again ordered to do it. Quite wet, our cousin entered the house, reprimanding Babe for soaking him with the hose. It later turned out that Sam's brother had wet his pants.

As far as studies went, Sis didn't like math but was very good at art. She won a boardwalk Easter Sunday prize for her hand-made Easter outfit. She also shocked the neighborhood when she wore a fishnet bathing suit.

SISTER'S COLLEGE DATES

Sister Julia, to this day, has never had an argument with anyone. Today, at 93, she enjoys her independence, assists her less healthy friends, loves being the adopted "grandmother" to a kindergarten class, swims almost daily, and still drives. She was a beautiful girl (and still is a beautiful woman). My brother and I would grade the many college dates who called on Julia. We liked the Dartmouth guys the best as they would toss a football with us while Sis was getting ready. Pipe-smoking Princetonians we didn't care for, nor the stuffy Harvard undergrads. Sis went to Girls High and later Pratt Institute in Brooklyn. After graduation she worked for a commercial artist, Al Weisberg, with whom she eloped. At least the mother of the bride did not have to pay for a wedding. More later about Sis's family.

BOY SCOUTS

The Boy Scouts had great appeal to me. I belonged to Troop 1 Riis Park (later Troop 112 Queens). We met in Dr. Barker's basement. I had the only Seamanship merit badge. I didn't become an Eagle Scout as I never went to Scout Camp and, therefore, could not receive the required Camping merit badge. Later, I spent 12 years as chairman of Troop 21 in Woodmere, Long

We liked the Dartmouth guys best—they would toss a football with us while Sis was getting ready.

Island. This troop had the wonderful support of the old Hewlett family. Richard was in the troop until at age 13 he focused on sailboat racing.

The Matthews were one of the memorable Scouting families. "Matty" Matthews was among the active troop parents. His son Peter was a few years older than Richard. Peter was struck by polio as a young boy, but became an Eagle Scout through sheer fortitude. He would go on hikes with a backpack — on crutches. Peter developed phenomenal upper body strength, and by age 13 slowly began to walk without crutches. By 15, he was running, and in his senior year he started at fullback on Hewlett's undefeated football team.

BEACH DAYS

In the summers, Babe and I became beach boys. I worked for Mrs. Laverty, wife of the chief lifeguard. Each day I would set up beach chairs and umbrellas for the local residents. Working with me was Gerard Sullivan. In order to encourage our customers to leave the beach early, we often would start a rumor of a pending thunderstorm.

THE SULLIVANS

The Sullivan family lived on 130th Street, close to St. Francis de Sales. The father was a New York Police lieutenant. Gerard's brother, Joseph G. Sullivan, attended St. John's Prep where he was star tackle and football captain, and the national schoolboy shot-put champ, winning a trip to the Olympics and a scholarship to Notre Dame. He was a lifeguard on our beach during the summers while his brother and I worked the beach chairs. My brother became Joe's boat boy (helping him launch, row, and land the life guard catamaran) and worshipped him. Joe was clean living - no drinking, smoking, or cursing. He hoped one day to become a priest.

When Babe was about 12, I took him to an Olympic-size pool to teach him to swim. I had a cold so did not plan on entering the water. Instead of holding onto the side of the pool as a beginner, Babe climbed to the top of the 10-foot diving board and launched himself into the pool. I had to jump in and pull him out. However, on the beach he could do all sorts of acrobatic tricks — without going out beyond the breakers.

Our lifeguards used large catamarans for rescue work. Joe Sullivan,

That year at the Army-Navy game they had a memorial service at Yankee Stadium.

before he went on duty, with Babe's help would launch the cat. Babe would row and Joe would swim. One day Joe said, "Now, it is your turn to swim." From that point on they would alternate. Babe became a lifeguard at 18. By that time Joe had entered Notre Dame on a football scholarship.

Joe and Babe corresponded with each other. Joe replaced the famous Moose Krause at right tackle. Joe would send Babe souvenir programs signed by the players. When they came to New York to play Army, Joe invited Babe to visit the team in the locker room. Joe took a lot of kidding because his teammates had thought "Babe" to be a girl. What a girl.

Joe, in his second year (1934), was elected captain of the team. For Christmas 1934, Babe sent Joe a belt with a silver buckle with the initials "JGS." Soon after this, Joe contracted pneumonia followed by mastoiditis. He was taken to New York Hospital. After three operations, on March 20, 1935, captain-elect Joseph G. Sullivan passed away. He was 22. My brother was in shock. He locked himself in his room for days. Joe was buried with the belt. That year, at the Army-Notre Dame game, they had a memorial service at Yankee Stadium. Joe's dad would not attend but listened to the ceremony over the radio. Two days later, he died of a heart attack. In my brother's home there is a section devoted to memorabilia that Joe sent him including an autographed football and a favorite photo of Joe in uniform. Sixty-four years later, the Sullivan story took a strange turn.

On March 21, 1999, 64 years after Joe Sullivan's death, I was reading <u>The New York Times</u> Sunday sport section. I read a headline "Family Football Saga: Saint, Sinner and Son—Notre Dame Legacy Lives in Prison Yard." The story covered the entire page. I was shocked to see a photo of Joe, the same photo Babe has in his home. Robert Doyle's article began: "Kelly Sullivan was 6 years old when his mother, Gail, drove him and his 10-year-old brother Ramsey to Clinton Prison in Danemora, New York, for their first family visit with their father." My God, the father was Joseph G. Sullivan serving two consecutive life sentences for three of some 30 mob-related murders – "the most dangerous man in America."

He is the nephew of Babe's Joe Sullivan. His father was Gerard, my friend from the beach chairs days. Gail did not know her husband was a hit man for an organized crime mob. She had thought he was a traveling salesman. She and the boys continue to pay regular visits to Joseph G. Sullivan.

Joe Sullivan, friend and neighbor of the du Moulins,
as captain of Notre Dame football.
He died of pneumonia at age 22.

*I*n my experience the old saying 'it pays to be honest' has worked for my family.

When Babe read the story he contacted Gail, and later prisoner Joe. Thus began a continuing monthly correspondence between my brother and Joe. Joe's letters are long and beautifully written. Babe and his wife Edith keep in touch with Gail and her boys, to whom he has given Joe's football and other memorabilia. In March 2004, Joe's oldest son Ramsey visited Edith and Babe du Moulin. On our birthday, Babe's and mine (both 12/31), Joe sends us cards.

MINIATURE GOLF

Back to the Rockaways: Money was always tight. I did a great deal of babysitting. My favorite sitting job was for my young neighbor, Freddy Engelman, whose dad was known as the Scarf King. At Christmas time, I would dress as Santa Claus and arrange to haul a bag full of toys up to his upper porch by rope. Father Fred owned two miniature golf courses. I worked at both of them. One course was in Breezy Point; the other, at Rockaway Park, also had a sad old horse for the young children to ride.

When cleaning the greens, I found a roll of bills amounting to $400, more money than I had ever seen. Late that day George Bernhardt, a summer resident and member of the American Stock Exchange, came by and asked if anything might have been found on the green where he had been putting. After he described the bankroll, I gave it to him. I was thrilled when he gave me $10. From that time until I started work in Wall Street, each year he would take my brother and me to Yankee Stadium where we saw Babe Ruth and the mighty Yankees play. Later, when I worked on "the Street," he would invite me for lunch. In my experience, in the long term, the old saying "**It pays to be honest**" has worked for me – and my family.

SHORT-CHANGED

One day Mom asked me to buy some fish giving me a $10 bill. I walked one mile to Rockaway Park and ordered fish costing $3.25. The shopkeeper gave me change for $5. I said I had given him a $10 bill. Home I went with the fish and $1.75. Mom and Grandma forgave me. From that day, even to today, I will check the last three numbers appearing on a bill that may have seven numbers. Over the years this has paid off – at the 21 Club bar, the Long Island Railroad ticket office, at restaurants. Short-changing a customer is not an unusual ploy. One example: Once I treated Mom and Sam Lauterbach to hamburgers and cokes. I gave the waiter a $20 bill, but he came back with change for $10. When I questioned him, he said the check-out clerk had short-changed him. I had marked the last three numbers on the tablecloth. I gave them to the waiter who returned with the rest of my change. My late friend Arnold Green insisted that I also check off the last three numbers on one-dollar bills.

EARLY BELLE HARBOR

In 1908, Belle Harbor had few homes. From the first house the family owned we could see but a few homes between ourselves and Ft. Tilden (about a mile and a half to the west). It was there that several 16-inch battleship guns with 144-foot long barrels were placed during World War I to guard the approaches to New York Harbor. As children we would hike there, climbing over the man-made mounds from which the barrels projected.

The Boggianos were a large family who were neighbors in Belle Harbor. To this day Babe keeps in touch with Robert, a retired medical doctor. Oldest brother Ed was a New York police sergeant, and George was a semi-pro basketball player who played for St. Rose of Lima. I didn't miss many of their games. They owned a number of small bungalows opposite Rockaway Playland and a bar, Bogianno & McWalters.

Adele steers while her son Ed looks on (1940).

I can remember the bad smell we would get when the wind blew from the North, across Jamaica Bay, from the "perfume" factory where they would kill horses. Today it is Floyd Bennett Navy Air Field, across from which, on Flatbush Avenue, was (and is) aptly named Dead Horse Creek. When I was in my teens I would take the ferry to Floyd Bennett Field, named after Admiral Richard Byrd's pilot. There I would help clean the planes of many famous aviators including Frank Hawks and Wiley Post. For two dollars I had my first biplane ride. In my high school yearbook, they predicted that I would become an aeronautical engineer. Seventy-two years later, my grandson Douglas Morea took up aerospace engineering at the

S am was an avid skier, having started around 1915. What a wonderful effect he had on all our lives.

Naval Academy from which he graduated on May 28, 2004. Doug is now in Texas where he will become a Navy jet fighter pilot. My schoolmates had picked the wrong generation.

MOM'S LICENSE

Mom was the first woman to receive a New York State driver's license. Her picture appeared on the back cover of The New York Daily News standing in line. When a reporter asked her name, she was afraid to upset the family by saying du Moulin and said Adele Miller, the English equivalent. The other cover photo was of Bill Tilden, the champion tennis player. Mom drove for about 60 years, including annual trips in the 1950s and 1960s to visit Babe's family in Boston for Thanksgiving. Richard often went with her. He recalls 15.9 cents per gallon gasoline on the Berlin Turnpike in Connecticut.

When Mom was in her seventies, she drove out of her house at Beach 139th Street in Belle Harbor. At the first intersection, a young policeman pulled her over and told her she had driven through a red light. Mom responded that for 50 years there had been no light at that corner, and furthermore she had never received a ticket in those 50 years of driving. The policeman noticed the special notation on her license as the first female driver in New York State, and indicated that he did not want to be the first to give her a ticket. The next day she drove through a red light again, and he did give her a ticket.

Mom was active in civic affairs, the American Red Cross, her Sisterhood, and school where she was a substitute teacher. After any tragedy in the poorer sections of the Rockaways, she would drive her old Dodge around town picking up clothing and food for families in need.

SAMUEL LAUTERBACH

In our early teens, into our lives came a remarkable gentleman, a quiet, reserved person of great integrity. This was Mom's bachelor cousin Sam Lauterbach. He lived in Manhattan and was an avid sailor. In the early 1900s he was an officer of the Yacht Racing Association of Jamaica Bay (YRAJB) headquartered in Sheepshead Bay. In 1915 Sam helped create the Rockaway Park Yacht Club (RPYC), which lasted through World War II. For a number of years I was treasurer. When the club liquidated I was given a beautiful half model and the signal cannon.

Sam was also an avid skier, having started around 1915. What a wonderful effect he had on all our lives. In summer he would sleep aboard his 45-foot yawl *Thora* moored off the bulkhead at the RPYC. *Thora* had been built in Gloucester in 1902 and Sam acquired her around 1916. She had twin engines/ twin screws and was maintained meticulously by an old German sea captain, Harry Groth. We all sailed, but I had the greatest interest. Mom and Babe loved to fish.

RUMRUNNERS – THE *THORA*

During winters the *Thora* would be tied up to a dock in Arverne on the far side of the Long Island Railroad swinging trestle. Surrounding the *Thora* were several gray-painted power boats – sleek, powerful rumrunners. Prohibition was in full swing, having been established by the 18th amendment to the Constitution in 1920. Bootlegging and speakeasies flourished – lives were lost in gun battles. Finally, when F. D. Roosevelt became president in 1933, Prohibition was ended by the 21st amendment.

In 1927 I sailed with Cousin Sam and Captain Harry to Block Island. We departed from Jamaica Bay, and after transiting the East River we moored at the old Port Washington Yacht Club in Manhasset Bay.

PORT WASHINGTON YACHT CLUB AND BLOCK ISLAND

We had a crystal radio set on board *Thora*. That night was the first radio broadcast of a prizefight. Handsome Georges Carpentier of France lost in a heavyweight bout. Members of the PWYC, in rowboats, surrounded *Thora* while Sam relayed round-by-round action. Next morning we were off to Block Island.

Rum-carrying schooners and other vessels, from as far as Europe, would lurk near the three-mile limit (later 12 miles) advertising in their rigging what they had to sell – and the cost. Fast powerboats from Block Island

Sam Lauterbach skiing in upstate New York (1930).

Sam Lauterbach's THORA, *the gaff-rigged yawl Ed sailed on as a young man with his friend, Arnold Green.*

would dodge the Coast Guard and bring the liquor to shore. Sam would obtain his liquor after which we would sail home. Sam provided friends and family with the goods, from "supplies" he purchased in Block Island.

A native Block Islander friend of Sam's, Searles Ball, drank more than a bit. You could easily pick out his home from the water. He had painted one side of his roof green with red trim; the other side of the roof was red with green trim. The Ball family was one of the early settlers of Block Island. Since Colonial days, the Island has been famous for wrecked ships. In World War II, anti-submarine vessels were based there to search for enemy submarines that attacked merchant ships approaching New York, Connecticut, and Rhode Island.

Block Island remains a family favorite. Ann and I have property there, and have spent many summer vacations on the island with our kids . Block Island Race Week has been one of our family's favorite racing events. Dad and Mom often stayed at Spring House with the Greens during race weeks. Grandson Ed spent the summer of 2007 running the Block Island Maritime Institute, introducing inner city kids to sailing. – **R. du M**.

WORKING ON *THORA*

As a kid in the 1920s, I would work on *Thora*. I polished brass, particularly the binnacle. My right index finger to this day is flattened as a result. *Thora* was gaff-rigged. In raising and lowering the mainsail I always handled the throat from the starboard side of the mast. When Captain Harry said, "Let her go!" I would do just that. One day I happened to be on the port side of the mast, where the peak halyard was. When time came to lower the sail, I just let the halyard go. Down came the peak, the gaff jaw broke, and I received a blast in German. Obviously, a lesson learned – the hard way.

One other "catastrophe" I remember related to the sterling silver tableware from *Thora*. It was stored in our basement for the winter. I wanted to surprise Sam and Captain Harry by polishing it. I read somewhere that if you place the silver in a bucket of oxide or was it oakite, and left it overnight, it would have a fine shine in the morning. On the laundry shelf, I picked up a box of Clorox and put it in the bucket with the silverware. Next morning, I went to the basement. Lo and behold, there was no more silver – only a bunch of lead skeletons. Honesty, a few tears, and my obviously good intentions got me through that crisis. My good friend Kippy Vaughan tells me that baking soda and aluminum foil in an enamel pan of boiling water would have been a correct solution.

SCHOONER *ATLANTIC*

One Saturday, Sam took me over to the marine basin in Brooklyn bordering on Gravesend Bay. He led me on board the famous graceful, three-masted, 185-foot schooner *Atlantic*. In 1905, in the first of ten New York Yacht Club transatlantic races, under the command of Captain Charlie Barr (skipper of two successful America's Cup defenders) she won the race establishing a transatlantic record of 12 days, 14 hours for heavy displacement vessels. This record lasted until the Rolex 100th anniversary race, May 21, 2005, when with as many as 18 large sailing vessels participating, *Mari-Cha IV*, a 140-foot schooner, finally broke *Atlantic*'s record by two-and-a-half days.

During the winter months, I would chop logs that I found on the beach. Sam and I would take the wood to Captain Harry Groth's modest home for his fireplace and wood stove. Some cold nights, we would walk the beach, shining a flashlight into the water, along the shoreline. The light would attract what we called "frost fish" (I don't recall the real name). We would scoop them up by hand and place them in a burlap bag. They were good eating.

HURRICANES – 1934, 1938

Hurricanes were exciting and frightening, particularly in the Rockaways, as we were situated on a sandy peninsula. From our Belle Harbor home we would walk the block and a half to the beach to watch the gigantic waves

As a kid in the 1920s I would work on Thora. I polished brass, particularly the binnacle.

I had a crush on my American History teacher, which must have enhanced my interest in the subject.

and the wild surf. On September 8, 1934, a major storm was forecast. My brother was assigned to help Captain Harry take the *Thora* through the LIRR trestle for safety. But the Coast Guard had asked that all seaworthy craft standby, as an 11,000-ton cruise ship, the *Morro Castle*, was burning off Asbury Park, N.J., and they might need seagoing yachts to help in the rescue. Eventually 137 passengers and crew perished in the *Morro Castle* disaster.

By the time the Coast Guard cancelled the standby due to the approaching storm, it was too late to go to *Thora*'s original safe haven. Instead Captain Harry decided to motor to the lee side of the Marine Parkway Bridge, anchor and wait out the storm. He and Babe played pinochle to pass the night. Meanwhile, at home, we all were concerned about where they were. I agreed to walk to the Coast Guard station on 169th Street (one and a half miles) to seek their help. When I opened the door of the station house, the door blew off. The next morning *Thora*, Captain Harry and Babe were located and safely escorted back to the yacht club mooring.

The hurricane of September 28, 1938, which cost over 400 lives, caused *Thora* to break away from her mooring at the Rockaway Park Yacht Club, where she was wrecked. A friend, Robert Walsh, managed to jump on board and salvaged some of the gear including an old barometer that was hung on board my various *Lady Del*s. *Thora* was sold by the insurance company for $500 and towed to a dock in Mill Basin, Brooklyn. She was bought and repaired by an old seaman and his wife who lived on her for many years. Sadly, *Thora* was unfit to ever sail again. Years later on the first *Lady Del*, Sam, my friend Tom O'Sullivan, Richard, and I would sail to Brooklyn to look in on an old sad *Thora*.

HIGH SCHOOL – JOB SEEKING

Far Rockaway High School was a bus ride of about 5 miles each way for me. I had a crush on my American History teacher, Grace Young, which must have enhanced my interest in the subject. I was a good swimmer and a good rope climber; I did not participate in other formal sports. In 1932, I graduated from FRHS, the shortest kid in the graduating class. Within three years I grew to over six feet. Over the years, many of my friends would show me off to their children who were discouraged by their short stature. The school newspaper was called "The Chat." The student editor got into hot water by placing a headline across page one that read: "It Is Not The School – It Is The Principal of The Thing."

That summer I began to job seek. The country was still in the Great Depression. We were okay: we had good food, a roof over our heads, a small victory garden and we saved our pennies. Finally, at year's end, two job opportunities arose. The first was a job in a garage in Brooklyn with a weekly starting salary of $5.00. Tempting. But Cousin Sam Lauterbach's accountant had been recently made managing partner of the Wall Street firm, J. S. Bache & Company, founded in 1879. It was one of the largest brokerage firms and was barely surviving the Depression. Sam mentioned to him that I was looking for employment. I was given an interview after which I was offered a job as a "gofer." I was sent down to the office manager who explained the starting salary would be $6.00 weekly. When he learned I commuted by the Long Island Railroad he raised the salary to $7.00. Without hesitation I accepted. My decision to accept this job, rather than the one in Brooklyn, was based primarily on the fact the salary would be 40 percent higher at Bache. I started on January 3, 1933. The unemployed, many in business suits, were still selling apples for a nickel on the street corners.

Ed aboard Thora, *about 1933.*

N.Y.U. - Bache

In September 1932, I enrolled at the New York University (NYU) Washington Square night school. When I told them I wanted to take up accounting, money & banking, typewriting/shorthand and celestial navigation, the interviewer was nonplussed. I explained that I did not want a degree but that my mother suggested the typing/shorthand and my cousin suggested the first two courses. Celestial navigation was my idea. I must say the typing was a great asset throughout my life. Without it, I never would have written any books.

Once I began working at Bache & Company, where they called me "Little Eddie" at least for another year or two, I took a bus to the LIRR, a train to Brooklyn, and the subway to Wall Street. I had to be at Bache by 9:00 a.m. – and often 8:00 a.m. The four nights I went to night school, I took the 10:27 p.m. train home, and got to bed by 11:30. For the first year, Mom gave me my lunch. At 5:00 p.m., I would walk from Wall Street to NYU at Washington Square to save the nickel subway ride. It all didn't

Ed with his mother, Adele, and Sam Lauterbach,
then Commodore of Jamaica Bay Yacht Club.

seem so hard at the time, and I must have liked it. After all, I did start a real job at 18 that would last 47 years. Remember Cousin Sam's motto, "**A Sticker Never Gets Stuck**." Today, however, is very different; relatively few people remain with the same organization for a lifetime.

Jules Bache was the senior partner, nephew of the founder. He was a major figure in the world of finance, and had a beautiful white-marble mansion at 814 Fifth Avenue. He was the major stockholder of Chrysler Motors, a company that resulted from the merger of his Maxwell Motors and Dodge Motors.

The firm had suffered heavy losses during the Depression. Jules Bache was the only partner with sufficient funds to carry on the business. He hired Louis Schapiro who he called "my boss" in order to "clean house." Schapiro was a tough executive who was a banker, accountant, and lawyer. During World War I, Henry Ford had hired him to ensure that the Ford Motor Company would have accurate records relative to their dealings with the U.S. Government. It was quite a dramatic move by Henry Ford who was a well-known anti-Semite.

Our office was located on the first two floors of a large office building at 42 Broadway that I believe is still there. It was a great viewing platform from which to watch our heroes as they received ticker tape parades up Broadway. The Cashier's Department was under a glass dome, above which was open air. During the depression days, several brokers committed suicide crashing through the dome into the Cage itself. Meshed wire was subsequently placed over this dome.

CASHIER EMBEZZLEMENT

A major position of trust in the company was that of cashier. George Phalen was the popular cashier for over 25 years. He was also manager of Bache's hardball semi-pro baseball team, part of an active Wall Street League. He hired pros as employees who would join the team. He avoided vacations and for good reason. For several years he had been cooking the books. The loss, when finally uncovered, was $625,000, enough to break the firm in those dark days of 1929 through 1932. The firm had a blanket insurance policy of $500,000 with the U.S. Fidelity & Guaranty Co. of Baltimore, which was paid to Bache. Our accountants at the time, Barrow, Wade & Guthrie, were sued for $125,000 and settled for $62,500. Phalen wound up in Sing Sing where he became a trustee. Because of his contacts, he was allowed weekends off to visit his New York friends. He even invited his old Bache baseball team to play against the prison team.

I had a tiny desk in the Partners' Section, right in front of Jules Bache's office, so I was a first hand witness to all of the exciting events of that period. I had worked my way up to $11.20 a week when Franklin D. Roosevelt set the minimum wage at $16.00. You bet I voted for FDR – again and again.

STATE BANK OF BINGHAMTON

Another crisis: the firm had a small branch in Binghamton, New York, managed by James J. Malane. His old friend, Andrew J. Horvatt, controlled the State Bank of Binghamton and was its president. Horvatt had a margin account (borrowed money from Bache to buy common stocks) and eventually opened other margin accounts in fictitious names. As the market continued its decline in 1932, these accounts were called for margin. Horvatt, short of funds, merely entered the bank's vault and "borrowed" customers' money to meet the margin calls, leaving his IOUs. This happened at the same time George Phalen was stealing funds. In March of 1933, Franklin Roosevelt declared a national bank holiday. No bank would be allowed to reopen until bank examiners gave it a clean bill of health. When the examiners checked the State Bank, they found Horvatt's personal IOUs in lieu of cash. J. S. Bache & Co. was sued by New York State for $900,000 plus interest. My boss, the managing partner, wanted to hire one of the top lawyers from Wall Street to defend, but Jules Bache insisted on using ex-state senator Clayton R. Lusk for his upstate political clout. Lusk asked for a non-jury trial. A panel of three judges was selected. After more than a year of court proceedings, clippings of which I cut out for my boss, Bache lost the case. By that time interest was $300,000. Jules Bache stood for all of the $1,200,000 loss as he was the only partner with available funds. That was half the firm's capital. Ironically, we were not covered by insurance as this loss was incurred during the same period as Phalen's embezzlement. As a result we had no insurance coverage. Thereafter, Schapiro had to go to England and convince Lloyds of London to sell us insurance, as no American underwriter was willing to cover us.

Why did we lose in court? The court held Bache liable because its manager failed to question the phony accounts opened by Horvatt who ended up in jail. This led to the adoption by the New York Stock Exchange of the Credit Card System – and taught me this valuable lesson: **Know Your Customer**.

Arnold E. Green

In June of 1933, Arnold Green joined Bache. We met, became friends, and found we had a common interest in boats. After a while, I asked him how much he had been paid when he started work for Bache. "Ten dollars per week," he answered. I had been told the starting salary was $6. He asked if I had a college education and I said "No." Arnold said he did, and that probably accounted for the difference. Months after I started, I was asked to set up salary records covering our branch employees. First thing I did was check to see if anyone had had a lower starting salary. Yes! There was a man in our San Antonio office who came in every afternoon to clean the boardroom. He got $2.50. I felt better.

One day I heard Mr. Bache say, following lunch with Ben Fairless, CEO of U.S. Steel, that "things could get no worse" according to Mr. Fairless. Mr. Bache also roared out that the bricks and mortar of his Chrysler Motors

One day I heard Mr. Bache say, following lunch with Benjamin Fairless of US Steel, that things could get no worse.

Ed dressed for work at Bache & Company in Manhattan, 1938.

plant was worth more than the stock, which was selling at $5.00 per share. In March of 1933, Bache published a very successful pamphlet called "The Worst is Known." In it they listed 20 stocks including Chrysler at $5.00 per share urging the investor to "buy now." Arnold and I did not have cash to buy stock except on paper. We wouldn't borrow, so we bought 100 shares at $5 on paper. When Chrysler rose to $10, we became nervous with our paper gain. After it reached $15, tripling our investment, we sold out. The next year it topped out over $130 per share. The dividend alone that year was $14 per share. Mr. Bache had purchased over 100,000 additional shares. I was happy with my $16 salary and our paper gain. My investment "wisdom" will be demonstrated later in this book when talking with Marvin Carton of Allen & Co.

WALL STREET POOLS

Before Franklin Roosevelt brought in the Securities Exchange Commission, "pools" were not uncommon on the Street. A legal-size document would be drawn up. Each participant would sign, stating how much he would put into the pot (pool). A broker would be selected to start buying a particular stock. He would slowly increase his rate of buying, and the stock would begin to move (up). Tape watchers and later the public would start to buy when they noticed the stock's upward movement. As the stock went higher on greater activity, the broker would reduce his buying and begin selling. If the pool was handled well, the poolsters would be out of the stock by the time the bottom fell out and John Q. Public was taken to the cleaners. The New Deal of FDR, through the Securities Exchange Commission, supposedly ended this scam.

ARMY DAY PARADE

Jules Bache had two male secretaries – very austere and proper. In Mr. Bache's 814 Fifth Avenue home, he displayed a very valuable art collection, now in a special section of the Metropolitan Museum of Art. The annual Army Day Parade up Fifth Avenue took place on an April Saturday. I loved a parade and was very patriotic. In those days, we worked half-days on Saturdays. I approached Mr. Bache's secretaries and asked if they would give me a pass to 814 Fifth Avenue. They assumed it was to see the art collection and gave me a lecture about the importance of knowing art and how impressed they were with my interest. They gave me a beautifully embossed invitation for the date I mentioned. When the day came, I arrived at the door of 814 Fifth Avenue, rang the bell, and the butler welcomed me and said to make myself at home. Up the circular stairway I went. On the way up, I nodded to Gainsborough's The Blue Boy, entered the living room, and opened the French doors leading to a tiny granite balcony. For hours I watched the Army Day Parade, making believe I was General John J. "Black Jack" Pershing. I did this for a number of years before I went off to war myself. The secretaries never did get wise. Later Mr. Bache's grand-daughter married General Pershing's handsome blond-haired son.

THE HONORABLE GEORGE LAMBERT

Jules Bache was a staunch Republican. It was 1936, an election year, with Kansas governor Alf Landon running against FDR. The London Times had asked the Hon. George Lambert, oldest living member of the British House of Parliament, to report to them each day on the American election. He was Mr. Bache's houseguest at 814 Fifth Aveue. Nightly, for about ten days, JSB would invite conservative economists, Republican politicians, industrialists, and bankers as dinner guests. This would give Mr. Lambert the opportunity to learn, firsthand, about the election – however, it sure wouldn't give him an objective view.

One of my tasks was to escort Mr. Lambert, during each lunch hour, on a walking tour of the Wall Street area. One of my favorite haunts was the Battery Park Aquarium where, at noon each day, an attendant prodded a very large electric eel. The creature's anger and excitement would light an electric bulb. As we began our first walk, I found it very difficult to tell him anything about the sights as he kept talking about his constituency in Devonshire. Mr. Lambert strutted with his thumbs hooked into his vest, speaking in a strong and too loud English accent. I felt embarrassed as we walked by many homeless people sitting on the park benches. I was bitterly disappointed when he didn't seem impressed by my electric eel – he just kept talking.

Since I knew some shorthand (never finished the course), I was delegated to take Mr. Lambert's notes. Late each afternoon I would cable

The **Queen Mary**, *without escort in WW II, was the first ship to carry a full division of 15,000 soldiers overseas.*

them to <u>The London Times</u>. The notes, of course, reflected the opinions of only anti-FDR Republicans. His final cable was sent the night before the election. In view of his age and position, he was permitted to board the first *Queen Mary* on election eve. (The Cunarder always sailed on a Wednesday.)

Lambert's final cable stated that Alf Landon would win by a landslide. The results were quite the opposite. FDR won by a landslide, losing only in Maine and Vermont. You can be sure Mr. Lambert was never asked by <u>The London Times</u> to report on any future political event.

As an historical note, this *Queen Mary* was the first ship in World War II to carry a full American division of 15,000 soldiers overseas without escort. With many thousands of wounded on board she would safely, on her own, return to New York. She used her high speed combined with zig-zag maneuvers to avoid U-boats. One returning serviceman was Eleanor's first cousin Norman Hyams who was wounded on the Murmansk run. More on this in a later chapter.

RUSSELL SAGE COLLEGE

Annually, the Russell Sage College in Troy, New York, would send a group of girls to Bache to learn about Wall Street. I was their tour guide. We would meet in the conference room where I would explain how orders were first passed through our busy and noisy Wire Room (never daring to take them there), then telephoned over to the floor of the N.Y. Stock Exchange and, after execution, sent back to the branches through our Wire Room. We then would walk over to the Exchange. Arthur Broderick was our very distinguished senior floor partner, who sported a well-groomed mustache that made him easy to pick out from the balcony. I suggested they observe our booth, see the phone clerk give Mr. B. an order, watch him proceed to the post where the stock would be traded, and then return to our phone clerk where the order would be relayed to our Wire Room. All eyes were staring at Mr. B. when he suddenly reached down and began to vigorously scratch his private parts. I was very embarrassed while the girls snickered. That was the last time I escorted the Russell Sage undergrads, or, for that matter, any group to the Exchange.

In recent years, I have urged that each of my grandchildren contact my nephew Ted Weisberg of Seaport Securities and arrange to be taken

The official wedding photograph of Ed and Eleanor du Moulin.

Gee, when I saw her in a bathing suit with her beautiful legs, I was even more attracted.

onto the floor of the New York Stock Exchange…and always remember that someone may be watching them.

TORONTO TRIP

Jules Bache was the president of Dome Mines (gold) in Canada. He was to address the stockholders in Toronto. I had been at Bache about two years when I was asked to deliver his speech to him in Toronto. This was my first business trip. I flew there in coach, spent minimum amounts for meals, and slept overnight in a very cheap motel. After submitting my expense voucher to the Accounting Department, I received a call to talk to them. Fearfully (thinking I spent too much), I met the accountant who explained to me that my expenses were too low, that they expected their employees to travel in proper style, and that I was setting a bad example.

ELEANOR

In 1937, Eleanor Lewis was employed by Bache as secretary to the partner-in-charge of the Research Department, who was a graduate of the very first class of Harvard Business School. Years later he told me how impressed he was when Eleanor spelled "eleemosynary" correctly. Neither he nor I could.

Afraid of becoming too involved with a particular girl, I would kind of play the field, sometimes getting my dates (and me) quite confused. One day Mom suggested I take a daughter of one of her old classmates to a senior prom in New York. I agreed but was taken aback when she turned out to be quite plump. She wore a long dress and wide sash. When passing through a revolving door, her sash got caught. I admit I was tempted to let her work her way out of it while I headed home. I reconsidered, and did the right thing. It should have taught me a lesson about dating Mom's friends' daughters. It did not.

When I first saw Eleanor walk by my desk, so slim and pretty, something happened. I didn't know until later that she would take that path just to pass my desk. We would share an exchange: "Good morning, Miss Lewis." "Good morning, Mr. du Moulin." One day, I received an interoffice phone call from her asking if I knew the tune of "Scheherazade." Hell, I couldn't remember my own high school song. Surprisingly, I did recall, from following college football, that the University of Illinois song was the tune of "Scheherazade." I immediately responded humming the tune of "We're Loyal To You Illinois…." This really impressed her. Later I learned she came from a musical family and played a great piano.

We began dating, but not exclusively. She did come to my home, and we went to the beach. Gee, when I saw her in a bathing suit with her beautiful legs, I was even more attracted. The years went by very fast. When I entered the service in 1941, I decided this was the time to close in. When I had liberty, I realized I could no longer play the field. Now, things are getting serious.

I MEET ELEANOR'S FAMILY

During one liberty I was invited to meet her family and stay for dinner. I was in my uniform, bosun's mate 1st Class USCGR (U.S. Coast Guard Reserve). After dinner, we went into the living room. I had been on duty for two weeks, and was glad to relax on a love seat while Eleanor played the piano, surrounded by her family. As she played, one classical piece after another, I would identify the piece after only a few notes had been played. The family was very impressed until I announced that I actually could read the title and movements from across the room. (I have been blessed by extraordinary long distance vision that would also serve me well at sea.)

Eleanor's mother, sister Dorothy, and uncle all made me feel most welcome. Eleanor's father was out-of-town. He was in the entertainment field and was a fine musician. In his earlier days, he was part of a vaudeville troupe, one act of which was called "The Three Lyres." They appeared in major theatres worldwide including the Palladium in London. During World War I, he was part of the U.S. Navy band.

SKI TRIP CANCELLATION

Most every Christmas-New Year holiday, before the war, I would go on a ski trip. Eleanor understood this. She had her own New Year's Eve plans. However, this particular year there was no snow. On New Year's Eve, I was home with my mother and Sam. Mom suggested I call a daughter of another old friend and if she were not busy, invite her down from New York City for the night. I called Marie who was not busy. I took the LIRR to Manhattan and picked her up. We got on the subway at 86th St. to head for Penn Station.

I hung on to a handstrap; in the other hand was Marie's suitcase. And who was seated in front of us but Eleanor! In those days it was safer for young girls to ride the subway. I sure was embarrassed. Eleanor got off at 8lst Street with a grim face heading for Al and Horace Hagedorn's party at the Beresford (2007: still there). On returning to my office, I tried to phone Eleanor but she wouldn't talk to me. It was several days before she gave me the chance to explain. That was the last time I would go out with another girl.

SOFTBALL

Bache had a softball team entered in a Wall Street league. During the season we would bus or subway to Manhattan Beach to play. I played short field. One Friday, when I left home, I packed my softball uniform. When I started to put on my blue pants, I realized they were my mother's blue culottes. They were too baggy, so I put a bunch of rubber bands around them and played ball. I lived through it.

Eleanor and a group of Bache girls would root for us. One night, after the game, Eleanor and I walked to the stone jetty. For the first time, we kissed. She said she heard bells ringing. Rather then let her think it was my kiss, I unromantically explained it was a bell buoy at the entrance to Sheepshead Bay.

MORE ARNOLD GREEN

Arnold Green turned out to be my closest friend for over fifty years (indeed, until he passed away in 1988). Arnold lived at 941 Park Avenue with his attractive widowed mother, Mabel, and two younger brothers. Arnold worked in the Bache Credit Department. He was a very modest, quiet man with a great sense of humor. We sailed together and later, when he married Muriel, Muriel became Eleanor's closest friend. Since Eleanor's death in 2000, Muriel and I keep in close touch.

Arnold was probably the brightest person I knew. He played piano, a great deal of J. S. Bach which I didn't particularly like. Arnold's mother Mabel and I were good friends. Arnold did not like formal dinner parties but would be pressured to attend many of these at home. He did, but with a long face, much to Mabel's annoyance. Often, on Friday nights, I would

> *When I started to put on my blue pants I realized they were my mother's blue culottes. I lived through it.*

stay at the Green apartment. On a Saturday morning, we would leave early, in old clothes, to head for a College Point shipyard to work on his sailboat. The landlord asked Mrs. Green if she would arrange for Arnold to take the service elevator in view of his worker's attire. It was fine with me, but Arnold refused on the basis that he led a clean life, whereas some of the elevator passengers were fur-coated kept women.

Since I worked directly for the Managing Partner, employees would come to me with problems, seeking my advice. One day Arnold approached me, quite upset. He had asked for a secretary. One was hired at a salary higher than Arnold's. He wanted to discuss this with my boss. I thought he had a good point. He was soon ushered into the boss's office. The door was closed. Several minutes later Arnold came out and told me he was fired. I then learned that **one should not give ultimatums without considering the consequences**, even if done in a quiet and respectful manner. It wasn't many weeks before Arnold was hired by a mutual friend and wound up working for Thor Eckert & Co., a shipping company. In later years, after World War II, he returned to Bache.

HORACE HAGEDORN

Talking of advice – one of Arnold's oldest friends was Horace Hagedorn. Horace was a fun-loving individual. Both were practical jokers. Often, on Fridays, we would meet at the Dublin House on West 79th Street (2007: it is still there) for beer and hamburgers. On one Friday, when Arnold and I went to the men's room, I noticed Arnold took the round white urinal soap out of the urinal, washed it, dried it, wrapped it in paper, and put it in his pocket. Later when Horace went to the men's room, Arnold slipped the onion-like soap into Horace's hamburger roll. Horace soon returned, and after taking a bite and quickly spitting it out, he turned on Arnold, who as quickly explained that he had washed it first.

One day, Horace called and asked if he could join us for lunch. He had a problem. Horace was employed by an advertising firm, and had an idea for a radio show, but his boss had told him that, as an employee, any ideas would belong to the company. The question was: should Horace quit and take a chance on the success of his idea? We asked him what he was earning. "$10,000 a year," he answered. We were earning less than $5,000.

Horace established a foundation that supports many Long Island charities to the tune of millions of dollars a year.

"You must be nuts, Horace, to give up a job paying that much." Against our advice, Horace quit, and with the help of the famous reporter Quentin Reynolds, sold the idea to Philip Morris. It was "The Big Story," featuring real life adventures of reporters. It played for years on radio, television, and was a great success.

Horace married Peggy O'Keefe and raised a large family. His later success was the development of Miracle-Gro home fertilizers. From an investment of $2,000 after WWII, Horace grew it into a quarter-of-a-billion-dollars-in-sales, family owned business, generating profits of $34 million annually. In 1995, the company merged with the much larger New York Stock Exchange-listed Scott Company. Horace received sufficient Scott stock to control the company. With the bulk of the stock, Horace established a foundation that supports many Long Island charities to the tune of millions of dollars a year.

Ed contemplates the fish head while his brother
Babe does the cleaning.

HOW ARE YOU DOING?

One calm day, while sailing on the first *Lady Del* with Mom, Sam Lauterbach, Eleanor and Horace, we passed quietly through the fishing fleet off Rockaway Point. We would usually hail the anchored fishing fleet, calling across the water, "How are you doing?" It so happened Horace, without my noticing, had gone forward to relieve himself on the portable head (from Abercrombie & Fitch). When I called across to one of the fishing fleet, "How are you doing," we were startled, and the surrounding fishing fleet quite amused, to hear this deep, loud voice from inside the curtained cabin yell, "I got a bucket full of shit."

Horace was my oldest friend, whose company I really enjoyed. My only regret is he never asked my advice again – only that once in the middle 1930s. Horace and his wonderful second wife, Amy (Peggy died around 1988), together became major, hands-on benefactors of many charitable organizations, mostly on Long Island. One of Horace's favorite charitable activities was to offer to pay poor kids' college tuitions should they be admitted to a college. He believed in working hard for success. A documentary film of Mr. Miracle-Gro was made in 2004 and shown on public television. "You have to put something back" was his favorite expression. My "young" friend of 72 years passed away February 1, 2005, at the age of 89.

90-DAY WONDER

In addition to going to N.Y.U night school, I took courses at the N.Y. Stock Exchange Institute. When I entered the service in August 1941, I was earning about $50 per week. Harold Bache, Jules Bache's nephew and a partner, had been an infantry captain in France during WW I and was very patriotic and civic minded. With war clouds gathering, he suggested I enter military service, explaining that the first in would likely be the first out, and that was the way it happened.

Having been brought up on the water and familiar with boats, I chose the Navy. At that time, there was a "90 Day Wonder" program at the end of which you would become a Navy ensign. The *U.S.S. Prairie State* was docked in the Hudson River. It was there you applied. This was early in 1940. The basic requirement was the equivalent of two years of college. No problem for me as I had 58 points (credits) from N.Y.U., and the Stock Exchange Institute credits should easily offset the two points I needed to equal 60. They wouldn't accept that, and I had to take two additional points at N.Y.U. They made me have my wisdom teeth removed. Finally, I was approved to enter the class of January 1941. However, in December 1940, the Navy changed the requirement to four years of college. I wasn't concerned as I had already been accepted. Woe was me. A notice arrived announcing that, in view of the higher requirements, I would not be eligible.

I had met a lot of fellows while standing in line: going through physicals, taking tests, etc. Fate played a hand. Many of my would-be "classmates" were assigned to the Pacific Fleet. One, I knew, from upstate New York, was killed on Dec 7, 1941 – during the sneak attack on Pearl Harbor. Had I been one of those shipped to Pearl Harbor, I might have been killed there – or released from service as a commander, four years later, if I survived.

Being rejected was a new experience. Now what? The U.S. Coast Guard had organized a volunteer reserve to help protect our local waters. Sam Lauterbach was involved as was I. My decision was to remain at Bache for the 1941 summer, race sailboats, and join the Coast Guard at the end of summer. I enlisted in August 1941 in the regular Coast Guard Reserve. As I felt it was my last "free" summer, I raced hard. I skippered Charles Simon's Victory Class sailboat *Blue Devil* (#3) to victory at Larchmont Race Week (1941). I gave the sterling silver trophy to the owner. Charlie died about 1993. The executor of his estate mailed me back that silver trophy. I then gave it to my son Richard to return to the Larchmont Yacht Club. Our family has continued a tradition of winning at Larchmont Race Weeks: Richard in his Blue Jay and Lightning in the 1960s, and his Express 37 *Lora Ann* in recent years; and his son Ed in Optimists and 420s in the 1990s.

CHARLES SIMON

Charles Simon grew up with Arnold Green and Horace Hagedorn. Like me, Charlie did not have a college education. He worked his way up at Salomon Brothers, a prestigious investment banking firm, to a very senior partnership. He had a sad married life, was quite moody, and generous to a fault. His favorite charities were the Animal Hospital and the American Indian Museum. If he read a book he especially enjoyed, over a dozen of his friends would receive a copy. When in England, he sent us all cashmere sweaters. Each time I invited him for lunch, at the last minute he would call and insist I had to have lunch at Salomon Bros.

The YMHA (Young Mens Hebrew Association) on 92nd Street in Manhattan had, for many years, a very popular program called Lyrics & Lyricists. It featured all of the famous composers and lyricists of our times. On Mondays in the 1960s, Eleanor and I would meet our Woodmere/ Hewlett friends Sigo and Norma Mohr and cousins Claire, Sam, and Al Lewis to enjoy the wonderful music.

Charles Simon donated a Center for Adult Life & Learning to the Y. We attended the dedication for the center with the Greens and Hagedorns. Walter Cronkite, the host, signed a copy of his new book for each of those attending. Later, in the large auditorium Charlie and Walter put on a show for the appreciative audience. When Charlie was a young boy, without family or financial support, he was sheltered at the YMHA at no cost. As a successful banker, it was his turn to pay back. This was similar to Horace Hagedorn's generosity.

This reminds me of another "give back" story. George Sirota was the son of a Lebanese peddler who had earned enough money to send George to Notre Dame. In 1929, the father lost all his money. George, in his second year at college, had to take on a number of extracurricular jobs to raise the funds for his tuition and board. He struggled, but kept up his studies and graduated. In time, George built up a small fortune trading commodities through the Miami office of Bache, and was sent by President Eisenhower to Lebanon to report on the progress of several U.S.-funded road projects. George established a fund of $100,000 in the early 1960s at Notre Dame to be used by any student who found himself facing the same financial problems as he had.

In 1977, Eleanor and I, along with Andrew MacGowan who helped organize the Enterprise syndicate to defend the America's Cup, visited Charlie Simon on Fire Island. He asked if the crew needed anything special. Andy mentioned foul weather gear. Charlie said, "Buy the best for the entire crew and send me the bill." We did, and ordered a set for him. Before leaving Charlie's home, Andy, quite innocently, admired a painting. Several weeks later it was delivered to Andy.

When my son Richard finished his Navy service as a lieutenant junior grade, he was trying to decide whether he should go to business school or go to work. I set up appointments for him to meet with Bache's economist and then with Charlie Simon at Salomon. Richard told me that the economist urged him to go to business school. When Richard asked Charlie, who never went to college, Charlie with a twinkle advised, "F—k business school – go to work!" Richard made his own choice, and never regretted his decision to attend Harvard Business School.

When Charlie died, there were wonderful eulogies given at Campbell's Funeral Parlor in New York City. Outside were ten limousines. At the conclusion of the service, it was announced that Charlie wanted, for the last time, to treat those attending to a party at the famous 21 Club. Over one hundred of us had a great time on Charles Simon, as usual. Charlie's last treat!

Portrait of Ed du Moulin at Bache & Co., 1940.

BACHE'S WIRE ROOM

Back to pre-war Bache: I became close to many employees and took a sincere interest in their problems. This interest in helping others would become a major theme in Eleanor's and my life.

One of my favorite places at 42 Broadway was the Wire Room, where I always felt welcome. Orders from and confirmations to our branches were

Eleanor was happy there and learned a great deal about foul language.

transmitted by Morse code (no internet back then!). One of the older order clerks took me under his wing. He knew I liked sports and was kind enough to invite me into his "fraternity." Saturdays, after the markets had closed at noon, if there was a major sporting event in the city, about 30 of the "chosen" would meet.

Here's just one example: Army-Notre Dame were playing at Yankee Stadium. Jack Hughes would collect $1.00 from each of us for which we would receive a 2x3 colored blank card, and attach a similarly colored ribbon to our lapel. We would subway to the stadium and proceed to a specified gate. At a signal, we would file through a designated turnstile, giving the attendant our blank 2x3 card. Once inside, we would eventually squeeze into a seat around the 50 yard line. I assume the $30.00 was split with the friendly gatekeeper. Not only did I see top football games, but also a wide variety of other events, including baseball games, Madison Square Garden basketball, horse shows, and hockey games. This was another lesson that it pays to **treat people nicely – it will come back to you**. This proved itself to me in extraordinary circumstances – while in service, while racing sailboats, during time spent managing America's Cup campaigns – as well as in our normal lives.

Harold Bache, J. S Bache's nephew, was the head of the Commodity Department. Over the years, he took a close interest in me, treating me like a son. He never married until after WWII. Soon after I entered service, my boss, the managing partner, left the firm. Eleanor was unhappy and decided to leave.

ELEANOR TO SALOMON

Charles Simon arranged for Eleanor to work at Salomon's Municipal Desk – one of very few women in that position on Wall Street. She was happy there and learned a great deal about foul language from the various traders. This would serve her well throughout her life.

While on liberty, I was invited to lunch at Salomon Brothers with Charlie and other executives. They asked me to consider working for their firm after the war was over. I thanked them and said that I first would have to consider returning to Bache. During the war years, Harold Bache kept in touch with me and others who were in the armed forces.

POST-WAR PLANNING

Once the U.S. formally declared war, the U.S. Coast Guard became part of the Navy and participated in every battle area of the war. While on convoy duty in the Mediterranean Sea, on board the 327-foot Coast Guard cutter *Ingham*, about one year before the war ended, Ed McCarrick, Bill Bryan, and I were chatting while off watch. What did we plan to do after the war? I said I would meet with Harold Bache who had become the managing partner, and insist upon being paid no less than $75 per week. If I didn't get it, I would work for Salomon Bros. Bill Bryan, a graduate of Colby College in Maine, said he was going to be Colby's Dean of Admissions. Ed planned to become a scout for the Brooklyn Dodgers baseball team.

We agreed to meet one year after the war at a downtown restaurant. The rendezvous was kept. Harold Bache had said OK to my salary demand. I said to myself that I should have asked for more, something like $80. Bryan did become Dean of Admissions at Colby, and Ed became a Dodgers scout. They made this informal agreement between them: if Ed found a young baseball talent, he would steer him to Colby College and hire him after graduation. Both Ed and Bill have passed away.

LOW-COST LUNCHES

In my early years at Bache, at audit time a group of us would spend time in our bank's vault, well below street level, where we would count the many millions of dollars of securities deposited by our customers. This was a tedious job. Its only compensation was a free sandwich lunch.

After I stopped carrying my lunch from home, Arnold and I had a few favorite eating places. There was Max's Busy Bee on New Street where we could pick up lunch for 15 to 20 cents. Then there was the wonderful Seamen's Church Institute near the East River. For 20 to 25 cents we could eat with the seafarers and view the wonderful old ship models. When we became more affluent, once a week, a group of us would go to Churchill's before 11:45 and get the "junior executive" lunch at the discounted price of 45 cents. We were at Churchill's when Hitler was threatening Poland. All of us pundits agreed he would not invade Poland – two years later each of us was in military service.

Another popular lunch spot for us was the Exchange Buffet, a

Skijoring at Lake Placid in the 1930s.

company listed on the Stock Exchange. Besides operating a popular and expensive restaurant on New Street where many of the higher paid brokers would gather, the company also ran cafeterias where the less affluent would select and eat whatever they wanted. On the way out, you would tell the checkout clerk the amount you spent. Let's say it was a Monday and you were short of cash, so you would eat 70 cents worth of food, but tell the clerk it was 25 cents. By the end of the week you had short-changed them between three to four dollars. And we kept track. When we received our weekly pay in cash on Fridays, we would spend about 50 cents on Friday's lunch, and on the way out pay the clerk the 50 cents plus whatever we owed from the rest of the week. The Exchange Buffet was referred to as "Eat It and Beat It," but few evidently did, as it was, before the war, a profitable company. It still existed after the war when many of us returned to Wall Street. Within two years thereafter it went out of business – too many customers were now "beating it."

During the lunch hour, Arnold and I would often visit the old ship chandlers on the East River waterfront or visit the Seamen's Church Institute, Seamen's Bank for Savings, or the India House to view the wonderful ship models and maritime oil paintings. The India House (upstairs) was a private club but the doorman would let us in to see their exciting collection. I dreamt that one day I would have my own ship model and a good oil painting of a fine sailing vessel. Finally, years later in 1960, Hans Kolstee, restorer for the Seamen's Bank model collection, called and urged me to inspect a ship model in Boston. In a heavy downpour, Eleanor, Richard, and I drove to Boston where we were shown a beautiful full-rigged model of a heavily armed British

East Indiaman (late 1770s), the *Asia*. A few years later, I found two old oil paintings of the sailing ships *Jane Dagget* and *Magi* that when restored by Georges Chappellier joined the *Asia* in the du Moulin living room.

SKIING AND SKI-JORING

Let's go skiing. Cousin Sam started skiing in 1915 at Lake Placid. His original skis had a binding that went through a slot in the center of the ski and tied around his boots—no safety release in those days! When I was about 20 (1934), Sam took Arnold and me on our first ski trip by train, the New York Central to Montreal, followed by the Canadian National to St. Sauveur in the Laurentians. I was hooked.

The next year Sam took me to the Ryans in Lake Placid. He suggested we go ski-joring. Fred Fortune owned a stable by Mirror Lake. Sam had previously ski-jored behind a steed named Blue Bells whose hooves were spiked for traction. Sam told me to hold the bar attached by rope to the horse and keep my skis parallel while he held the bar with one hand and the reins in the other. Just like water skiing? No way, as you shall see.

On the lake, there was mush snow alternating with ice patches. I locked my knees, held on tightly to the bar (my knuckles were white) and off we went. We were about three feet behind his/her tail. As my skis hit the ice patches they would jump forward; when they hit the snow they would fall back. Up and down the bar went.

Suddenly, disaster struck. My ragged motion had shaken Sam off the bar. The empty reins were dragging along and Sam was fast disappearing behind me, yelling something unintelligible. I held on even tighter and yelled to Blue Bells "Whoa-Whoa." In horse language it apparently meant something other than "Stop NOW!" Up went Blue Bell's tail to point straight at me. In seconds I was covered from head to toe with steaming horse manure. Blue Bells never stopped – where was he/she taking me? I must have been quite a sight (and smell) as we trotted down the snow-covered main street of Lake Placid and turned into the stable where Sam was waiting, along with an audience that cheered as I appeared on the scene, covered by frozen manure. The first thing Sam said was, "Didn't you hear me yell LET GO, LET GO?" I responded, "Hell, Sam, I never thought to do that. The bar was the only thing I could hang on to!" I slunk

Ed skiing at Lake Placid in plus fours.
Pointy skis were also in fashion.

into the Ryan's basement and had a long shower. After that experience, I wouldn't even go water skiing behind a boat.

THE CHIVERS BROTHERS

We were at the bottom of a ski slope when two magnificent skiers in green outfits came to a Christie stop where we were standing. I asked, "Who are these fantastic skiers?" They turned out to be the Chivers brothers, stars of the Dartmouth ski team. I said to Sam, "If I could have gone to college, that's where I would have liked to go."

About fifteen years and a war later, Richard was two years old. One of my associates at Bache, Harry Jacobs, was a fine skier and graduate of Dartmouth. At his suggestion, I filed a preliminary application for Richard at Dartmouth. And yes, that is where he went sixteen years after the application was filed. Through him, I vicariously experienced my dream of attending Dartmouth.

With confidence, Richard declared that he wanted to join their ski patrol. I said to Eleanor that I didn't think he would pass the test the first time. I reasoned that his ability to go slowly down a slope, under tight control, wasn't good enough. He was more adept at skiing fast. After he passed the test, on the second try, I gave him my old National Ski Patrol patch.

The next generation also picked up skiing as a favored sport, second only to sailing. Richard's daughter Lora has spent the last two years as a ski instructor in Jackson Hole, Wyoming.

The following year Lora's younger brother Ed also taught at Jackson Hole. — **R. du M**.

WALL STREET SKI CLUB

In the middle 1930s, a group of Wall Street skiers formed the Wall Street Ski Club. Viking Hedberg (NYSE) was our president, and I was an officer. It was a wonderful group of 75 to 100 members, a cross section of the Street. After work on Fridays, we would go to Grand Central Station where we had checked our ski outfits and skis. We would change into our ski clothes in a dressing booth for 25 cents, and check our civilian gear. We then boarded our specially chartered ski train complete with sleeping cars.

Early Saturday morning we would arise, for example, in places like

Brandon, Vermont, or North Creek, New York, where Gore Mountain is today, near Richard and Ann's ski house. The sleeping cars served as our lodging with the local inn for meals and partying. Sunday night the train would return us to New York, arriving around 6:00 a.m. Monday. We changed back into our business clothes, checked our ski equipment, ate breakfast and would be in our offices by 9:00 a.m. In total we spent about $40.00, that included fare and food. As Ski Patrol members we didn't pay for tows. Today, that same $40 hardly would cover a half-day ski pass.

The club would run ski races for novices to experts. A group of us were National Ski Patrol members, volunteering our services. This was before most areas had their own patrol or even emergency toboggans. We were quite proficient in handling sprains and a broken arm or leg. We were trained to use skis and poles to apply traction and to make toboggans out of four skis and poles lashed together. In areas which did not have tows, we used seal skins, attached to our skis, to help us climb the hills. As we moved the skis forward, the skins would be moving with the grain, so to speak, providing a smooth slide forward. Then as we switched balance to that leg, the fur would open up and hold the ski in place as we advanced the other ski.

When the war started, the U.S. Army formed the 10th Mountain Division. A number of our Wall Street Ski Club members joined, and distinguished themselves fighting on skis in Italy. This was a famous group of fighting men. Amongst them, Senator Robert Dole was badly injured, as was my friend from Knickerbocker Yacht Club, Andrew Lager, who died in 2004. Andy received a battlefield promotion to sergeant and won a Bronze Star.

When the war was over, we were not able to reorganize the Wall Street Ski Club. Many of us were too busy renewing our careers and raising families, but I am confident that most of the members eventually returned to skiing with their children, just as I did.

Ed with the 32-foot gaff-rigged sloop Lady Del, *purchased by Sam Lauterbach after* Thora *was wrecked in the 1938 hurricane.*

Palm Beach Suit

My sister Julia had a fine sense of humor. One evening in the 1930s we were having Friday night dinner around my mother's large circular table. For the hot days, I had bought an off-white Palm Beach suit. I had not worn it yet. While eating, the phone rang. It was for me. I heard a girl's voice, very soft and sultry. She introduced herself, explaining a friend of

LADY DEL *making knots in a fresh breeze.*

hers had spoken so highly of me. She was visiting her friend on 130th Street, and, if I were not busy, would I call on her? Of course I said yes. I would be there by 9:00 p.m.

Sis suggested I wear my new Palm Beach suit. When I left, everyone thought I looked just wonderful and wished me good luck. After a half-mile walk, it was now dark. I began checking house numbers, but there was no such house number as I'd been given. I rang the bell of one house where a dog pawed my handsome suit. The woman was no help at all. I began to smell a rat. When I returned home, everyone greeted me with uncontrolled laughter. I was not a very happy camper. At dinner, I had not noticed that sister Julia left the table and went upstairs. She had called me from there, putting on a sultry voice to deceive me. It sure worked. After I hung up, she had calmly rejoined the group.

MY SISTER AND HER FAMILY

Much to the surprise of my family Julia eloped with Al Weisberg, her boss in a successful commercial art company. I played the peacemaker. Al was a first class amateur photographer. They lived in Great Neck, New York, and raised Ted and Irene. Ted's children are Jason and Rebecca, who both work with Ted at Seaport Securities. Jason married a lovely English girl named Laurie, and they have a son Morgan. Jason is very athletic and does triathalons. He worked for Stars & Stripes during one America's Cup campaign. Irene's children are Ian and Jamie. Irene is an artistically talented woman. In her younger days, she did some cool cruising on a 24-foot sailboat, and raced with me on *Lady Del*. Jamie is a terrific singer and has entertained us at many family events. Ian is married to Denise, and they have a young son named Max.

LADY DEL AND *NYMPH*

After *Thora* was wrecked in 1938, Sam bought a 32-foot Gil Smith sloop built in 1919 at Patchogue, Long Island. She was a gaff-rigged centerboarder, drawing only two-and-a-half feet with the board up.

Sam's brother-in-law owned a sister vessel, *Nymph*. Sam's nephew

Paul Oppenheim was handsome and athletic. In his senior year at Cornell, majoring in architecture, he was driving back to school late one night with his left arm partially outside the car window. A truck sideswiped him, severing his arm. He had been left-handed, and yet managed to graduate with his architectural degree. To build his confidence, Paul sailed *Nymph* to Maine without any crew. He lived to be a very successful California architect. As a result of the accident, New York State passed a law requiring trucks to have corner lights at their maximum width.

On the Gil Smith boats, one could walk on the cabin roof, the sides of which had a canvas curtain that could be opened. On a too sunny or rainy day, folks could sit inside comfortably on the two bunks. Sam's boat was named *Lady Del* for my mother, Adele, the first of four *Lady Del*s. As she had no motor, we would sail her right into her slip. We learned to judge her headway after we lowered her sails and coasted into the slip, with spring lines ready.

Although I never wanted to fish myself, it was great fun for me to steer as Mom, Sam, and Babe trolled for blues off Rockaway Point. Sam and I raced *Lady Del*, usually doing quite well. We belonged to the Yacht Racing Association of Jamaica Bay.

The Sherburnes

We had wonderful neighbors in Belle Harbor. The Sherburnes were originally New Englanders who still hadn't accepted the British defeat in the Revolutionary War – their ancestors were Tories. I was an American history buff and would have exciting arguments with them. We came together when England went to war in 1939. The following year I began donating blood in the Blood for Britain drives. I continued donating blood for more than 25 years.

U.S. Coast Guard Bosun's Mate Ed du Moulin
in the fall of 1941.

PART II
WORLD WAR II

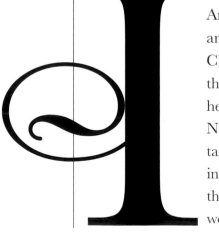n the early days of World War II in Europe, 1939-40, American radio and newspapers were full of stories about anti-British, pro-Nazi activities. Father Coughlin of the Christian Front was a pro-Nazi rabble-rouser while Father Fulton Sheehan was the reverse. Fritz Kuhn was the head of an active organization in New Jersey called the Nazi Bund. The Bund wore full Nazi uniforms, had military drills, and carried Nazi flags. Kuhn boasted of having met Mussolini. Emotions ran high. Organizations like the Anti-Defamation League and other anti-Nazi groups worked hard to contain the Bund.

From left: Sam Lauterbach, Ed, Arnold Green,
And Babe—US Coast Guard enlistees
in January, 1942.

I was approached by Steve J., a senior employee of Bache who was a member of Boyce's Tigers, a group of volunteers under command of a Colonel Boyce. They were being trained in civilian defense. In Central Park, armed with broomsticks for guns, they would practice man-to-man combat.

Steve was concerned about the activities of a very handsome anti-Semite, Joe McWilliams, the head of the Christian Mobilizers who, on Friday nights, would arrive in a horse-drawn covered wagon at 1st Avenue and 85th Street, in the heart of Yorkville, a German neighborhood. He carried a lantern and would call out, "I am looking for an honest Jew" (parodying Diogenes looking for an honest man). He gathered large crowds, referred to President Roosevelt as President Rosenfeld, called for the downfall of Great

I agreed to help him form a volunteer group that would join the Christian Mobilizers as "moles"

Britain, and urged the spilling of Jewish blood in the streets of New York. In the rear of the mob were New York City policemen who just stood by to control any action by objectors. Freedom of speech prevailed.

Steve was looking for volunteers with no connection to any anti-Nazi or Jewish organization to try to stop Joe McWilliams through legal means. I responded that there always would be some leader (like Lincoln) who would step forward and quell such movements. He asked me to go with him to one of the Friday night visits by Joe McWilliams, suggesting I first change into old clothes. I agreed and was very disturbed by what I saw.

Consequently, I agreed to help him form a volunteer group that would join the Christian Mobilizers as "moles". Three athletic and good friends - Larry, Arnold Green, and Mel - joined me. We changed to old clothes at Arnold's apartment at 941 Park Avenue, just a few blocks from Yorkville.

I was given the choice of taking steno notes at the outdoor meetings or joining the Christian Mobilizers Defense Unit. I chose the latter as I didn't like the idea of being mobbed at the outdoor meetings. I completed an application and was invited to attend an indoor meeting somewhere in Yorkville. It was crowded with a very rough looking bunch. Maybe I should have taken the steno assignment. I was issued a pair of brass knuckles with an instruction sheet on how to conduct streetfighting. This was followed by a lecture. My gut feeling was to make a hasty retreat. Later, the material given to me would be of value in the courtroom.

Eventually, Joe McWilliams was arrested along with others including John Zitter and John Olivo. Both had criminal records and were later deported. McWilliams went to jail. Most importantly, our actions helped stop the movement. Arnold was a great witness. He was able to retain, in detail, without notes, the chilling statements made at meetings, and memorize lists of names.

When asked by McWilliams' lawyer Frank Walsh what organizations he belonged to, Arnold responded "The Seuss Navy." He said he was an admiral and showed his "diploma," a beautifully drafted document by Theodore Seuss Geisel, the well-known creator of the Dr. Seuss series of books. When Arnold explained that he had received this at the Boat Show from Esso Oil Company, the entire courtroom laughed. Dr. Seuss was a Dartmouth graduate, so Richard later donated my own Seuss Navy diploma to the Dr. Seuss collection at Dartmouth.

Joe McWilliams may have gone to prison, but the Nazi Bund remained active, holding a rally in a packed Madison Square Garden decorated in Nazi flags. In the middle of the speeches, suddenly our National Anthem, loud and clear, resounded through the speakers. This was the action of another cell working behind the scenes to counter the evil work of the Bund.

JOINING THE COAST GUARD

Having a good bit of boating experience, I entered the Coast Guard in August 1941 as a bosun's mate lst class and was assigned to the base at Fort Tilden, New York. My first duty was to serve on a fast 40-foot motorboat, CGR-454, on loan to the Coast Guard by a son of a former high official of Standard Oil of New Jersey, in return for which he was made a Chief Petty Officer. He knew nothing about boats so I was assigned to operate it. Prior to Pearl Harbor, we were giving aid to England. Our particular duty was to standby in Perth Amboy where ammunition was loaded on barges that we would then escort to Gravesend Bay for loading onto ships heading for England.

Ed (left) with Julia and Babe, and Julia's daughter Irene.

My skipper and owner of the boat, Dick W., had only one thing on his mind – girls. Dick was in service to escape alimony payments. I had to be especially careful as I was in for the duration. Dick would stow a woman in the aft cabin and lock the door in case any officers came by. Then when we went on missions, he would join her while the one seaman and I would handle the boat. Eventually he was caught showing porno films on the top floor of the Coast Guard base. That resulted in his release from service, and also the release of his boat.

NEAR DISASTER

Late November in 1941, I was ordered to return the boat to Larchmont. On the scheduled day, there was a sou'easter storm raging. Dick decided to ride along, so his mother drove him to the Coast Guard base with his very big brother (a football player at Trinity) and his girlfriend. Fortunately, I had asked Arnold Green, a civilian then, to go with me. Sam Lauterbach had urged me not to go due to the storm. Meanwhile, Dick's mother drove back to Larchmont.

Under pressure from Dick, I decided to depart. Off Coney Island,

running parallel to the shore, several large waves broke over our vessel. There was an open cockpit at the bow with a door leading aft. One wave landed in that cockpit, broke the door, damaged the steering gear, and let in a lot of water. We all had donned lifejackets except Dick's brother, who panicked. His girl was seasick, prone on the cabin sole, and Dick was in shock. Suddenly, the brother in a heavy overcoat climbed through the aft wheelhouse window onto the cabin roof, where he freed the small wooden tender. The wind catapulted the boat along with the brother overboard. I had to slap my former skipper in the face to get him to assist.

Miraculously, with no steering but the help of the twin screws, we managed to pull alongside the man overboard. As the boat heeled, Arnold and I pulled him on board quite waterlogged and shivering. We were approaching the breakers. Arnold crept forward and pitched the anchor overboard and it held. We tried without success to attract the attention of a police car driving on the boardwalk. We then decided to reverse our course for the shelter of Sheepshead Bay. Arnold went forward and cut the anchor line with an axe. Dragging two lines with buckets to help us steer, we managed to work our way into Sheepshead Bay where a Coast Guard cutter, in answer to our radio call, met us and escorted us back to our base.

Without Arnold, I would not have tried to make the delivery that day. If it were not for him being on board, the brother would have drowned and we probably would have ended up on the Coney Island beach. We went to my home to dry out and wait for Dick's mother to pick up her kin. Sam was quite annoyed with me for using such bad judgment.

On shore, Dick was a polished gentleman. My mother was quite impressed with him. Little did she know about his escapades, nor did he show her an old Far East news clipping with his picture which he proudly carried in his wallet. He had been shot by a Navy officer who, upon his return home, found Dick in bed with his wife. After his discharge from the Coast Guard, through his connections, Dick became an army lieutenant stationed in Miami. He kept in touch with Mom and Sam but I told them never to tell him where I was stationed. For a time I was on anti-submarine duty out of Miami, walking distance from where Dick was stationed, but we never met again.

My Brother's War and Mine

My brother Ted (Babe) enlisted in the Coast Guard shortly after Pearl Harbor and spent almost two years on the 165-foot cutter *Tahoma* assigned to patrol duty in the North Atlantic between Greenland and Iceland, cold and rough duty. During the early period of the War in those waters, the American destroyer *Reuben James* was torpedoed. Her depth charges were not set on safe, and as she sank they exploded adding to a heavy loss of life. A popular folk song was later written about the *Reuben James*. In those same frigid waters, the American troopship *Dorchester* went down with a loss of 900 troops. On board were four chaplains – two ministers, one priest, and one rabbi. They gave their life jackets to others and arm-in-arm went down with the ship. Today, in Valley Forge, there is a Four Chaplains Chapel in their memory.

After ammunition and escort duty between Perth Amboy and Gravesend Bay in November-December 1941, my next assignment was on a patrol boat in Lower New York Bay and Ambrose Channel. A metal anti-submarine net, with a gate, was installed across the harbor entrance near where the Verrazano Bridge is now located. After the battleship *Missouri* was commissioned, she was degaussed off Ambrose Light (to neutralize the magnetic field surrounding a ship to avoid magnetic mines). We were part of her escort. While on patrol, on Sunday morning December 7, we heard over the radio that Pearl Harbor was under Japanese attack, the Day of Infamy. Our feelings were similar to what we experienced decades later, when the September 11, 2001, national tragedy occurred. The following day in 1941 we were officially at war.

Ellis Island and the *Isla de Tenerife*

I was ordered to Ellis Island, issued a mattress, a 45-caliber pistol, and leggings. Now I found myself in strange territory. That very first evening, my name was called, "Bosun's Mate du Moulin, report dockside with full gear, prepared to go to sea." Nervously, I fumbled with the leggings. With pistol at my side, I careened down to the end of the pier. It was dark and cold, and lined up were 20 seamen with old Springfield rifles. I was the 1st class petty officer in charge of these men, with a junior lieutenant in command. None of the seamen had ammunition since they hadn't yet learned to fire a gun.

A light moment with Eleanor (top), Ed, Dorothy (Eleanor's sister), and Babe.

*A*n excited sailor
shook me awake to
tell me there were
strange noises coming
from the bow.

They were raw recruits. We boarded an 83-foot subchaser, sped out of the harbor through Ambrose Channel with orders to seize a Spanish ship, *Isla De Tenerife,* and bring her back into the harbor. Later we learned that she carried contraband for German submarines.

Around midnight, we pulled alongside and ordered the captain to stop and lower the gangway. I assigned the seamen to various parts of the ship to stand guard, but much to my chagrin, they didn't know the bow from the engine room. As best I could, I directed each one, while our officer went looking for the captain. Under escort by our 83-footer, the ship finally dropped anchor off Staten Island. The enlisted men and I remained on board. After setting watches, I turned in.

About 0300, an excited sailor shook me awake to tell me that there were strange noises at the bow. I quickly put on my peacoat and watch cap. When we arrived at the bow, we could hear a metallic sound. I knew exactly what the "strange noise" was, and explained that the ship was swinging with the change of tide causing the chain to scrape against the ship's stem. I left him scratching his watch cap.

Isla De Tenerife's officers were all members of Franco's Fascist Party. The crew, including older, matronly workers who wore long black dresses, were Loyalists taken out of Spanish jails to work the ship. We remained on board for thirty days. I contacted my mother who arranged to collect clothing and other things for me to distribute to the women.

One late night, warmly dressed, I started my usual check of the ship. I stopped to talk to one of these older Spanish women standing on the deck without hat or coat. I called on my high school Spanish and said "Madre calor," suggesting she was warm-blooded standing in the cold, coatless. Very agitated, she responded, "Mi no madre calor – mi madre caliente – mi no fucky-fucky." That was the last time I strayed from the English language except for one other occasion:

In Bizerte, North Africa, in 1944, some of my shipmates wanted me to ask a drunken French soldier where we could get a drink. After all, with the name du Moulin, I should know some French. I asked him "Où est le vin?" He answered, "Où est le cinquième armée de France?" Next morning we waved as the French Fifth Army sailed for Italy. Yes, we did find a seedy bar – it was no Dublin House.

THE CORSAIR FLEET

The four war years were not dull. My duties were varied but always on the water. I had no land jobs. My long experience sailing and "messing about in boats" led to four assignments where I would be involved in commissioning a new vessel. There were many goodbyes; certainly they were better than one long goodbye.

The Navy's commander-in-chief was Admiral Ernest King who did not have much regard for the British, whose Royal Navy intelligence told him that the Germans had relocated their U-boats (submarines) to the U.S. east coast. King refused to believe the British, so he kept our big cutters and destroyers deployed in mid-Atlantic. Therefore German U-boats, with little or no opposition, were sinking a tremendous amount of shipping within a few miles of the shore, particularly ships silhouetted by the lights along the Long Island and New Jersey coasts.

On January 15, 1942, a 10,000-ton British tanker was sunk off Fire Island. By the end of that month, 14 ships (including nine tankers) were sent to the bottom along our coast. For the first six months after Pearl Harbor, less than a dozen U-boats sank more Allied shipping off our east coast than the Japanese Navy could claim for the entire war in the Pacific – two million tons. The approaches to New York Harbor were particularly hard hit with a heavy loss of merchant marine crew. The British urged Admiral King to establish a picket line of seaworthy sailing and powerboats to harass the U-boats, protect war shipping interests, and save lives.

The Cruising Club of America, an old and prestigious outfit, offered to volunteer and man their schooners, cutters, and other yachts. Probably because it was a British idea, King delayed much too long taking advantage of the offer. Finally, on May 15, 1942, he assigned the task of forming a picket patrol, later dubbed the "Corsair Fleet," to the U.S. Coast Guard. Most of our Navy vessels had been sent to the Pacific, while new anti-submarine vessels were not yet available for local convoy or anti-submarine duty. There were some planes, including the Civil Air Patrol, and a few blimps from New Jersey that would help. The Coast Guard picket patrol bases with which I was most familiar were at Greenport and Fire Island, Long Island. The larger sailboats (many schooners) were assigned to Greenport and did patrols for as long as three weeks at a time. Seaworthy vessels with less draft were assigned to Fire Island. It was to Fire Island I was transferred from the Fort Tilden Coast Guard base.

THE ROLLING *BETTINE*

In 1941, the Coast Guard purchased a 47-foot, round-bottom motor sailer named *Bettine*, built by John Alden. It was ketch rigged with twin engines and a boxlike wheelhouse. It was dubbed "The Rolling *Bettine*"– and it did roll, roll, roll. Maximum speed was about 10 knots. Her number, CG-7240, was later changed to CG-47008. Before the Coast Guard purchased her, we took her out on a test run during heavy weather off Rockaway Point. A heavy sea crashed on her foredeck and broke through the large glass windshield. Fortunately, the inspectors and I were wearing heavy coats that kept the broken glass from cutting our chests, although there were face and hand scratches all around.

Access to the twin engines was under the cabin sole, so one engine was flooded out. We needed screwdrivers to pry open the engine-room hatches as there were no handles to lift them. The engine was restarted. New shatterproof glass and pull handles were later installed. I was informed that I would be her skipper. This act of confidence was based on my not-quite disastrous experience with Dick W.'s boat off Coney Island.

On board CG-7240, the Rolling *Bettine*, the U.S.C.G. installed a cabin heater stove, a 30-caliber machine gun mounted on the foredeck, a radio, and sound gear for detecting U-boats. Later, several small depth charges were placed aboard. We did drop

The Rolling BETTINE, *the 47' motor sailor by John Alden, in U.S. Coast Guard trim.*

one, once, but at our top speed of 10 knots we couldn't get far enough away from the explosion. When it went off, we were nearly lifted out of the water. You can be sure we normally set them on safe.

We were also issued 1903 Springfield rifles and I had my 45-caliber automatic. The Coast Guard was going to remove both masts. After I pleaded with them, citing stabilization issues, they left in the mainmast, making her a sloop with a not-too-large mainsail. I carried a trysail for really bad weather and a jib – anything to reduce the rolling! Her yachtie white hull was quickly changed to wartime gray. This was to be my home for about 14 months.

PANISH CONTROLS

The Rolling *Bettine* had Panish controls to put the engine into and out of gear, as well as acting as throttles. They operated with a six-second delayed action. It took a lot of practice before I became fairly adept in close maneuvers. While I was in New York on liberty I left my 18-year-old coxswain, Tom O'Sullivan, in charge. The executive officer appeared on board and ordered Tom to move the boat across the basin as they were expecting heavy winds. Tom told the officer that he wouldn't do it explaining that the controls were too complicated. The exec again ordered him to do it, reminding him that as a coxswain he was supposed to be able to handle boats. Tom started the engines, and off he went, smack into the other side – no major damage except to Tom's confidence.

On my return, I was ordered to proceed to Bayshore and replace the Panish with standard controls. The next day the job was completed and the new controls were operational. There was a very heavy fog. The route from Bayshore to the Coast Guard base was quite tricky and the Great South Bay not too deep. I had marked my chart carefully and had full confidence in my course directions. Off we went through the fog. A short while later, we ran aground, stuck on one of the many sand bars. I hated to radio the base and announce my fighting vessel was hard aground. When asked where I was located, I said that if I knew, I would not be stuck. Hours later, the fog lifted and they sent a boat to tow me off the sandbar.

There was no radar and GPS was years away. What happened? Did I make a navigational mistake? It turned out that when they replaced the

A short while later we ran aground, stuck on one of the many sand bars.

controls, instead of all bronze, there were some ferrous parts used that had affected the compass. What a lesson. Today, I check the fillings my sailing friends have in their teeth before I let them near the compass.

ON PATROL

I was assigned a machinist mate, a coxswain, and one seaman. My orders were to patrol Opal 75, a 15-mile square grid, 60 miles southeast of Fire Island Inlet. Each patrol was to last for 96 hours, four days. We were issued arctic clothes and plenty of food. After the incessant rolling and the long winter nights, we were pretty tired by the time we returned. The point came when we were assigned two Coast Guard Auxiliary volunteers. When we entered the war, the original U.S. Coast Guard Reserve was changed to Auxiliary. After the first patrol with the very seasick and useless volunteers, we reverted back to the original crew of four. There also was the question of their status should a submarine capture them as they were not regular members of the armed forces.

My crew consisted of Coxswain Tom O'Sullivan; 2nd Class Seaman Ed Soukup from an Oyster Bay, Long Island, oystering family; and 1st Class Seaman Charles Powell from Detroit. Soukup would intentionally foul up just to avoid a promotion, his reason being "As a 2nd Class seaman I ain't supposed to know nothing." He didn't want any responsibility and believed neither he nor the boat would survive this duty. He arranged to have his paychecks sent to my wife Eleanor. When his account reached $300 he bought a beautiful deep sea fishing pole and reel. If he were to die, Seaman Soukup wanted to be holding this pole! Off duty, he would sit at the stern trolling for tuna and bluefish. With our Springfield rifles we would shoot at sharks but never managed to hit one.

With the *Bettine*'s lack of serious weapons, we strategized about how we might deal with a U-boat. We prepared a life ring tied to a long line with a loop on the end. Our plan was to sneak up to the periscope from behind, loop on the line, fall back, and follow the ring as it was towed behind the submerged U-boat, even after the periscope had submerged. We would radio for an aircraft and help spot the target for them. Then someone asked what we would do if the periscope turned around just as we were about to loop on the line. Tom, who was a fine young artist and later became a combat artist, had the solution. He drew a picture of the bow of a charging destroyer with a big bow wave. Tom would place this picture in front of the enemy periscope.

One night the lookout spotted a periscope! Equipped with line, life ring and picture we approached slowly from behind. We dropped the loop over the periscope and pulled it tight -- at which point the waterlogged tree and its "periscope" branch rolled over. That was the closest we ever got to implementing our plan.

To help pass the time, O'Sullivan was challenged by Powell to an eating contest: first to give-up or throw-up would lose. They ate tall saltine sandwiches filled with peanut butter, then grapefruit rinds. At some point, Powell asked if I would give him a Gillette double-edged razor blade and a glass of water. With widening eyes, O'Sullivan watched as his opponent chewed the blade into tiny pieces that rested on his tongue. In a flash, he tossed down the water and swallowed the metal. Tom admitted defeat and so Powell became "the slumgullion champ of the Rolling *Bettine*." None of us threw up. I always wondered if Powell ever suffered from bleeding piles.

Periodically, we reported by radio to our base, "NRBG," to advise them we were on patrol. We had no sextant and dead reckoned for the patrol period. We would go upwind slowly under one engine. When we figured we were at the end of our grid, we would start downwind on one engine with the jib tightly trimmed to the centerline, dragging a drogue to slow us down. With no speedometer, we had a bag full of small blocks of wood. We would drop one from the bow and time it when it reached the transom, 47 feet away. By application of the formula $S \times T = D$ we determined our speed. Every wind shift or change in speed was entered in our log.

The main effectiveness of the offshore picket patrol, or Corsair Fleet, was to discourage submarines from rising nightly to charge their batteries. If we had any unusual indications, such as the smell of diesel fuel, floating objects, or motor sounds, we would report that immediately. If a sub was actually sighted, or even suspected, planes and/or a blimp would arrive on the scene. Patrol boats from other grids would be brought together to fan out, searching with their sound gear. Ships continued to be torpedoed and seamen picked up. Throughout the long months of patrol, we never did run across survivors.

If a sub was actually sighted, or even suspected, planes and/or a blimp would arrive on the scene.

THE WEATHER

The scariest part of our duty was to be caught in a real storm. We became used to rough days and nights. Initially, we would be ordered to return to base if the forecasters at 17 Whitehall Street in Manhattan thought it necessary. They often did not realize the actual conditions we were facing. In my case, at full speed, it would take us about eight hours to reach the treacherous Fire Island Inlet. In an easterly blow or heavy winds from the south, the Inlet became impassable unless you were able to arrive at high tide, during slack water.

On board, I had four different methods of judging the weather including the barometer, cloud formations, wind direction, and old sailors' weather wisdom. If three of the methods predicted a bad blow, I became concerned. I would know what the conditions would be at the Inlet at my estimated arrival time. If I couldn't arrive by that time, I would plan to either head for Greenport, Sandy Hook, or New York Harbor. I never had to do this.

In late November 1942, the CGR-3070 *Zaida*, out of Greenport, was caught in a major storm and went missing. The Navy Hunts the CGR-3070 by L. Thompson tells the story. *Zaida* was owned by the famous sailmaker George Ratsey whose ancestors had made sails for Admiral Nelson. *Zaida* was miraculously located Christmas Eve off the Carolina coast, almost a month later. And a 50-foot, very high-sided Elco out of Fire Island, commanded by Bill Pray, was caught in another storm. We thought she was lost but she did turn up two days later, off New Jersey, badly damaged.

After many bad experiences, the Coast Guard decided to allow each skipper to make his own decision to head for port if he thought bad weather was in the offing. At first, I was pleased. We soon realized that this solution had its problems. None of the skippers wanted to chicken out and be the first to return to base. An example follows: The ocean was peaceful, the sky was blue with no special cloud cover. However, my barometer was falling with the wind slowly backing. Three of my four formulae warned of approaching bad weather. On board I now had two additional regular Coast Guard crew – six of us in all.

Let me explain how I received the additional men. Late one night, we were approaching New York Harbor under sail and power. Several times a day the Navy recognition signals would be changed. They were to be used if challenged by the patrol. If you didn't answer with the correct signal, you would be taken as the enemy and fired upon. On patrol, I slept in the wheelhouse and not in my bunk. Around midnight, with one man at the wheel and another as lookout, we were thrown a challenge. Both crew on watch were not overly alert after the four days' patrol. I woke with a start – bullets were flying overhead and our mast was shot down. Quickly, we illuminated our little vessel and Morse-coded the proper response. We

Coast Guard cutter INGHAM *battling a storm in the North Atlantic.*

had been mistaken for a sub because of our wheelhouse shape and lack of response. After an inquiry (not a court martial) we were assigned the two additional crew.

Let's return to the beautiful day when my weather notes convinced me of the possibility of heavy weather ahead. I had figured out the time I had to arrive at the Inlet to get through it safely (slack high), around 1700. In spite of the razzing of the crew, at 1000 hours I advised my base that I was returning. I was very uncomfortable but I bit the bullet and entered the Inlet as planned. We advised the base that we were anchoring, prepared to return to our grid if the weather remained benign. We ate dinner, listening to the radio. The evening was beautiful. I was sweating and the crew was on my case. At 2100 hours, over the radio we heard, "All vessels return to port." One hour later we were tied up to our dock. I was ordered to report to our commanding officer, Lt. Commander Simpson, in the morning. Armed with my weather notes I reported to the commanding officer. Meanwhile, Bill Pray was unable to make the Inlet in time, and suffered in the storm.

Commander Simpson asked me how I forecasted the pending storm. I showed him my weather notes. He seemed satisfied, perhaps even impressed, because this led to my promotion to chief bosun's mate. Simpson later was

Commander Simpson asked me how I had forecast the impending storm. I showed him my weather notes.

placed in charge of a fleet of 83-foot U.S.C.G.-manned subchasers that took part in the Normandy invasion. They rescued many hundreds of soldiers who were in danger of drowning after their landing craft were sunk. My friend Victor Romagna from Port Washington, a member of The America's Cup Hall of Fame, served with the Greenport Picket Patrol and was in command of one of these 83-footers at Normandy.

DEAD RECKONING

To make sure we would be able to find the entrance buoy to Fire Island Inlet after our four-day tours of dead reckoning, we spent a day identifying and charting the fish nets along the shore for about 20 miles running east. On our return from patrol, particularly on poor visibility days, we would set a course that would take us east of the inlet, carefully sail the boat close enough to identify an outer fish net stake (which would carry a lettered number), and then work our way west until finding the entrance buoy off Fire Island Inlet. I had marked the charts in red so they would stand out. But at night, when the red chart light was on, the red chart markings disappeared. This was quickly corrected.

Another convenient navigational aid was the 10-fathom (60-foot) line running parallel to the Long Island shoreline. We would locate it with our leadline (we had no fathometer) and then run parallel with the shore. During the two winters on patrol, the CG-47008 would often get loaded with ice that we had to carefully chop away. Handling the lead line under those conditions wasn't too pleasant.

One day while on patrol out of Fire Island, we were ordered to locate a 52-foot picket patrol vessel that had been rammed by a fishing boat at night. At daybreak we found her with her stern low in the water. You could barely see the depth charges. We pulled alongside, only after making sure their charges were set on "Safe." We slowly proceeded, in fairly choppy seas, to Fire Island Inlet where we were met and relieved of our tow.

SKYLINE ILLUMINATION

During darkness, from many miles at sea, we could see the New York City skyline. The illumination from the city enabled the subs to easily target ships running close to the shoreline. Up until the blackout was finally established for New York and Long Island, 190 ships were lost. By early l943, the submarine warfare had abated.

In my library are many photographs and stories of the Corsair Fleet. Joseph Cooper, who wrote <u>Lands End, Waters Edge</u>, about Long Island Sound yacht racing, also wrote for <u>Nautical Quarterly</u> about the coastal picket patrol (Corsair Fleet). Many Long Island Sound sailors, two of whom were parents of Richard's present crew [2007], sailed with the Corsair Fleet -- Jim Moore (son Steve) and Don Browning (son John). One day, I plan to donate my Coast Guard memorabilia to the New London Museum. One outstanding book helps to understand the terrible shipping toll off the Jersey and Long Island shores during l942-3, and that is <u>Operation Drumbeat</u>, by Michael Gannon, Harper & Row, 1990. Also of interest is <u>Shadow Divers</u> by Robert Kurson, the story of the U-869, not discovered until 1993 in 200' of water, 60 miles off New Jersey. Another good book about the submarine warfare is <u>Bloody Waters</u> written by my friend John Waters from my ship, the *Ingham*.

NEW 83-FOOT U.S.C.G. SUBCHASERS

By 1943, new 83-foot U.S.C.G. subchasers were replacing our Corsair Fleet. On March 20, 1943, I was ordered to commission the CG-83413 at the U.S.C.G. Depot on Staten Island. The crew included three petty officers and nine seamen. She was outfitted with two 600HP Sterling engines, four 300-pound depth charges, a 20mm gun, hedgehog (which projected a barrage of rocket charges over the bow), and small arms. Top speed was 17 knots with a range of about 300 miles. They had a tiny room, placed as low as possible, in which the sound detection gear was located. To my surprise, she was equipped with the all too familiar Panish controls on the flying bridge and below. I made sure my bosun's mate lst quickly became proficient with their use.

The 83-foot subchaser Ed commissioned.

LANDSICK

During the three weeks preparing the 83413, I would take the Staten Island Ferry, then the subway, to visit Eleanor and her family. Several times I felt faint during my days on shore. One evening, I rang the doorbell of Eleanor's apartment, and as the door opened I did faint. Next day, I reported to the Marine Hospital on Staten Island. After a thorough exam, it was suggested that I had a deviated septum. Eleanor said, "No way!" and made an appointment for me to see a nose and ear specialist. He examined me, handed me a booklet to read in his office, after which he wanted to talk. I read about the balance in the ear that causes car or seasickness. He asked how long I had been on offshore patrol and asked if I got seasick. My answer was no. He said my septum was fine, and suggested that until I got back to sea, I should be careful not to stand too close to the edge of the subway platform. If these spells continued once I returned to sea, then he recommended that I should report to the medical authorities. His diagnosis? He thought I had a case of "land sickness" following so much rocking and rolling on the ocean. And once I shoved off, the dizziness never happened again.

ENGAGEMENT AND MARRIAGE

On St. Valentine's Day in 1942, from a phone booth, Eleanor and I became engaged. When I next had liberty, I was stunned by all the excitement that action had created. This must be serious. I made such a pest of myself, Mom said to Eleanor, "For God's sake, marry him." Finally, we set the date: August 30, 1942. I had pressed for an earlier date, but August 30 it was. It was a small wartime wedding. Arnold Green and Sam Lauterbach were my best men. Brother Babe was somewhere in the North Atlantic. I was lucky to get a week's leave. After the ceremony, Eleanor and I took a train to Albany where I had reservations for the night at the DeWitt Clinton Hotel. We checked in. I wanted to go to our room but Eleanor wanted to eat. After dining, she insisted we take a walk, and then stop for coffee. Eventually, we went to our room. Two o'clock in the morning, there was a knock on the door. The bellhop delivered a telegram from Charlie Simon. It said he hoped he wasn't disturbing us.

In the morning we trained to Lake George where we stayed at The

Ed and Eleanor du Moulin at the time of their engagement in 1942.

Antlers. The week was a blur but a very happy one. Then back to New York. We rented a one-room apartment at the Cameron on 86th Street which we could share on my off days. After a month, we gave it up. I hadn't realized that Eleanor and her wonderful sister, Dorothy, were struggling to maintain their family's apartment. Their father and uncles had developed the popular hair product Vitalis. In 1929 it was sold to Bristol Meyers for over a million dollars. Eleanor's father, the vaudevillian, was on the road most of the time and had squandered his share. I had great admiration for the two girls.

After returning from our honeymoon, Mother urged me to make funeral arrangements in the event of my death. She did not want Eleanor to go through the pain that she had when my father died so suddenly and so young in 1918. Through my marriage to Eleanor, Mom really acquired another daughter. There was a deep mutual love between them. Eleanor and I decided not to have children until after the war was over.

DESTROYER *TURNER*

Before I left Fire Island, I recommended that Tom O'Sullivan become a combat artist, which role was granted him. For the balance of the conflict, he sketched various actions. On January 3, 1944, he was on board the CG-83306 on patrol out of Sandy Hook, New Jersey. The destroyer *Turner* (DD-648) was part of a convoy task force that arrived safely from Gibraltar. Before entering New York Harbor, she anchored several miles off Ambrose Lightship. The crew was preparing to transfer ammunition to the Naval Magazine at Fort Lafayette, Brooklyn. At 0600 (about two hours before sunrise), the first of a series of explosions occurred. Mom, living in the Rockaways, was awakened by the blast. The ship was aflame. Tom's wooden subchaser was the first to arrive. Men were jumping into the burning oil-covered water. Without hesitation, the 83-footer came alongside the bow, where many sailors, blinded by the oil and smoke, jumped or slid on lines to the wooden deck, which was much lower than that of the DD. The death toll was 155 sailors.

After taking on as many injured sailors as they could, the 83306 sped to Sandy Hook where ambulances were waiting. Later, Tom made a number of sketches of the action for the U.S.C.G. archives. He and others received Letters of Commendation for their rescue efforts. After the war, Tom became my

The destroyer TURNER *exploding (top), and* BETTINE *patrolling in shark-infested waters – two examples of Tom O'Sullivan's dynamic combat art work.*

lifelong friend and crewed on all my sailboats for the next 35 years. Every Christmas and birthday Tom sends us original, hand-drawn cards.

MARCH WINDS

One day in early March, when it was blowing like stink and snowing, I was ordered to take command of a beautiful 72-foot clipper-bow power boat, CG-7222, and proceed to a location to standby for further orders. To me, March was the most difficult month on patrol – "March winds bring April showers." I admit I was more nervous about a strange boat and crew than the weather. As night fell, one of the sailors whispered to me, "Don't be worried, the Lord will take care of us. Do you believe?" My response was that I was not sure He could help, as I had to do the navigating to our destination, but that I did believe in the Golden Rule. At that moment, I couldn't remember what the Golden Rule was. When I was ready to take a short nap, my friend said to use his bunk. I slept surrounded by crucifixes and pictures of Jesus. At some point we were called back to the base. My friend and historian John Rousmaniere was writing a book on religious experiences at sea. I sent him a more detailed story.

CG-83413 AT SEA

Just before departing Staten Island, a brand-new U.S.C.G. Academy ensign was assigned as commanding officer of "my" subchaser – I was the officer-in-charge. He was nice enough but was fairly green. We picked up an old tramp steamer with orders to escort her to Norfolk. This we accomplished with no incidents. We usually were in front of the vessel, sometimes circling her, always with the sound gear manned and lookouts posted. Along the East Coast, navigational buoys had been removed. However, we had a confidential chart that showed the location of many sunken merchant ships.

We could "ping" off them with our sound gear to determine our position.

Another subchaser relieved us of our ship so we could refuel in Norfolk. We were assigned as escort to an even older, rusted tramp. After departing Norfolk, at a specified point we were to turn south. At dusk (the most dangerous times for submarine attack are morning twilight and evening twilight) a lookout spotted a sub with conning tower partially exposed off our port quarter. Our radioman tried unsuccessfully to reach the Norfolk station so a plane could be dispatched. Our prime duty was to protect the ship we were escorting. We made a sharp turn to our left while the ship proceeded south. The sub submerged quickly heading north. We dropped a few depth charges and sped back to escort our tramp steamer. We were positive that the sub, with a limited supply of torpedoes, would not waste one on our tramp. As for the radio failure, it was attributed to the area in which we were. We were relieved of our tramp and entered Morehead City, North Carolina, for refueling. Our next refueling stop was St. Augustine, Florida. Finally, we tied up at the U.S.C.G. base in Miami, our new permanent base.

At this time, the Germans resorted to "wolf packs," where several subs would operate together. In response, we developed "killer groups." One day a sub surfaced and shot down a Navy blimp off Miami. We were one of several subchasers that tried to locate that sub without success. Several of the blimp crew were killed. Twenty-five years later, I cut a clipping from <u>The New York Times</u> commemorating the incident.

We had a confidential chart that showed the location of many sunken ships.

St. Augustine

I learned a good lesson in St. Augustine. On the way south from North Carolina, one of the crew was throwing up in the small head but didn't bother to clean up the mess. The crew complained to me. When we docked in St. Augustine, I lined them up and asked the perpetrator to step forward. No one did. I announced that there would be no liberty until the matter was settled. Silence – no confession. At that point, I realized that I couldn't carry out my order – an ultimatum. I was preventing ALL of the crew from a deserved liberty. Except for those who had the watch, the liberty party departed. The only accomplishment was that the head remained clean in the future. Lesson learned: **Do not give orders that cannot be carried out.**

Once I was no longer in full command of the 83-footer, I decided to apply to the Coast Guard Academy in New London for a commission, which I did soon after reporting to the Miami duty officer.

MIAMI TO NASSAU

Nassau, capital of the Bahamas, is about 180 miles east of Miami. We were ordered to escort the duke and duchess of Windsor back to their home there. It's about an 18-hour run. They would not fly. Their vessel was to be escorted by two U.S.C.G. 83-footers and several Navy 110-footers. Our station was off the port bow. In case we were attacked, we had attached the recognition signals to a weighted plate to jettison if there was risk of their capture. As it often is in a northerly, the Gulf Stream was rough. Night fell – we all were blacked out. The worst duty was to operate the sound gear deep in the bowels of the boat. The seamen had that duty with half hour watches. Some would go below with a bucket, spend a half hour throwing up, be relieved, come topsides, empty the bucket and then take the wheel and steer. In one case, I had to hold the helmsman by his belt he was so weak.

Around midnight, I spotted some flashes off our port quarter and managed to read an "OS." I assumed this was an "SOS" transmission. Permission was asked of our convoy leader to investigate. Reversing course, at top speed, we headed in the direction where the flashes had been. Suddenly, our boat was lit up like a Christmas tree. There, above our heads, was a Navy blimp blinking a recognition signal at us. We were unaware that our convoy included a blimp. Hastily, we responded with the correct signal.

Soon we sighted a cluster of little red lights in the water. We got permission to use our 12-inch searchlight. On it went. There, in the water was the bow only of our sister ship CG-83421. The small red lights were attached to men in life jackets. Dozens of coconuts were floating nearby. The chief machinist of the CG-83421 collected them as we hauled the full crew of 13 out of the water (near Great Isaac Light, where the depth is several thousand feet). Luckily, most of the 13 crew had been sleeping on deck, which was more comfortable than sleeping below. A few broken teeth were the extent of their injuries. We rejoined our convoy. When we arrived in Nassau, we were told to look sharp as the governor and the duke

Eleanor and Ed photographed when she visited his
Coast Guard duty station in Florida.

and duchess of Windsor wanted to personally thank our crew. They shook hands with each of us and praised our action.

Sometime later, in Miami, a court martial was convened. One of the Navy 110s had cut the CG-83421 in half. One possible reason for the collision was that our compasses would swing wildly when we dropped from the crest of a wave. That night the cruiser *Cincinnati* had passed through that area. Their log showed that conditions were not rough. Perhaps not to a 555-foot, 7,000-ton cruiser, but to us on an 83-footer, it was mighty rough. I do not recall what the final verdict was for either vessel's skipper.

ELEANOR IN MIAMI

While I was in Florida, before heading to the Coast Guard Academy, Eleanor was able to be with me for a short spell. I received a note from her, after she returned home, stating that she had decided to give up smoking as I had asked her. After she left me, I regretted pressuring her about that. After all, we weren't together, why deprive her of that pleasure? So I shipped her a cartoon of cigarettes from the Ship's Store. Her letter and my carton of cigarettes crossed in the mail. After the war, around 1980, she finally did give up smoking cold turkey.

Eleanor had always wanted an alligator pocketbook. While in Miami I bought one and shipped it to her. Eleanor put it in a bureau drawer and said she would not carry it until the war was over. When I finally returned home for good, two years later, out came the pocketbook. The alligator skin had separated. I sent the bag and skin to Bache's office manager in Miami and he got me my money back.

SPARS

While I was waiting for my assignment to the U.S.C.G. Academy, a salty regular Chief Bosun's Mate Mike Peabody and I were ordered to train SPARs (U.S.C.G. Auxiliary women) in the art of rowing a large pulling boat. Mike was quite unhappy. I was not too pleased. This meant rowing past the Anti-Submarine Training Center to the whistling "encouragement" from the sailors along the shore. One afternoon, a barge was being towed in the same direction we were going. Mike and I steered our boats close to the stern of the barge, ordered, "Up oars," and nonchalantly allowed our boats to be dragged along in the barge's wake right past the office of a high Navy official. We received an order not to repeat that performance.

U.S. COAST GUARD ACADEMY

My brother was still on the *Tahoma* in the North Atlantic when he also applied for admission to the U.S.C.G. Academy. We both were ordered to report to New London for the October 1943 class. Rooms were assigned alphabetically, four to a room: C. du Moulin, E. du Moulin, J. Dunn (Kentucky), and H. Earle (Rhode Island). Jack Kramer, the number-one ranked tennis player, was across the hall and a Paul Donnelly in the next room. For the first

Ed at the helm teaching Coast Guard SPARs (women recuits) how to row a pulling boat.

month we were not permitted to leave the grounds or receive visitors. At night, we stood outdoor security watches. It was a very cold winter, and we knew firsthand. Arnold Green had joined the Coast Guard and had preceded us to the Academy, where he had been a top student. Upon graduation, he was asked to remain as an instructor in navigation and seamanship. Arnold and Muriel therefore lived in New London. When we would pass him by, we had to salute but were permitted no conversation with a senior officer. When we got our first liberty, we rushed over to Arnold's tiny apartment where Babe smoked a cigar and, of course, I had the pleasure of Eleanor's company. We ate like kings.

One Saturday, our class was to attend a concert at nearby Connecticut College. We marched into their auditorium to the music of a string quartet. After a while, Babe disappeared with a couple of his buddies. Not too long after that, in the middle of the recital, from high above the stage, snow began falling. I had a funny feeling that Babe and his pals were creating this blizzard of falling bits of paper. It was as I thought. Luckily, they escaped discovery but there was quite a bit of muffled laughter. I never went to another string quartet recital.

After the first month in New London, we had to choose whether we wanted to be deck or engineering officers. It was no surprise when

The New Zealanders had arranged to adopt every one of the 1000 orphans.

brother Babe chose engineering. It disturbed me as we would no longer room together nor would I be able to help him. As it was, my roommates and I helped Kramer. Babe struggled with the electricity course. He was well liked, even admired, by his instructors who gave him several chances to pass. After lights were out, he would spend hours in the bathroom cramming.

Babe Goes AWOL

A questionable policy at the Academy was that if you were dropped (bilged), you would temporarily be assigned to do menial maintenance work on the Academy grounds. Babe, a machinist's mate with impressive wartime experience, told me that he would go AWOL (away without official leave) if that happened to him. It happened, and he went AWOL. Weeks later he was apprehended and placed in the brig (military jail) in Manhattan. I was allowed to visit him. He was in real trouble, which got worse when a petty officer ordered him to do cleanup work outside his cell. There was an argument and Babe hit him.

Captain O'Connor, who was in charge of the Engineering Department at the Academy, had Babe brought before him. The captain was impressed with his wartime service and the effort Babe had made at the Academy, and agreed that his treatment by the Academy was inappropriate. Babe was asked what assignment he might like. The answer was "To get back to sea." The Captain invited him to go to New Jersey. Babe rode in the front seat with the driver. Completing construction was the *General Randall*, a 27,000-ton, fast troop transport, fully Coast Guard manned. He offered Babe an immediate berth on board which Babe readily accepted.

Babe served on the *Randall* in the Pacific from early February 1944 until the end of the war. While punching a bag on deck, Lt. Commander Wood noticed that Babe's sweatshirt said "Rockaway." Wood asked his name and where he lived. Commander Wood's home was on our street in Belle Harbor. Babe said that he had known that but had no intention of introducing himself. He was complimented on the fine condition of his engine room.

I graduated from the Academy as an ensign on February 23, 1944. I decided that before I gave an order to any enlisted man, I would think how my brother would react. It made life much easier for me.

THE *GENERAL RANDALL*

The *General Randall* operated without escort in the Pacific where she carried 5,000 marines and/or soldiers from one battle area to another. On a voyage in 1944 they were docked in Bombay, India. While there, brother Babe bartered some of the ship's bedsheets to buy gifts for the family. Another time, a number of nurses and medical people climbed aboard. On October 7, 1944, the English delivered over 1,000 young Polish boys and girls, accompanied by a priest and several nuns, to the ship.

These children were mostly Catholic refugee orphans who had traveled overland from Poland to Bombay to escape the war. Some died en route, while others died on board the *Randall* and were buried at sea. Each Sunday, Mass was held on the afterdeck. Also on board were hundreds of New Zealand soldiers, many wounded, who were being returned to their native New Zealand from the European front. Some were Maoris who were particularly helpful with the children. Everyone entertained the children. All kinds of toys, bracelets, and other gifts were made by the crew for their young friends.

GENERAL RANDALL *(above), the ship that delivered 1000 Polish orphans to New Zealand (below).*

On October 27th, the *Randall* spent a day in Melbourne, Australia, before arriving in Wellington, New Zealand, four days later, where the prime minister greeted and thanked all hands for their humanitarian efforts. The New Zealanders had arranged to adopt every one of the 1000 orphans upon arrival, a wonderful humanitarian act. In 1987 when Eleanor and I were in Australia for the America's Cup, we spoke to many of the Kiwis who knew some of these orphans, now adult New Zealand citizens. New Zealand should be proud of the role they played in 1944.

One of the 1000 orphans boarding
the GENERAL RANDALL.

BABE AND HIS TOOLS

I returned home from the war before my brother. One day, Mom, Eleanor and I were sitting on the porch in Belle Harbor when an American Express truck pulled up. Two men struggled with Babe's GI mattress and deposited it in the basement. Weeks later, when he arrived home, we asked what was in it. He said he had patiently sewn as many of his machinist tools from the *Randall* as he could into the mattress. I trust that the Statute of Limitations will protect him if this story leaks out.

PAUL DONNELLY'S WAR

Back to the U.S.C.G. Academy. I became friendly with classmate Paul Donnelly, who also was a chief bosun's mate with an unusual number of wartime ribbons. He had been a regular Coast Guardsman before the war. Before Pearl Harbor, in return for British bases in the Caribbean to help us protect the Panama Canal, President Roosevelt had given 50 World War I destroyers – the famous "Four Stackers" – to England to help combat the U-boats. Our Navy retained several of them; they were converted into fast APDs, troop transports. The four midship torpedo tubes were replaced by four small landing craft. Each "tin can" (destroyer) was assigned 150 Marines. The landing boat group was commanded by an experienced Coast Guard chief bosun's mate. Paul reported on board the APD-3 *Gregory* which was part of Transport Division 4, which included a sister ship, the *Little*. Paul landed their 150 Marines on Guadalcanal with the first assault wave.

Around 0100 on September 5th, the two APDs went after what they thought was a Japanese sub shelling the shore. A Navy Catalina dropped flares that unfortunately illuminated the APDs. Instead of a sub, the shelling was from three modern Japanese destroyers and a cruiser. In short time the lightly armed *Little* and *Gregory* were sunk. Then the Japanese fired on the sailors in the water. Some swam to nearby Guadalcanal. Paul's skipper was wounded and drowned. Paul was rescued by a Navy ship heading for Hawaii. Weeks later he was landed, unhurt, in Honolulu. Meanwhile, he had been reported as "missing in action." Unfortunately, the censors failed to remove the identification number on the bow of the sunken *Gregory*. A photo appeared in a Philadelphia newspaper showing the bow protruding above the surface with its number clearly visible. Paul's family, not having been notified of his rescue, assumed he was dead. For years after the war we kept in touch with each other. He worked for Scott Paper.

MORE OF THE U.S.C.G. ACADEMY

At the Academy, by the time December came around, I had been landlocked for three months. In late December, my friend Paul Donnelly and I were assigned to an 83-footer along with 15 other cadets and a senior officer for a shakedown cruise. We were to spend several days and nights sailing around Montauk Point. As luck would have it, the weather was beastly. The forward hatch came loose and I went forward to secure it. I clearly remember freezing cold, very rough seas, solid water coming aboard. Miserable conditions. The senior officer and crew were seasick, most to the point of uselessness. It was Paul and I who spent most of the time on the flying bridge keeping the boat afloat. At one point, I threw up without any after effects – one of three times in my life. We managed to finish the shakedown, happy to return to base.

THE *INGHAM*

The top ten percent of the graduating class was assigned to the crack 327-foot cutters, the Coast Guard flagships. I was fortunate to be assigned to the *Ingham*, which was in the Brooklyn Navy Yard getting new armament. I reported on board March 14, 1944, and was assigned my cabin. The skipper was Captain Craig and his executive officer, who ran the day-to-day operations of the ship, was Lt. Commander Medd, a "mustang" (promoted up through the ranks) who had been in the old Lighthouse Service (taken over by the Coast Guard). One Sunday morning I was duty officer, stationed at the gangway, when Mr. Medd came aboard with a hangover. I greeted him properly, whereupon he curtly asked me to correct the Union Jack flying from the bow. I did not see anything wrong with it. In a nasty tone, he ordered me to the wardroom to look up flag etiquette in the Navy Regs. I said that I could not leave my post without being relieved. He ordered me below anyway. To my dismay, I learned that the Jack was upside down. The stars had to stand on their two feet, not on only one foot. I was soon to learn that Mr. Medd hated, on principle, reservists like me even more than full-time Academy officers.

President Roosevelt had given 50 World War I destroyers to England to help combat the U-Boats.

Another, the Campbell, rammed a U-boat followed by hand-to-hand combat

There were seven 327-foot class U.S.C.G. cutters, each named after a Secretary of the Treasury. They were about the length of a destroyer, but beamier (41 feet), far more seaworthy, slower (maximum 19 knots), and carried about 236 men. They were ideal for convoy duty and usually carried the convoy commodore who would be responsible for the convoy. The 327s were highly successful in their efforts against the U-boat, as well as in wartime sea rescues. One of the class, the *Alexander Hamilton*, was torpedoed off Iceland in January, 1942, and sunk. Another, the *Campbell*, rammed a U-boat followed by hand-to-hand combat until the U-boat slipped away from the Campbell's bow and sank.

Mr. LORAN

Before the *Ingham* was ready to go back to sea, I was sent to New Orleans to attend a "secret" school. There I became familiar with the long range navigation system, LORAN. After 10 days, I returned to the ship. Several days later, after another family goodbye, the *Ingham* departed New York with a retired submariner, Navy Captain Headden, as convoy commodore. Many years later in March 2004, I received a phone call from Jim Mertz, age 92, who commanded a destroyer escort (DE) in our convoys, asking the name of the commodore, and I was glad to provide the information. Jim passed away recently, having raced in more Bermuda Races than any person in history. Richard, who stayed at the Mertz' house during junior sailing days, was one of the eulogists at Jim's memorial service. Richard and his friend John Browning are hoping to challenge Jim's record. Later this year (2006), Richard will sail his 19th Bermuda Race, while John does his 20th.

Back aboard *Ingham*, the commodore's staff of seven Navy personnel crowded our bridge. We picked up our convoy in Norfolk with about 10 Navy and Coast Guard destroyer escorts. The 100-ship convoy would sail in a straight line at 10 knots, the speed of our slowest vessels, like the LSTs (Landing Ship Tanks). Surrounding the convoy were the escorts which would be on constantly zigzag courses. The *Ingham* led and every vessel maintained radio silence to avoid detection by the U-boats. Each of the convoyed ships had a small stern light on which the following vessel could concentrate and steer its course. The *Ingham* was the only ship with radar. During times of poor visibility, we would communicate by

TBS (transatlantic bullshit) which was a very short range radio. When the visibility permitted, Morse code messages were transmitted through blinking our l2-inch (diameter) searchlights.

In navigating, we had a template scaled to conform to our charts, which represented a single phantom "ship" equal to the convoy's width and length. Excluding the escorts, the convoy was probably about 2 miles long and 1 mile wide. As we passed through the Straits of Gibraltar, and along the African coast, we would navigate the convoy to clear land or other obstacles, with enough room to allow the escorts to operate safely around the perimeter.

The *Ingham* had a fully equipped sickbay with a ship's doctor and trained medics. Nearby and aft of the bridge were the Navigation Room and the

Photographed from an accompanying vessel, the 327-foot INGHAM, *in big seas during a North Atlantic convoy.*

*M*edd came to his cabin, grabbed him by the leg, and yanked him out of bed.

Combat Information Center (CIC), commonly referred to as "Christ I'm Confused."

For the first several days after departing Norfolk the weather was bad and no one could use a sextant to obtain their exact position. Normally, at noon each escort vessel would get its own position. Our navigator was Commander Del Wood from New Orleans. With our "secret" LORAN, each day he would TBS our noon position to the convoy signing the message "Loran." When we docked in Bizerte, North Africa, a group of navigators from other escorts came aboard *Ingham* to congratulate our navigator, Mr. Loran, for his accurate position after so many days of poor visibility. They had never heard of LORAN.

As we passed Bermuda, with clearing weather, a plane was sighted towing a target. This called for General Quarters and firing at the sleeve. In a GQ call, I became battery officer of the most forward gun – a 3-inch 50-caliber. The drill went smoothly thanks to my training in Shell Beach, Louisiana.

CAPTAIN BLIGH

The Executive Officer, Lt. Commander Medd, was a Captain Bligh, a very big, ruddy-faced bull. About the second day out, he ordered me to his office. He promptly locked the door and proceeded to yell at me, blasting reservists and threatening to beat me up. I was stunned. He had no specific complaint, would not allow me to talk and gave me a warning to stay out of his way. This was something that should have been reported to the captain, but no way could I do this without witnesses. I would just have to watch my step.

Besides my other duties, I was a junior watch officer, a job I loved. My station was on the wing of the bridge, be on lookout, and take turns conning the ship. My senior watch captain was Lieutenant John "Muddy" Waters, a regular (not reservist) graduate of the U.S.C.G. Academy, and veteran of two years on the *Ingham* serving in the North Atlantic. He participated in many rescues and the sinking of U-626.

He was upset one day because Medd came to his cabin, grabbing him by the leg, yanking him out of his bunk. In strong terms Lt. Waters advised Medd that it was a violation to lay a hand on a commissioned officer and told him if it happened again he would haul him before Captain Craig. Now I had a friend, which made me feel much safer. Medd had appointed the engineering officer, another old mustang, to be in charge of the wardroom. He would collect money from the officers toward the purchase of our food. We believed they cut our food supply and split the balance. We were kept on an unsatisfactory diet.

One night, after coming off an especially tiring night watch, still in my uniform, I entered the wardroom. Lt. Waters entered in his bathrobe to get some coffee. Medd came in and yelled at him for being out of uniform and accused him of something (I cannot remember what). Without thinking, I said it was not so. With that, the bull turned on me and said, "Are you calling me a liar?" I replied, "No sir, I'm just relating what really happened." Then he yelled and said he was relieving me of duty on the bridge and assigned me to the communications office.

I disliked working codes in the small communications office with its cipher machines, a chair on rollers, and no portholes. For ten days I rolled around and was miserable. Why, I do not know, but I was then ordered back to the bridge.

CHIEF SIGNALMAN

Chief Signalman Weiss came from Broad Channel, across from my home in the Rockaways, where his family operated a popular restaurant, Weiss', where I took my family for many years after the war. I never ceased to be in awe of his ability to communicate with other ships in Morse code via the searchlight. At nights while on the wing of the bridge, I would tap out love messages in Morse code to Eleanor. Of course with the light off. Some nights were beautiful with the moon illuminating the convoy and a million stars overhead. Eleanor had supplied me with a jar of hard candy sour balls. When I went on watch I would bring eight with me. Each half hour I would suck one slowly. It seemed to shorten the watch.

I also owed many thanks to Chief Weiss who arranged with the cook to place a cinnamon bun for me behind the bridge early each morning. I would walk behind the bridge, "checking the convoy behind me," and quickly pick up the bun, practically swallowing it whole before returning to my bridge wing.

Since we were the flagship of the convoy, we had been issued one of the newly invented British radars. We were able to view the convoy and escorts on the screen, and easily see our position as we zigzagged in front of the convoy. About 0200 one morning, Captain Headden, the convoy commodore, sneaked up and shut the radar off. It took me by surprise. I had to immediately react and continue the zigzag pattern without the radar's assistance, which was not that easy. The commodore's favorite expression when reprimanding someone was "Get your finger out of your asshole and your mind out of neutral." That expression came in handy many years later in sailboat racing.

The Number 2 gun above me was a big old 5-inch, 50-caliber. That gun's veteran crew had shaved their heads, except for an alphabetical clump of hair, leaving each man's head marked with a letter, adding up to V-I-C-T-O-R-Y. Chief Trei's total head-shave permitted him to be the period.

We had a number of calls to general quarters; all were submarine alarms (versus air or surface attack). Off Gibraltar, we listened to Nazi radio-personality "German Sally" report our convoy's passage into the Mediterranean Sea. She identified the *Ingham* as a large cruiser. Off Gibraltar we received fuel from a Navy tanker, transferred an officer by breeches buoy, and exchanged a load of mail. Running along the African Coast, our gun crews were ordered to sleep by their guns. The enlisted men carried their mattresses on deck. I did not have one as I had the comfort of a bunk. Thinking of my brother, I would buy chocolate bars in the ship's store for the crew to munch while on deck. In turn, there always was a GI mattress for me. German planes would fly low out of Africa, while others would come from behind the Balearic Islands.

Ed's gun crew at work on board the cutter INGHAM.

Barrage balloons would be flown from the decks of the convoy ships, while the escorts would put out smoke screens. The balloons and their cables would keep planes from coming in low but they would also protrude above the smoke screen so the planes knew exactly where the ships were. We suffered no damage from either planes or subs.

At dockside in Bizerte, North Africa, our Athletic Officer Bill Bryan arranged ball games. We picked up souvenirs of the German retreat, mostly from shattered tanks and planes as well as other remnants, such as helmets, of Rommel's forces. John Waters and I took our crews to the beach on the Mediterranean, where we all got sunburns, particularly on the tops of our feet. The temperature was about 112 degrees F. The open markets laid their wares out in the hot sun on wooden tables. The meats and vegetables were surrounded by hordes of flies, quite unappetizing.

Gibraltar – D-Day

Every day while on the *Ingham*, I wrote a letter to Eleanor and, almost as frequently, to Mom and Sam. The officers had to pitch in and censor each others' letters and those of the crew. The *Ingham* was passing Gibraltar when we received word that the Normandy Invasion was underway (June 5, 1944). I wrote a V-mail (Victory letter) to Eleanor to be sure she paid my Prudential insurance policy. I was trying to tell her I was not involved with the invasion. Eleanor and Mom were puzzled as I had no such policy. It finally dawned on them I was passing the Rock, Prudential's famous logo.

On the return trip we escorted some ships as far as Gibraltar. At that time in the Med, there would be a destroyer stationed about 20 miles ahead of the convoys as protection against unmanned glider bombs. We docked in Gibraltar harbor. The British battleship *Warspite* was there, her decks penetrated by one such missile. We were all glad to turn in early. I was sound asleep when an explosion awakened me. I grabbed my life jacket and bolted up the ladder. No General Quarters had sounded. A bunch of us gathered on the quarterdeck. Since Gibraltar was adjacent to Spain, the English were concerned about underwater saboteurs swimming across and attaching explosives to the hulls of ships in the harbor. Nobody had told us that patrols would periodically drop 25-pound depth charges to deter such divers. In my bunk, my head was a few inches from the steel sides of the ship so the sound of an explosion had been greatly magnified. The following day, the crew was given limited liberty to visit the wonders of Gibraltar. The trip home was uneventful. It was a great feeling to pass the Statue of Liberty and return to the Brooklyn Navy Yard.

Ingham and Arnold

During nights in the Navy Yard, when we were in our bunks, workmen would put asbestos blankets over us as they worked on our overhead, installing new electric lines and equipment – not the most restful night's sleep. We were at the shipyard for close to two weeks. I had invited Arnold Green to visit me and see a real ship. He was teaching lifeboat handling to the merchant sailors at Hoffman Island just outside New York Harbor. I was very disappointed when he didn't show up. The evening before we were to shove off, a cab arrived. Out came Arnold with a full seabag. What a bit of luck! He had been assigned to the *Ingham*. He and I had a long talk in my cabin. I filled him in on the problems I was having with the executive officer, and suggested he make sure that Mr. Medd didn't learn that we were close friends.

Meanwhile, Captain Craig did learn about some of Executive Officer Medd's actions. He invited Mr. Medd, Lt. John Waters, and a few of us junior officers to his cabin. We all had a chance to talk, with Lt. Waters taking the lead. The exec didn't take it too graciously. Captain Craig said we were fighting a war and just had to get along. We reluctantly shook hands at the Captain's urging. Several days before we departed, Captain Craig was replaced by Captain Zittel. We were stunned. I am sure Zittel was filled in by Craig. After I left the ship, one of my old shipmates wrote that Executive Officer Medd had been placed on an island in the Pacific. They finally had caught up with him.

Arnold became Assistant Navigator. Early each morning he would appear on the bridge with his sextant to determine the ship's position. I would do the same. Arnold would finish his calculations much sooner than I did. I had to follow my written notes. Arnold did not. I asked him how he arrived at our position so fast. He asked if I used the Red Azimuth tables. Of course I did. "That explains it," said Arnold. "I use the *Green* Azimuth Tables." He then showed me a notebook with that title. He had developed short cuts and modestly gave his name to the system.

New Orleans Interlude

My assignment during General Quarters was Battery Officer of the Number One gun. My only experience was anti-submarine warfare that included knowledge of small arms, depth charges, and a 20mm gun. Off I went to New Orleans to attend Gunnery School at Shell Beach, Louisiana. Eleanor went with me to New Orleans. Another honeymoon. When we arrived, friends recommended we look for lodging along St. Charles Avenue on which old trolleys ran. We checked a few places before we came to a beautiful white house with black shutters. We rang the doorbell and a lady in a clean white outfit answered. It was a funeral parlor. However, she told us to try the Chez Alcyone, a few blocks away. She told us that they only take in officers, and diplomats from South America, and one must pass careful scrutiny.

From her description, we easily recognized the impressive mansion with large white columns and large porches on the first and second floors. We gingerly rang the bell. An elderly, white-haired black servant opened the impressive door. We explained our situation. He asked us in. A few moments later, a very tall and stately woman introduced herself as Miss Wiltz. We had a friendly conversation and passed her inspection. She told us they had one room, recently vacated by an officer and his wife. She took us upstairs into an immense, high ceilinged room. In the old fashioned but sparkling clean bathroom a cord had been hung upon which to dry laundry. Eleanor asked the name of the previous occupants. Miss Wiltz said it was a lovely couple, a Coast Guard lieutenant and his wife, named Green. We almost fell over. Eleanor had guessed it might be them, as she and Muriel both always hung a string to dry clothes. That sealed the bargain.

Dinners were excellent. The sterling silverware was beautiful and the antique furniture was in perfect shape. We were offered cocktails before dinner. After dinner, most of the guests would sit on the porch in wicker rockers. We learned that the Wiltz sisters were daughters of a former governor of Louisiana. They ran this exclusive boardinghouse to help pay the taxes. The butler was nearly a family member, with them since they were young. They wore long white organdy dresses. Eleanor and I easily made friends with the other guests.

Eleanor and I enjoyed Pat O'Brien's in the French Quarter, where they had a great colored piano player (maybe it was Fats Pichon). Several of us

An elderly, white-haired black servant opened the impressive door. We explained our situation. He asked us in.

were going to Pat's one evening. We asked the sisters if they would join us. Sheepishly, they said they had never been down there. We convinced them to join us. One of the guests, an officer of the Hibernia Bank, phoned to reserve a table for six in the corner by the piano. The Wiltz sisters were in their long white organdies and wore two very big white brimmed hats. This was going to be a first for them, and for Pat O'Brien's. We ordered beer and some food. As the evening progressed, the "girls" were beginning to feel no pain and their hats became askew. All of us were having a great time. A generous tip was placed in our entertainer's bowl. We had to support our two tall and tipsy special guests as we worked our way to the cab.

GUNNERY SCHOOL AND THE PIANO

I had to check in to the gunnery school by 0900. The school was situated on sand and in the blistering sun. I would return to the Chez about 1800 with my khakis drenched with sweat. Each day, upon my return, one of the sisters would unlock a ten-foot-tall mahogany door to her living room (off limits to the guests) and present me with a cocktail. The room was about 40 feet long and 20 feet wide. Against the rear wall was an old player piano. I was told it had been in disrepair for many years. There were many music rolls (like "Charlie My Boy"). I asked if she would like me to try to repair it. She readily agreed. After my daily cocktail, I would crawl around the piano. It took me a week to have it working again.

I asked Miss Wiltz if I could play it after dinner. That would be just fine. She said she would open two large windows by the porch so the guests in the rockers could enjoy the "concerts." I would play really old songs. The guests loved my recitals and would wave to me through the windows, and later compliment me. About a week before we had to depart, I decided to spring the surprise by letting them know it was a player piano and not me playing. That evening, I was doing my usual nodding to those who would wave to me from 40 feet away. This time, I waved back, first one hand, then both hands, pumping the pedals all the time. At that point, everyone was peering through the windows. They were hilarious. Out came the liquor. We all turned in later than usual. The evening before Eleanor and I left we were thrown a wonderful party on the upper porch, complete with silly games. It was a sad departure the following day, as Eleanor was to leave for

New York and I to my ship.

With our close friends Clara and Bert Papanek, Eleanor and I did return to revisit New Orleans after the war and stayed in the French Quarter. We had met the Papaneks before World War II through sailing. He was active in the U.S. Coast Guard and entered the service early. As a Lt. Commander he was appointed skipper of the Destroyer Escort *Key West*. He saw extensive service in the Pacific. After the war and his death in the 1980s, Eleanor and I accompanied Clara to Norfolk where a new nuclear submarine was to be named for Bert's ship *Key West*. It was a moving ceremony for us.

The Papaneks had two children, Maida and Paul, who keep in touch with Richard and Ann. Maida's son spent time in the Navy and then went to college. Maida and Bill Cantle developed a marketing service that periodically brings one or both to the East. Paul is a successful commercial photographer.

ARNOLD AND HIS FS

Arnold had left New Orleans for San Francisco to report to an FS, a 175-foot Army freight supply ship. He was to be the navigating officer. The FS did not even have a gyro-compass, just a regular magnetic compass. Lashed down on the large open foredeck were all kinds of Army vehicles that would be subjected to salt water spray. They ran into bad weather and the FS was taking solid water over the foredeck. In the middle of the night, one horn after another started honking. The loading crew had not disconnected the wires. It was too rough to go forward to try to disconnect them. Arnold wrote that if a Japanese submarine had surfaced, they would have thought they were in a traffic jam in Times Square. Until the war's end, these "Island Hoppers" moved supplies from one island to another.

PROPELLER DAMAGE

Back to the Brooklyn Navy Yard and the *Ingham*. We finally shoved off (another goodbye) heading for Norfolk to pick up a convoy. On entering Norfolk Harbor, we hit an obstruction, bending one of our two large propellers. We were quickly hauled while a truck sped down, with police escort, from Boston (*Ingham*'s home port) bringing a replacement prop. The convoy commodore was transferred to the Coast Guard destroyer escort *Holder*. She took our lead position at the head of the convoy and they left without us.

I decided to spring the surprise by letting them know it was a player piano, not me playing.

ARNOLD AND HIS LIFEBOAT

Several days later, we departed Norfolk. Sailing alone without a convoy, we were able to make 15 knots. Off Bermuda, we again had gunnery practice shooting at a sleeve being towed by a plane. The captain ordered the launching of one of the ship's lifeboats while underway. Arnold was assigned to be the officer to direct the exercise. I stood by to watch along with many of the crew. The long time veteran "Coastie" Chief Trei side-whispered to some of his cronies to watch this reservist dump the crew in the sea. He had no way of knowing that Mr. Green, the reservist, taught this procedure to the merchant mariners. The launching was flawless. They rowed off and safely returned to the ship. When the crew hit the deck, there were cheers.

EMPTY THROUGH THE MUZZLE

Daily, at 1300, there was a ship's muster. Each officer would account for the men in his division, after which those off duty would review procedures. In my case, it would be with my gun crew. I would ask questions. One that was raised each time was the procedure to follow in the event the gun was loaded when the ceasefire order was given. I would order that the barrel be elevated to a 45-degree angle, aim at a clear part of the horizon, and obtain permission from Gunnery Officer John Waters "to empty through the muzzle."

And the time finally came when, after firing the gun and reloading, we were indeed ordered to cease fire. The gunner's mate advised me that there was a shell in the barrel. With aplomb, I gave the order, "Empty through the muzzle!" Suddenly, the gun went off and I jumped, unready for a gun blast. Only then did I realize that "emptying through the muzzle" meant actually firing the damn gun. In the Charlie Chaplin film "Modern Times" there was a scene in World War I where "Big Bertha," a giant long range German gun, fired a shell that just dropped out of the muzzle to the ground. Stupidly, that is what I had pictured as "emptying through the muzzle." How did we ever win the war?

The *Ingham* kept in touch with the slower moving convoy. Once into the Mediterranean we were ordered to drop off film and other supplies at Oran, North Africa. Inside the harbor were a large number of damaged

French warships that had been destroyed by the British fleet after the fall of France to prevent Vichy France from giving them to the Germans. This aggressive and defiant decision by Churchill had a major impact on FDR's belief that the British would never surrender to Germany. The one night we were in port, there was liberty for some of the crew and officers. Word had passed around that there were many lonely U.S. Army nurses stationed there. Arnold and I volunteered to stand watch while other officers went ashore. Both of us were newlyweds.

CONVOY ATTACKED

We were underway early. At full speed, we were closing on our convoy. Suddenly, the convoy was under attack by German planes. The planes managed to severely damage the *Holder*. We could see some of the action from astern and listened to the radio transmissions. One-half of the stricken flagship was successfully towed to port. Later the surviving half of the *Holder* was patched up and an oceangoing tug managed to tow her back to the United States. Half of another damaged vessel was successfully attached to the *Holder* half in a Philadelphia shipyard and she rejoined the war effort. Meanwhile, the *Ingham* took her place at the head of the convoy. Fate had played her hand. If we had not damaged our prop, the *Ingham* would have been the victim.

UNEXPECTED PRANK

One beautiful Sunday, Arnold and I, along with other off-watch officers, were sunning ourselves on the quarterdeck. My khaki shirt and pants were next to me. General Quarters sounded – "All Hands to Your Battle Stations." I grabbed my pants but couldn't get my legs into them, or my arms into my shirt. They were tied in knots! On a run, in my underwear, wearing a life jacket, my uniform in hand, I ran forward to my gun. Clothing protected you from hot shells and flashbacks. That was one concern; the other was being caught out of uniform. After the gun was secured, I was called to the bridge to explain what my problem was. This was a prank (and a pretty stupid one) of Arnold's, but I said I didn't know who had "short-sheeted" me. It was a U-boat contact that had led to the General Quarters call.

Only then did I realize that "emptying through the muzzle" meant firing the damn gun.

Time Off In Connecticut

We had a nine-day vacation after I returned from overseas in 1944. I had read a glowing advertisement in The New York Times about a resort in Lakeville, Connecticut. Eleanor and I arrived in town by train. I was in uniform. A friendly taxi driver, on the way to the resort, gently said that we might not be too happy there, that he would wait while we checked it out. It turned out to be a shattering prospect with seedy grounds and cabins. I told the receptionist that some of the mud houses in North Africa were cleaner looking.

At that point our driver said he would try to get us into a wonderful place. He drove us to the Wake Robin Inn. While we waited, he spoke to the owner. A lovely woman asked us in. She said the only vacancy was a room exclusively reserved for a professor and his wife, but she thought they would not mind. It was perfect in every way. We recommended it to our close friends, and years later we also returned. Cousin Sam had once told me, in a small town, if you want a good restaurant or place to stay, **talk to a local taxi driver.**

Return To Bizerte – Carthage

Back on convoy duty, our destination was once again Bizerte, on the African coast. One day, Arnold and I managed to find a sailboat in Ferryville, a town east of Bizerte. We had a good time doing our favorite thing – sailing. Arnold announced that he and three other officers had arranged for a command car so they could drive to Tunis and then visit Carthage – part of the ancient Roman Empire. I was asked to join them. We left at 0300 the following morning. It was a five hour trip. We passed camels, dirt huts, and Arabs. I had told them to let me off in Tunis as I preferred to tour the city. They could pick me up around 1800. Truthfully, I wasn't anxious to chance a quick plane trip across to Italy just to see the ancient Roman Empire. As I stood in the town circle, they departed, presumably for the airport.

I remembered Cousin Sam's suggestion of checking with a local cab driver. I approached one who said I could get a wonderful view of the Mediterranean from high on a cliff at the Club Inter-Allie. First I would have to become a member. He drove me to an officers' information center where I received my membership card for $1.00 while the cab waited for me. After about a twenty-minute drive, he pulled up to a magnificent stone

Ed using local transportation while on leave after a convoy to Africa.

mansion. Far below, in bright sunshine, was a perfect blue Mediterranean Sea. I relaxed and had a wonderful meal that cost very little. I arranged for the cab to pick me up after lunch.

THE CASBAH

My next objective was to visit the native quarter, the casbah. I was driven to the entrance and found myself in a smelly, crowded world, on a narrow (maybe 9-foot wide) street with open sewerage running along the side. Dirty children really did try to sell me sexy cards and offered to introduce me to their "soeurs" (sisters). It was a bizarre bazaar. After an hour or so, I reversed my course. Happy was I to breath clean air. What I did not know, until later, was that our armed forces were forbidden to enter the casbah. That was not my only mistake of the day.

At about 1800, Arnold's command car pulled up and we drove back to our ship. My friends had had a great time in Carthage, viewing the ruins where the Christians were fed to the lions. Arnold took photographs. It wasn't until the next day that I found out that Carthage was not in Italy but only ten miles outside of Tunis. I should have studied more ancient history. When I saw the slides, I asked Arnold to give me a set so I could make believe I was there. Once home, I showed them to the family and, in explaining the scene, I said this is where the Christians ate the Jews. I couldn't figure out why the laughter until I was reminded it was the lions that ate the Christians. We also got many good photos of German prisoners under guard, wrecked planes, and our ship at the pier.

TRIP HOME

Among the ships we were escorting on our return to the States was the patched up half of the *Holder* under tow. Our captain sent a signal message saying that it was an unusual sight to see a Coast Guard vessel at the wrong end of a towline. After passing through the Straits of Gibraltar, en route back to the States, there was submarine activity. A few miles away there was a small aircraft carrier that was covering our convoy. They not only located the U-505 but they **CAPTURED** her. The Navy managed to get on board and prevent it from being scuttled. Today, the U-505 is a permanent exhibit at the Chicago Museum of Science.

Dirty children tried to sell me sexy cards and offered to introduce me to their sisters.

Transfer To Duluth

On July 13, 1944, while still in the Gibraltar area, Arnold and I received transfer orders. The two of us would have 10 days leave when we docked in New York. We were then to proceed to Duluth, Minnesota, to help commission 175-foot ice breaker/weather patrol ships, Arnold to the *Sundew* and I to the *Woodrush*, both under construction. Eleanor was still working; Muriel Green was not. Eleanor decided to remain in New York until I learned how long it would be before my CG-178 would be ready to go. The Greens and I left by train. In Duluth, we checked into a hotel. Muriel located a nice upstairs apartment owned by a Mrs. Harding. It was not too far from the shipyard. We learned that the *Sundew* would be commissioned before the *Woodrush*, the latter by early March 1945.

Eleanor agreed to join me in several weeks. While in Duluth, we met some wonderful folks, one an older lady who was a buyer for Oreck's, a fine Duluth department store. We kept in close touch with her until her death some years later. Another person arranged for us to use his private club. When Arnold was at the shipyard and during his trial run, Muriel and I would be together. Tongues were wagging. We spent a great deal of time playing cribbage. She played better than I did.

Arnold's *Sundew* left on a week's trial run. Muriel and I went to "our" club, movies, and dinner together. Soon after Arnold left on his ship, Muriel returned to New York and Eleanor arrived in Duluth, having resigned from Salomon Brothers. On November 17, 1944, I surprised her by getting on her train in Superior, Wisconsin. We embraced and together rode the ten miles to Duluth. Our reunion was another honeymoon. Eleanor quickly adjusted to the new life, as she did wherever we went, and to the bitter cold. Some were confused by my relationship with Muriel when after her departure, along came Eleanor.

We did some interesting sightseeing. We were impressed with the massive open ore mines in Hibbing, Minnesota, the home of Bob Dylan. The avenues were extremely wide and tree lined. The schools were new and first class. The town had been moved and rebuilt by U. S. Steel as the open pits were encroaching on the old town. I think of these safer, open pit mines every time there is a mine disaster where the miners have to work thousands of feet below the surface.

SUNDEW'S COMMISSIONING

The commissioning of *Sundew* had attracted many local politicians, crew families, and most of the Coast Guard personnel. On the foredeck was a long boom resting horizontally – it could lift 15 tons. When one of the civilians asked what was it for, Arnold coolly explained that if the ship grounded, the boom would pick the bow up. I was caught off guard as I had not thought of that idea. It took me a few seconds to realize that Arnold was spoofing his audience, of which I was one. A short while later, Arnold left on his ship, heading down Lake Superior for the Sault Ste. Marie Locks, 320 miles from Duluth, then past Chicago and down the Mississippi.

Winter was soon to be upon us, with Minnesota temperatures 25-30 degrees **below** freezing. Walking from the nearby Duluth Hotel one evening, Eleanor wound up with frostbitten legs. After that it was heavy stockings. We did manage to survive one outdoor night ice hockey game.

WOODRUSH – CLEVELAND FIRE

Before Eleanor arrived, I would spend weekdays at the shipyard watching the progress of the construction of *Woodrush*. On September 22, 1944, we had our sea trials. Our destination was Cleveland, Ohio. Everything ran smoothly and we looked forward to seeing the sights. As we secured our ship to the town dock on Lake Erie, we were greeted by a city official. He informed us that a large fire was raging, and that they needed all the fire fighting equipment and crew that we could spare. The captain set a watch and ordered the remaining 60 of us to get into our dungarees, and gather together our portable equipment. Trucks were on hand to take us to the scene. We were speeding down a main avenue, with a hook & ladder ahead of us, when a large hole opened up in the middle of the avenue, ensnaring the fire truck. We skirted it and continued on, the sky filled with heavy black smoke.

The charred ruins of the Cleveland gas fire of 1944 in which 125 lives were lost.

The fire was located by the lakefront along an avenue with a tall wire mesh fence. We saw completely burned cars and bodies along the road. Inside the fence were a series of large gas tanks, some of which were burning fiercely. We were directed to a tank that had not yet caught fire. Our job was to prevent it from catching fire. It looked like a battlefield – brick buildings had been turned to rubble. All around us were water-filled mud holes, the craters caused by the explosions, with burned bodies floating in some of them. A total of 125 lives were lost. The city supplied us with sandwiches and drinks, and the next day we were trucked back to our ship. The following morning we were thanked by city officials before steaming back to Duluth. That is all we saw of Cleveland.

DAMAGE CONTROL

I was appointed Damage Control Officer of the *Woodrush*. A team of seven enlisted men and I were ordered to the Damage Control School at Fort McHenry in Baltimore, Maryland, for four weeks training. What a learning experience that was! I got along very well with my crew, some with lots of sea duty. I will relate only three drills that I shall never forget. The first was to dive to the bottom of a circular vertical tank, maybe 30-feet deep, with portholes at different levels for others to view. As the officer-in-charge, I would be the first to perform the exercise. I was given the choice of either building a wooden box or assembling a set of pipes. In grammar school I was good at working with wood, so I chose the wooden box. With a breathing lung, a bag of wood, hammer and nails stuck in a tube around my wrist, down I went. There were the piercing eyes watching their fearless leader. Comfortably seating myself about 30 feet below the surface, I put the hammer on the bottom where it stood with the handle pointing upward. Next, I opened the bag. All the wood pieces quickly floated to the surface. A diver delivered a second bag to me. At that point, he did not have to remind me that wood floated. He did explain how to place the wood, one piece at a time, under the narrow steel shelving strengthening the tank walls. I would then nail one piece to another and rotate until the sides were finished. The bottom of the box was easy. Up I went with restored confidence. The crew that followed had no problem.

Next, we entered a large pool in which a 25-foot beautiful model of an army transport was floating. It had guns, superstructure, lifeboats (all removable) on deck. It had a large list to port, having been hit by a torpedo. We were to right the ship. No big deal. I instructed the crew to remove weight, including guns, from the low side. Slowly the ship righted herself. As we proudly climbed out of the pool, there was a large splash. Our transport had continued righting itself until it turned over on the other side. We had a fine view of her bottom, props, and rudder. Back into the pool we went with the instructor, who explained that we should have removed weight incrementally until it attained stability with no list.

We were then marched over to a section of a Liberty ship in which an oil fire was raging. I was to lead the men into the hold and extinguish the fire. The bulkhead temperature was, I believe, 1300 or more degrees F. We all put on oxygen masks. As the intrepid leader, I was given a long-armed spray nozzle. With the men holding on to each other behind me and in single file, I was instructed to move the spray from side to side as we filed into the inferno. In we went, with the spray actually keeping the flames from us. I felt woozy. Next thing I know I was dragged out into fresh air. When I moved the spray arm from side to side, I was squeezing the oxygen out of my pouch that was on my chest. The moment came when the oxygen was exhausted, and I had passed out.

By the time we left the Damage Control Center, we were quite confident that we would make a good damage control team. We had learned how to use damage control equipment such as air pressure rivet guns, how to shore up bulkheads and many other procedures that could save our ship and lives. The crew had a good time, partly at my expense.

ABOARD THE *WOODRUSH*

Back in Duluth aboard the *Woodrush*, I was experiencing some discomfort when climbing up the ladders from my cabin to the bridge. Eventually, Eleanor and I went to Chicago where I went through a hemorrhoid procedure. That had been my only real hospital experience in 90-plus years, until stricken with MDS in July of 2005. The Navy doctors did a reasonable job as I was never seriously bothered with that problem again. The Marine Hospital was in an awful part of town that made it unpleasant for Eleanor, so the experience was worse for her than for me.

By December, Duluth Harbor became frozen. We had the very best arctic gear, including facemasks, to keep us warm. All lake shipping had ended until the following spring. Our job was to keep the waters between Duluth and Superior open, a distance of about ten miles, until several Navy supply vessels were completed. There was a toll bridge over this waterway. To avoid the ten cent toll on the bridge, cars would drive back and forth between Duluth and Superior on the ice - a convenient short cut. They would have to be careful, however, not to fall into the area we had cleared. Some commuters ignored warnings and dropped through the ice.

Each morning at 0800 we would leave Duluth, slowly breaking the ice. We would usually stop midway and walk around our ship on the ice. The average thickness was 18 inches. Late in the afternoon we would break ice on our way back to our base. For weeks we made this daily round trip. The Navy ships (net tenders) were finally completed and commissioned, and ready for departure.

The Coast Guard icebreaker WOODRUSH.
Her crew helped fight the Cleveland fire.

MID-WINTER CONVOY

Around January 15, we opened the ice lane and led the two new vessels into the open water of Lake Superior. It was snowing and the visibility quite poor. We had 320 miles to go before arriving at the Sault Ste. Marie locks where the large Coast Guard ice breaker *Mackinaw* had been doing the same duty we performed – keeping a lane open for our Navy ships, which would then proceed past Chicago, down the Mississippi to New Orleans, and then on to the Pacific.

The Duluth papers were filled with the story of our mid-winter convoy, the very first mid-winter transit in the history of the Great Lakes. I doubt if it ever was repeated. The average temperature for our trip was 28 degrees below zero. We were chopping ice from the rigging, bulwarks, and deck all day long. Daily we would blowtorch the outlets for the fire hoses. We sure would have welcomed LORAN or GPS, and especially radar, as it was most difficult to see our little convoy through the snow.

*T*he **Ingham** *had a long history: launched in 1936, retired in 1986 after 50 years of amazing service.*

TRANSFER SOUTH

In March of 1945, with the worst of winter past, I received orders to proceed to Miami. Eleanor left for New York on March 20 and I arrived in Miami on March 27. Then I returned to New Orleans where, on May 9th, I attended Merchant Marine Communications School. Once again, I was to help commission a new ship, the U.S.C.G. manned supply ship *Codington*, AK-173. On June 9th, on board the *Codington*, I went from New Orleans to Beaumont, Texas, where I had a 10-day leave. Eleanor came down and we stayed at the Hotel Edson in a room overlooking the railroad tracks. During the night, freight trains would go past with over 100 cars. We counted. We were glad to get out of there, but it was sad to say goodbye once again to Eleanor.

The *Codington* was commissioned on July 23rd, a very hot day. We did look sharp in our white uniforms. We sailed to Gulfport, Mississippi, where we started to load her up. I was happy to once again have Chief Bosun's Mate Mike Peabody (remember teaching the SPARs to row?) also assigned to the ship. I was Damage Control Officer and he would be my right hand. We loaded all sorts of equipment, including many thousands of cases of beer in their small plastic bottles. It was many years after the war that small bottles of beer were finally put on the market. Under direction of Chief Peabody, the beer was carefully stowed behind wooden bulkheaded sections. A wooden door was the point of entry and I was the guardian of the keys. I wisely permitted Chief Peabody to quietly remove a few bottles each day for the comfort of the CPO's mess.

THE ATOMIC BOMBS

The atomic bombs were dropped on Nagasaki and Hiroshima, and a few days later on August 14, 1945, President Truman announced that Japan had surrendered. The next day *Codington* headed down the channel to begin her long journey to Cebu in the Philippines. You may recall earlier in this narrative when Harold Bache advised me to get into service early so as to be among the first out. Well, miracles of miracles, just before dropping our Gulfport river pilot, alongside came a Navy launch carrying a lieutenant from Philadelphia with orders to relieve me. I was ordered to report to New Orleans on August 23rd for discharge as I had sufficient points to qualify. My ship arrived in Cebu after I had returned to Bache & Co. on October 1.

I often wonder how much beer was left by that time.

As for the atomic bombs, as horrified as I was by their power, I still believe it was the right action taken by Truman. My brother, Arnold Green, and I would have been part of the Japanese invasion force. Untold hundreds of thousands of Americans (and certainly more Japanese) would have died. We were fully aware of how the Japanese ruthlessly fought to the bitter end on Okinawa, Iwo Jima, and other islands. Certainly, on their home ground they would have fought even harder, if that were possible.

THE *INGHAM*

Before returning to New Orleans and my discharge from the Coast Guard, let me relate the further saga of the *Ingham*. After I left her, she was converted to an AGC, a communication and command vessel. She carried Admiral Barbey and General Eichelberger on board, landed General Douglas MacArthur back on Corregidor ("I have returned"), and participated in a number of other landings. Had it occurred, she would have been in the thick of the invasion of Japan. The *Ingham* had a long history: launched in 1936, and retired September 1986, after 50 years of amazing service.

Today, she can be visited at the Patriot's Point Maritime Museum in Charleston, South Carolina. Arnold's and my uniforms are laid out on our bunks. She is manned with lifelike mannequins throughout the ship and a display of interesting memorabilia including one of her commissioning pennants (given to me by Chief Signalman Weiss). Captain John "Muddy" Waters was responsible for *Ingham*'s permanent place for future generations to view. Her 50-year record is unsurpassed in Naval or Coast Guard service in peacetime and wartime. After the war, and until "Muddy" Waters' death, we remained close friends. He was the author of several books: <u>Bloody Winter</u> and <u>Rescue at Sea</u>, both of which are excellent reading. Richard and young Ed du Moulin have visited the retired *Ingham*.

In June, 2006, nine weeks after Dad's passing, grandson Ed, as co-captain of the Georgetown University Sailing Team, helped his team win the Team Race Nationals in Charleston Harbor by winning the final race of the series, finishing under the bow of the Ingham. — **R. du M**.

Edward (sail number one) and Andrew Campbell crossing the finish line 1-2 in the final race of the Nationals. Chris Behm was the third skipper.

ELEANOR'S COUSIN NORMAN'S WAR

One more war story. Eleanor's first cousin Norman Hyams, who is still alive at the age of 96 [2007], lived an usual life. At 17, he joined the Marines and participated in the Nicaragua landing of 1927. He next joined the Merchant Marine during which time he spent many years traveling the world. Periodically, he would visit Eleanor's family, the Lewises. He was always sparkling clean and neat, and would lecture Eleanor and Dorothy about how they should behave, and warn them of everyday dangers. Then he would go off for another year or so on his own high-risk adventures!

When England went to war, he was disappointed that America remained neutral. Therefore he joined the Canadian Navy and saw heavy action in Europe on a destroyer that, after being damaged, returned to Canada. Shortly after Pearl Harbor, Norman left Canada, without checking out, thereby becoming a deserter from the Canadian Navy.

He immediately joined our Navy as a Gunner's Mate, and was assigned to the Liberty ship SS *Nathaniel Greene* in 1942. There were several convoys to Murmansk, Russia, in September of 1942 that were set upon by German U-boats and German planes flying out of Norway. Only 11 of convoy PQ-17's 35 ships arrived in port – 24 were sunk with very heavy loss of life. Equipment losses included 450 tanks, 300 crated airplanes, and 380 trucks. The next convoy, PQ-18, Norman's convoy, arrived in Murmansk on September 12, minus 13 ships and without Norman.

Norman and his crew manned the old 3-inch 50-caliber gun at the bow. Realizing how ineffective such a gun was against twin engine Heinkel dive bombers, Norman used dangerously short one second fuses and elevated the barrel vertically to meet the diving Heinkels. The strategy was successful, although also risky for the gun crew. Incredibly, Norman's gun crew shot down eight Heinkel bombers before the ship was heavily damaged and Norman injured. Norman's right arm was hit by shrapnel and nearly severed. He was placed on board a British destroyer and removed to a Scottish hospital where he had the first of many operations removing shrapnel (and parts of his turtleneck sweater) from his arm, and transplanting nerves. Later, Eleanor and I visited him at the Brooklyn Naval Hospital. In total, Norman was in and out of hospitals for 17 months. It was there the Canadian Navy caught up with him as a deserter, but charges

Ed and Eleanor, left, and Norman and Blanche Hyams with children Cathy du Moulin, and Carol and Paul Hyams, visiting the Statue of Liberty in the mid 1950s. Rich took the photograph.

were dropped and he was honorably discharged.

Norman received a Commendation letter from our Navy and the Order of Glory from the Russian government that included a lifetime pension and, should he move to Russia, a home. The *Nathaniel Greene*, though damaged, arrived safely in Murmansk. She was one of only nine merchant ships to receive the "Gallant Ship" award during World War II. The Murmansk toll included a number of Merchant Marine cadets. My late friend Victor Tyson, an 18-year-old Kings Point cadet, survived the sinking of his ship in the PQ-18 convoy. The film <u>Action in the North Atlantic</u> with Humphrey Bogart was the story of the *Nathaniel Greene*.

RUSSIA RENEGES

Each year, Norman visited the Russian Embassy to pick up his "lifetime" check. World War II was over, but the Cold War had begun, and Joseph Stalin was not too happy with America. In 1948, Norman went to the Russian Embassy for his pension check, only to be told that he no longer would receive it. I contacted the <u>New York World Telegram</u>, and a few days later a reporter visited Norman. The next day's headline was: "Reds Are Just Indian Givers. U.S Hero Finds Drinks on Joe Soon Evaporate." Only one good thing came out of it. Norman and his bride Blanche were on a long waiting list for an apartment in Stuyvesant Town. The real estate agent read the article, contacted Norman, and told him he would get his apartment immediately.

PART III

HOME FROM THE WAR

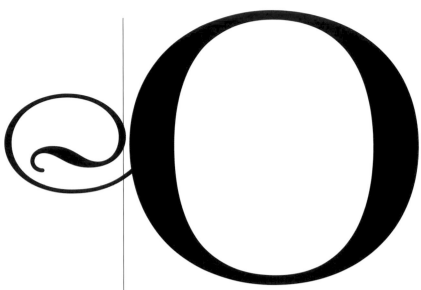

On August 23, 1945, having been relieved of duty on the *Codington*, I returned to New Orleans for my discharge. I went directly to Chez Alcyone where I received a warm welcome. I was given a parcel they were holding for me, which was kind of strange since I had been unlikely to ever return. What was in this package? When Eleanor and I were staying there, I had admired a certain dress of hers that she frankly didn't like. She had decided to leave it hanging in the closet, from where the Wiltz sisters retrieved it. I tucked the parcel in the bottom of my seabag. Chez Alcyone was my home for two weeks, during which time I had my physical exam. Finally, I received my discharge on September 6, to be effective October 18.

I departed the next day to a wonderful homecoming. When I unpacked my gear, I took Eleanor's discarded dress and hung it up with her other clothes. It wasn't discovered until several days later, reminiscent of the film, Gaslight.

The upstairs tenants my mother had in her home in Belle Harbor had moved out, so Eleanor and I moved in. We were extremely happy there, and this became our first family home. Eventually Richard, in 1946, and Cathy, in 1949, arrived and "moved in" with us.

Portrait of Eleanor with the old Dodge stick shift car that Ed taught her to drive, with difficulty.

ELEANOR AND OUR STANDARD SHIFT CAR

Shortly after the War, Mom overheard me offering to teach Eleanor how to drive a shift car. She suggested I not do so, but have her take lessons from a professional. However, by nature, I was a calm and patient person and I was deeply in love. Why should there be a problem? Mom said a husband should never try to teach his wife how to drive, particularly a shift car. Our house was halfway between Newport Avenue and Rockaway Beach Boulevard. Off we started in the old Dodge. Halfway to the corner, I was trying to explain how to push in the clutch, shift gear and gently release the clutch. The car was jerking my head off. I began to raise my voice. Suddenly in the middle of 139th Street, Eleanor jammed on the brake, opened the door and stepped out. Loud and clear, she said "---- you!" I was shocked, and surprised by her choice of words. Then, I remembered she had experience working on the Municipal Desk at Salomon Bros. A local bus driver was hired to teach Eleanor. Eleanor got her license. Mom had been right.

A Growing Family

Both Richard and Cathy were born in the Women's Hospital (St. Lukes) on 110th Street in Manhattan, a short distance from the unfinished Church of St. John the Divine where I often visited. For part of his childhood, Richard could not figure out why, as a male, he was born in a

Ed and Eleanor with their children Rich, and Cathy.

Eleanor and Richard (left), Babe's wife Edith (top), and Adele holding Edith's son Gary.

woman's hospital. He eventually figured it out by the time he went to college. For Richard's arrival in 1946, Eleanor and I were at the Park Theatre in Rockaway Park, with our WWII friend Tom O'Sullivan, when Eleanor said that we better get to the hospital. We abandoned the most popular war movie of the day, The Best Years of Our Lives, with Frederic March. Cathy's turn came while Eleanor and I were visiting Murmansk veteran Norman Hyams and his bride Blanche, who were living in Stuyvesant Town.

WINSTON CHURCHILL

To me, the greatest statesman of the twentieth century was Winston Churchill. When my son Richard was not yet two years old, I learned that the prime minister was coming to the United States and was to land at Floyd Bennett Field very early in the morning. Eleanor, with Richard in her arms, and I patiently waited along an empty Flatbush Avenue just after dawn. The "Big Man" had to pass our location en route to New York. Suddenly, along came an unescorted black limo. The car slowed down to a crawl as it passed us, the window opened, and there was Winston. We exchanged the "V" for victory sign. It was a real thrill, and Richard claims he can remember the big round face peering out of the car window.

MOM AT COLUMBIA PRESBYTERIAN

In the 1950s, Mom began to age. Living with her, we were too close to catch it early. However, our friends from New York who spent summers across the street urged us to have Mom checked by her local physician, Dr. Boggiano. He diagnosed the problem as nerves. But Mom, who had been driving since the 1920s, was driving down the middle of the avenue. Nor could she fix her hair properly. Given her unflappable disposition, none of us could believe it was nerves. We took her to Columbia Presbyterian Hospital where a famous brain surgeon, a Dr. Ransahoff, said it might be a blood clot on the brain, or perhaps cancer based on a prior stomach problem. While she was at Columbia for further examination, and I was at my office, I received an emergency call from Dr. Ransahoff who urged me to see him immediately. He said he was sure it was a blood clot and needed my signature in order to perform an emergency experimental operation. There was little time as Mom was rapidly weakening, so I agreed.

The morning after the operation, I visited Mom who was bandaged and quite sedated, but on the way to full recovery. I asked Dr.Ransahoff how he had determined that Mom had a blood clot. He said it was "baseball." Mom, being the astute baseball fan she was, had been asked by Dr. Ransahoff to tell him where the Dodgers stood in the National League at various points in the season. Mom's memory was accurate up to a certain date, whereupon she got confused. The doctor asked her for more details about what she did that day. She recalled that her upstairs tenant had been shopping, and had complained that there was something loose in the rear of her car. The doctor called the tenant, who said that Mom, while bent over to check the muffler, had hit her head and fallen. Mom never remembered that fall, but the Doctor guessed that is how the clot started. A brilliant surgeon and detective!

One month after her release Mom drove Richard to Boston to visit Edith and Babe du Moulin. She was also a regular at Ebbets Field to watch her beloved Dodgers.

The *Triton*

One day my mother read a small item in <u>The New York Times</u> stating that the famous Captain Edward Beach, skipper of the newest nuclear submarine U.S.S. *Triton*, just launched at New London, was seeking books for the sub's library. Mom gathered a carload of books from family and friends and shipped them to New London. She received a beautiful photo of the *Triton* commissioning, autographed to Adele du Moulin by the captain. In 1960, the *Triton* completed the first submerged circumnavigation of the world – a journey of 36,000 miles in 84 days. Upon her surfacing, Mom received a beautiful letter, posted from the vessel, in which the crew and captain thanked her for the many books she had sent. These memorabilia are with Richard.

BACHE & COMPANY

My career at Bache & Company started in 1933 and spanned a period of 42 years, including my years in the service. This was the only company I ever worked for, and I purposefully never worked for compensation after I retired in 1975.

POWER STRUGGLE

While I was in the Coast Guard and the war was nearing a close, Harold Bache's father, Jules S. Bache (JSB), passed away. The major part of the firm's capital was in JSB's estate. The Street guessed that another firm would take over Bache or JSB's son-in-law, Cliff Michel, would run the firm. However, everyone had underestimated Harold's determination to carry on. I was a witness to the power struggle that was taking place upon my return to the firm.

THE RYAN FAMILY

Our oldest commodity client was John Ryan & Sons. The Ryan family had left Ireland during the Irish Potato Famine and settled in Troy, New York, where we had one of our oldest offices. From scratch, the Ryans built a highly successful business dealing in burlap. Later they entered the cotton business, headquartered in North Carolina. Harold Bache invited the Ryan brothers to join Bache, whereupon they invested several million dollars to replace Jules' capital. Mr. Michel then left to become a partner in C.M. Loeb Rhoades & Co.

James Ryan, serious and money-oriented, became the protector of the Ryan capital. Amiable John Ryan spent most of his time running the John J. Ryan & Sons Carolina enterprise. The most interesting of the brothers was Frank, a world traveler who was handsome and had a great personality. He had been closely associated with Wild Bill Donovan, the director of our WWII Office of Strategic Services, the famous OSS, the highly secret spy organization founded by FDR in 1942. Frank was also friendly with Edward Stettinius, head of U.S. Steel and later Secretary of State. When the conflict was over, Frank Ryan and Stettinius formed the World Commerce Corporation (WCC). Through his wartime contacts with the Vatican and Spain (one of his duties was to keep Spain from entering the war on the German side) Frank negotiated large barters between Italy and Spain and other nations. WCC operated in the shadow of the Marshall Plan. I remember a great article in <u>Readers Digest</u> on the WCC.

When the Ryans joined Bache, they brought with them William J. Flynn who had grown up with the Ryan boys. Bill was a fine athlete who had sparred with heavyweight champion Gene Tunney, and later taught the Ryans boxing. Bill was the most handsome man I ever met. He was tall with broad shoulders and very narrow hips. Many of his Bache associates wondered if he wore a corset – much like wondering what the Scotsmen wear under their kilts. Once, at the Colony Club in Palm Beach, he was dining with the Hollywood stars Gary Cooper, Walter Pidgeon, and Buddy Rogers. Cholly Knickerbocker, a New York gossip columnist, described Bill as the best looking of the group. Bill would play an important part in my career at Bache.

JOSEPH KENNEDY

The final coup by Harold Bache was to receive, from former ambassador Joseph Kennedy, one million dollars.

The final coup by Harold Bache was to receive from former Ambassador Joseph Kennedy, father of the future president, a million dollars. Joe Kennedy thereby became a special partner. To protect his interest, Joe Kennedy introduced the firm to his financial advisor and close friend, James Fayne of Boston. Mr. Fayne also became a Bache partner. He was extremely intelligent and a true gentleman. Over the years, we became quite close. On one occasion, I was with him when Joe Kennedy called him, quite distraught. He couldn't get over the loss of his son who had been killed in a plane crash in England. I was impressed with the manner Jim Fayne consoled him. He also confided in me Jack Kennedy's plans to run for president.

With the Ryan and Kennedy major investments, Harold Bache was able to replace all of Jules Bache's capital and carry on the firm. It astounded the Street.

BACK TO WORK

After my discharge from the U.S. Coast Guard, my first meeting with Harold Bache was very productive. Being the first service man to return, I received a really warm welcome. I purposely wore my uniform. My salary was set at $75 per week. More important was my new assignment. Harold made two suggestions: (1) become part of the Operations Department, or (2) start up a new Investment Advisory Department. I quickly chose the latter. Why? Since the firm did not have such an operation, I could be judged more easily on the results of my efforts. I really didn't have much of an idea as to how such a department was to function.

My desk was located next to our large Research Department. I had easy access to their library and security analysts. I also purchased several books on investment supervision. My next step was to get introduced to several of the leading firms specializing in this phase of the investment business. After checking, I selected the firms of Lehman Brothers, Delafield & Delafield, and one of the large banks. They were very helpful and gave me the confidence to set up shop. I ordered good stationery embossed with Investment Advisory Department. This officially established me as the head of a Bache department. I quickly doubled the staff of the department by hiring a secretary.

WIRE HOUSE

Bache was a "wire house" – the second largest on the Street – with a large number of branches in the U.S., Canada, Mexico, and leading cities of Europe. At that time our salesmen were called "customers men." There were only a handful of women "customers men," but there were a few. Our customers were mostly traders/speculators. They were not interested in having their accounts supervised for which a fee would be charged. I found this out on my first field trip to Philadelphia to sell our advisory service through the sales force. After the market had closed, the manager arranged a meeting at which I distributed beautifully prepared pamphlets to the salesmen and gave a short talk. The first question was "Have you got any hot tips?"

THE 21 CLUB

My first accounts were those of a number of the firm's partners. One of our senior partners was a close friend of ex-marine Colonel Mac Kriendler, owner of the famous 21 Club. He made an appointment for me to meet Mr. Kriendler at the 21 Club to try to sell him our advisory service. I was invited to join him for lunch with "Prince" Mike Romanoff, a well-known bon-vivant. It really was not my element. After lunch, the prince departed. Colonel Kriendler gave me a copy of his security portfolio. It listed about 125 well-known companies. I asked him how he had come to invest in such a large, diversified list. He explained that he always purchased stock of his customers, most of whom were the chairmen or chief executive officers of our major companies. He agreed to subscribe to our service and looked forward to our report. Before leaving, he gave me a 21 Club tie.

On a later occasion, after I had become a general partner, I invited my partner John Huhn to join me for a drink at the 21 Club bar. After ordering our drinks, I gave the bartender a twenty-dollar bill. He promptly gave me change for a ten. You may remember that I always memorize the last three numerals, except for one-dollar bills. When I told the bartender that I had given him a twenty, his partner said no, it was only a ten-dollar bill. I stood on the brass foot bar, leaned over the counter and told him what the numbers were. He promptly gave me my correct change. I related the story to Colonel Kriendler's friend (the Bache partner) who passed it along. Later, I was told that Kriendler had gathered all the bartenders together and read them the riot act.

From left to right: Eleanor and Ed, Sam Lauterbach, Al Weisberg, Babe. Seated: Adele, Julia, and Edith.

ANALYSTS

One of my first innovations was to establish an Analysts List. Up until then, the firm would recommend stocks to buy, on a continuous basis, but rarely kept a record of when they were recommended or when they might be sold. I established a committee to supervise this list. I acted as chairman but the key person was the senior analyst. It required a great deal of diplomacy in dealing with the senior analyst. My concern as chairman was to be sure the process would be followed, rather than be involved in which securities they might recommend.

The outside firms I studied had investment advisory committees to periodically review the accounts that paid for the advisory service. The committee I established at Bache included the partner-in-charge of research, the senior analyst James Fayne, and the firm's economist. As chairman, I set the agenda, submitted the various portfolios for review, and conducted the meeting. The committee would set the basic investment policy of Bache. Since I never studied securities, nor was I particularly interested in doing so (this was the role of the others), my main interest was the coordination of the program. I was good at it. To minimize jealousies, the senior analyst's desk and mine were placed front to front. He was upset that I, as manager, a non-expert in securities, was in charge.

MUTUAL FUNDS

Mutual funds were first beginning to be recognized on Wall Street as a popular product for a growing investing public. A young ex-GI, George Meyer, had been hired under the G.I. Bill of Rights. I asked Mr. Bache to assign him to help develop a sales department for mutual funds. It was a satisfying feeling to see George develop as the years went by. My first step was to print a letterhead. Thus, I was in charge of the Investment Advisory Department, the Mutual Funds Department, and responsible for the coordination with the Research Department. George spent his full business life in mutual funds and became a leading figure in that field.

INSTITUTIONAL TRADING

My old friend Charlie Simon invited me over to his investment firm, Salomon Brothers, to show me how his Institutional Department operated. I was intrigued with their "block trading" section. They had a card file. On each card they would list large blocks of securities (stocks and bonds) that would likely interest certain buyers. They also had lists of issues which institutions or large investors might be interested in selling. When a large order to buy a certain security would come in, a trader would check the card file and call potential sellers. If a trade were made, it would mean large commissions from both the buyer and seller. I presented this idea to the Executive Committee at Bache. It was readily accepted. One of the old traders who knew how to close a trade was assigned to work with me. I worked out a few trades myself with the trader doing the actual transaction. Thus the Institutional Department was born. Later, Harry Jacobs, another WWII veteran and Dartmouth graduate with imagination and drive, took on this activity. He eventually became the President and Chief Executive Officer of Bache after it became a corporation. I felt good to have helped Harry get his start. The institutional activity eventually became a major division of the company. Although the Investment Advisory Department never became an important source of income, it sure opened the doors for me. Another letterhead for the newly formed Institutional Department – and I was coordinating (managing) four departments. Later, A. Glen Acheson, brother of our Secretary of State, took over the Institutional Department.

Ed chopping driftwood at Rockaway Beach in the late 1950s.

FLYNN & DU MOULIN

The Ryans wanted to give their friend William J. Flynn, who had been hired by Bache, greater responsibility. The firm approved Bill as head of the domestic Branch Division, consisting of over 60 branches in the United States, with about 900 sales personnel. It was the main source of the firm's income. Bill Flynn wanted an assistant – and what Bill wanted he got. The next thing I knew, Mr. Bache told me that I was to become Assistant to Mr. W. J. Flynn. I hadn't met him, but I did know who he was. This was a great opportunity. Bill and I developed a warm and trusting relationship throughout his association with Bache. We discussed things frankly. I was not a college graduate, which was fine with Bill. Among college graduates, he least liked Princeton grads. They didn't move fast enough, they smoked pipes, and were generally stuffy. We had a number of Princetonians who were branch managers. I must admit that their offices were not very successful, although they had good social graces.

As mentioned before, Bill Flynn was extremely athletic and handsome, and spent much time going out with well-known socialites. He was a member of the exclusive Meadow Club on Long Island where he would spend many weekends, leaving early on Fridays to beat the traffic. He and I spent a great deal of time traveling the branch system. I would cover for him when he would leave early for his weekends. One of us was always available for the not too infrequent emergencies.

*T**he new office had air conditioning and provided no facilities for pigeons.*

GREENSBORO

Bill Flynn would send me to a branch he thought we should close. That meant that I was to study the situation and report back to him. I would make appointments with town leaders to get their impression of what our problem might be and what they would recommend. An example was our old office in Greensboro, North Carolina. The manager had been there since before 1929. He became an alcoholic after the New York Stock Exchange seat he bought for $600,000 before the 1929 crash was later sold for under $100,000.

Our office was on the second floor overlooking the main street. Since there was no air conditioning, the large windows were always open. On the window ledges, pigeons would sit watching the traffic go by. Their rear ends hung inside the window ledges, over the floor that was, understandably, covered with pigeon excrement. This was fine for those who wanted the sidewalks clean but sure didn't enhance our office décor. Had the pigeons been interested in watching the market tape, the floor would have been clean at the expense of the passersby below. In contrast, the office of Merrill Lynch, our only competition, was clean and efficient looking.

My next step was to call on Neil Van Story, chairman of Wachovia Bank & Trust. He was very frank and helpful. Mr. Van Story admitted the office was a disgrace but like all the townsfolk, he knew and liked our manager, fully recognizing his problem. To demonstrate the problem, Mr. Van Story picked up the phone and called our manager to ask if Bache would advance him $900, as he was going away for the weekend. Our manager told him that he would first have to get an approval from our New York Credit Department. Mr. Van Story said never mind and then called Walter Ridenhour, manager of Merrill's office, who said the money would be over in ten minutes. That was an example of the difference in service. Mr. Van Story urged Bache to stay in town and offered to help find a good location at a reasonable rent and suggested that we "retire" our manager in a decent way. I then called on Mayor Ben Cone (Cone Mills) and he also urged us to stay. On my return to New York, Bill said go ahead. A year later we opened a modern office with a manager who was a lifelong friend of our old manager. The new office had air conditioning and provided no facilities for the pigeons. It turned out to be very successful.

A strange irony when, in 2004, the Wachovia organization took over Prudential Securities, the successors to Bache twenty-five years before. Mr. Van Story must be smiling from above.

BEVERLY HILLS

Our large Beverly Hills office was exciting but had to be supervised carefully. Many of the customers were famous Hollywood stars. On one visit, I noticed a familiar face sitting behind a desk in a small office. I was told he handled a large number of stars' accounts as an investment advisor, but not as a Bache employee. In the WWII movie *Mrs. Miniver*, he had played Greer Garson's son. On the side, this actor, Richard Ney, had designed a shirt with an ascot attached to the collar. He gave me one and asked if I would wear it flying back to New York. For a while it sold in some of the more fashionable stores in New York. Ney wrote several treatises on Wall Street that were not taken too kindly.

On a later trip, I had arranged to have a meeting of regional managers at Trader Vic's. I had eaten before in Trader Vic's tropical and dark atmosphere. About ten of us were there. With confidence, I suggested, as starters, we try the Bombay Special drink with hot hors d'oeuvres. The very sophisticated Chrysler office manager, a heavy smoker and hypochondriac, was seated next to me. The drinks were served. On the center of the table was placed a large metal platter filled with the hot hors d'oeuvres. There was a romantic glow with a wisp of smoke. I took a bamboo sliver in my hand, speared a hot hors d'oeuvre, blew out the flame, and ate it. My guests followed my example. A few moments later, the Polynesian waiter approached the table screaming "no eatee, no eatee – STERNO!" Those who hadn't swallowed the delicacy, immediately spit out what was in their mouths. Everyone laughed, except our Chrysler manager. He was visibly upset and immediately started to put a cigarette in his mouth. I wasn't looking for more trouble, so as he took out a match, I grabbed his arm and with authority said: "What are you trying to do, blow us up?" That night he had to call the hotel doctor as he was so upset. We had no ill effects, although for several days we imagined the ends of our noses had a glow, and we were reluctant to pass gas. So much for my sophistication – I never went to college!

COUSIN ELENA GOODALE

My mother had an ailing and elderly distant cousin, Elena Goodale, who for 40 years lived in a first class Beverly Hills hotel with a nurse. My grandfather Charles Isarr and the Goodales had been involved in the South America import markets. Each Christmas, Mom sent Elena a small gift and note. When my brother returned from the Pacific in 1945, he called her to see if he could drop in. She thanked him but said she didn't have visitors. When I was out there, I contacted her with the same results. We did send her flowers.

One day I received a phone call from our Beverly Hills manager. He read to me an article in the Los Angeles Times that told about the passing of Elena Goodale. Listed were a number of large charities to which she donated substantial sums, many dealing with animals. It also mentioned Mom, my sister, brother and me. Mom eventually received a large sum of cash, and the three of us each $25,000 – a lot of money then. Mom's only sister received a much smaller amount. She was upset, but the answer was that Aunt Lucille never had paid any attention to Cousin Elena.

Months later, we received about eight large barrels of the most beautiful silver, Venetian glass, fur coats, large sets of old imported dinner service, and beautiful jewelry. Mom gave much of it to her three children, sold a great deal, and gave the fur coats to friends (she would not wear fur). Years ago, we took a dinner plate to Tiffany's who said a single plate was worth $100. Elena is buried in a churchyard near 135th Street on Broadway in New York.

MATCHMAKER

I always have enjoyed trying to bring people together (a matchmaker) in one form or another. We had a very old office in Tulsa, Oklahoma, much like Greensboro. In the old-fashioned boardroom sat tape watchers, dressed in clothes as if they had just come in from the oil fields. As part of the modernization program, this office was near the top of the list. We wanted to broaden our customer base, develop more institutional contacts, and install new leadership.

One day I read in The Wall Street Journal that Henry Gray, with top New York investment banking firm Eastman Dillon, was to attend a formal banking affair and that he was engaged to marry Mildred Phillips, daughter

Ed ready to hit the road in the 1950 Chevrolet coupe he used on business trips for Bache.

of Frank Phillips, the founder and largest stockholder of the Phillips Oil Company. She was also running the Phillips Foundation. Phillips Oil's headquarters was in Bartlesville, Oklahoma, a relatively short distance from Tulsa. (In later years, Richard would frequently call on Phillips Oil to negotiate tanker charters.)

I arranged to attend the event and eventually located Mr. Gray. He was tall and handsome with a full head of carefully groomed gray hair. I introduced myself and asked him, quite directly, would he be interested in managing Bache's Tulsa office. He said that he might be. In a matter of days, he came to our office and I introduced him to Bill Flynn. He was soon in our employ and within a year was married, moved to Bartlesville, and became our manager. Our office was moved into modern quarters. For the opening, I went to Tulsa. Henry insisted I stay at their (Mildred's) fine old mansion. We had a delightful dinner, after which we all attended the dedication of a beautiful, new indoor stadium, a gift of the Phillips family. The highlight of the evening was a basketball game featuring the Phillips Oilers. We sat in the box of the Phillips' chairman. Although I had been familiar with the famous Olympic champs, until they trotted on to the court, I just didn't realize who the team was. The new Tulsa office became a prestigious and profitable one. Imagination and persistence really paid off.

PARTNERSHIP

In 1952, the firm planned to take in four new general partners from the ranks. I had no thoughts of a partnership, certainly not then. To my amazement, I was offered a general partnership. Later, I learned that Bill Flynn had told the Ryans that I deserved to be a partner along with the others. This was my reward for backing up Bill and doing things in his name, like sending flowers to branch staff on appropriate occasions, and covering his flank.

My knowledge of the inner workings of a partnership was quite limited. At the end of my first year as a partner, Mr. Bache told me that I was to be given a $20,000 bonus. Each year the managing partner was given a sum of money (the float) to be distributed by him to the various partners as he saw fit. I was in shock – it was a huge sum to me. We had moved during 1949 from Mom's house (it had become crowded with baby Cathy and toddler

Richard) to Mora Place in Woodmere. We had very little furniture.

Across the street lived Stanley and Rose Rich, who welcomed us to the neighborhood. They have been wonderful friends for over 56 years. Stan is a CPA and a financial advisor with an outstanding education (Yale & Harvard). He was a young naval officer interpreter in the South Pacific toward the end of WWII. He became my lifelong all-around, family and financial advisor – not only for me, but also for my children and many of my friends. After hearing the good news about my bonus, I rushed home to tell Eleanor and Stan. I excitedly told them, "Now we can buy all the furniture we need!" Stan commented, "Now you can't even buy Eleanor a brassiere!" Stan explained to me that bonuses from the float had to be left with the firm to help build its capital and, of course, mine too. That was the good news; the bad news was that we barely had the cash to pay the income tax on the bonus. For many years thereafter, I would ask Stan if I could buy Eleanor a brassiere "now."

MY FIRST BORROWING

When I became a partner, I had no capital of my own. Mr. Bache suggested I speak to a wealthy cousin of Eleanor's who was following my career. After discussing it with her, I met with her cousin Maurice. He asked how much I would like to borrow. Being a Depression kid, I asked if $25,000 was reasonable, figuring it would take all my life to pay him back. Without blinking, he wrote me out a check in that amount. I insisted on paying him interest. He said I could repay the loan any time. When I proudly advised Mr. Bache of the loan, he asked why I had not said $200,000? It did not take long before I was able to repay the $25,000 to Maurice.

Mr. Bache was at Cornell when he entered the Army in 1917. He never graduated but maintained close ties with the university. Around 1955, he recommended that I attend the six week Executive Development Program at Cornell. I hesitated, as I was very concerned that Bill Flynn would run into trouble in my absence. Harold Bache wanted Bill to go to our major Detroit branch that had a problem – the manager had locked himself in a hotel room for a week on a drinking spree. Bill had an important date and decided to forego the trip. I had urged Bill not to cross Harold and offered to go in his place. Bill said no, that I must go to Cornell so I would

Eleanor and Ed sailing the first Lady Del, *1954.*

not damage my relationship with Harold Bache. Bill also thought it was a wonderful opportunity, and I should not worry about him.

CORNELL

Eleanor, Richard at age nine, Cathy at age seven, and I drove to Ithaca. We rented a Cornell professor's home on North Sunset Drive. The class had about 45 executives from all over the United States and abroad, including some from the FBI, State Department, and firms like du Pont. The family had a great time swimming in Lake Cayuga and visiting the waterfalls. We also acquired a rabbit the kids named Crusader.

About ten days into the program, I received a call from Harold Bache. He had just fired Bill Flynn, who had not followed his instructions to take care of the manager on the drunken spree, and Mr. Bache announced that I was to run the branch system upon my return. Even though I had had a premonition that this could happen, it was a real shock. When I offered to quit the course and return to the office, Mr.Bache sharply rebuked me and said that I must see it through, that he would take over himself until I returned.

I found it very difficult to keep my mind on the curriculum. I kept in daily touch with Mr. Bache, outlining my plans and making long checklists. **I always keep checklists**. My first boss at Bache taught me to maintain checklists to avoid forgetting items and to keep my mind clear. I heartily recommended this to my grandchildren. Richard has always kept checklists throughout his successful shipping and sailing careers, and so does my grandson Chris.

The training I received at Cornell was invaluable, particularly in view of my new responsibilities. I learned about the difference between line and staff (more later), and the advantages of regionalization. On my return, my primary objective was to establish regional managers, each one of whom would be responsible for a group of branches. We departed Ithaca having had a wonderful and exciting summer. Crusader did not make it back with us; he "somehow" escaped from his outdoor cage the night before our departure.

EXECUTIVE COMMITTEE & BOARDS

Being in charge of the major source of the firm's income, I became a member of the Executive Committee and Board of Directors. My first Executive Committee meeting was quite an event. On the way to the meeting, to be on the safe side, I stopped by the partners' bathroom to which I had been given my own key. In closing my zipper, it broke. I stepped into my partner Bob Hall's empty office and called my secretary to bring me a stapler, pronto. When she arrived, I shocked her by quickly punching staples to hold my fly together. During the meeting, I kept one leg crossed over the other. Without realizing it, I was pulling on a loose thread on my sock. After the meeting had ended, and I started walking toward my office, one of the partners asked me if I always wore one sock. Sure enough it looked that way as the upper part had separated from the lower.

Meanwhile, I received a beautiful letter from Bill Flynn. He appreciated our relationship and wished me a bright future. We exchanged letters over the years until his death. I owed him a lot.

Ed speaking at a meeting of the Mt. St. Stephens Club in Montreal, 1961. Seated far right is Bache partner, John Roosevelt, FDR's son.

BRANCH VISITS

Before a branch visit, I would list the names of the employees along with personal information. It was important to spend a few moments with each individual. If I asked the manager how things were going, the usual answer would be all fine. That was plain b.s., as there were always problems with certain customers, the New York office, or something or someone. I would then ask the manager to review with me any open items with New York. Usually some had gone unresolved far too long, so I would bring them back with me and make certain they were cleaned up. Before leaving, I would bring the branch staff up-to-date on the firm's progress and answer questions. Then I would take the manager to lunch or dinner, and I would pick up the restaurant check. I quickly learned to have him tell me what tip I should leave. As a New Yorker, I would likely leave a tip larger than the manager would, which could be embarrassing to him. **When in Rome, first find out what the Romans do, then do it.**

I tried to limit my days on the road to ten days a month. After all,

Eleanor was raising our two children and I wanted to spend as much time with them as I could. I would plan to bring gifts to them on my return. I learned to inventory such gifts rather than depend on last minute airport shopping. On a trip to our St. Petersburg office, time was running out, so I asked the manager if she would send me two of the stuffed alligators you could find all over town. Several weeks later the package arrived. Eleanor was with Cathy. When they opened the package, two small live, snapping alligators scampered out. The girls jumped on the couch with lusty screams. One of the neighbors enticed the critters back into the box. Later, I built a pen for them which Eleanor insisted would have to be outside. They eventually succumbed to the winter cold. Eleanor, who was a lover of all animals, was much relieved but the children were saddened. We got them another live rabbit instead. Once again, he/she escaped from the pen I built. It took a while before I could live the alligator episode down.

The Cocktail & Dinner Circuit

After I became a partner, Eleanor and I found ourselves invited to many partners' cocktail parties or formal dinners in Manhattan. This meant traveling to the city and leaving Richard and Cathy with a sitter. As time passed, we had to reciprocate. Eleanor would hire someone to help serve, but she would do all the cooking. By that time, we had moved to a more formal home in nearby Hewlett Harbor, but within the same school district. Most of the city affairs lasted late into the evening. Though we met interesting people from all over the world, we really didn't enjoy this life.

Promotion Dilemma

About 1964, Mr. Bache called me to his office. He had been like a father to me for many years. Mr. Bache complimented me on the job I was doing, and then said he would like me to also be responsible for the Sales Division and the Fiduciary & Control Division in addition to my running the Branch Division. What a promotion this would be! I asked if he would give me a few days to think about it, to which he agreed. Here I must emphasize that he had a very bad habit that I describe as "bear hugging a person to his death." If he liked someone, he would give that person more and more responsibilities. The result, too often, was that the ambitious

Eleanor and Ed.

favorite would become impossibly overworked. In time, the "jackals" would get Mr. Bache's ear, resulting in the promising protégé winding up with a nervous breakdown, demoted or released. Fortunately, Eleanor, who knew the partnership intimately, had great common sense and understanding. I always consulted with her before making any important decision that would affect us both.

The following week, Harold and I met at 9:30 in the morning. I told him that I realized he had presented me with a wonderful opportunity. With my knowledge of "Line and Staff" garnered at Cornell, I then said I felt I could accept the challenge, if I were able to bring Wally Auch, the young, talented, successful branch manager of our Detroit office, to New York and have him run the Branch Division under my direction; retain Robert Hall, an Oxford scholar and ex-banker, to continue to run the Sales Division; and have Tom Lynch, who was a department head in the F&C Division, to head that division and report to me. Harold said, "No, I want YOU to run the three divisions!" I could feel the bear hug descending upon me.

I explained to Mr. Bache that at Cornell they emphasized the difference between line and staff. I was working around the clock to run the Branch Division of the firm, so how was it possible that I could take on two more divisions and RUN them too? Remembering that Mr. Bache was an Army captain overseas in 1917-18 and should understand my next bit of logic, I explained in World War II General Marshall was in overall charge of our armed forces. He had operated out of Washington, and under his command was General Eisenhower, responsible for the various army groups. Eisenhower did not run the divisions under him – he had General Patton, General Montgomery, and other generals run them, reporting to him. I suggested to Mr. Bache that he was asking me to be a General Eisenhower and, at the same time, be a General Patton and a General Montgomery. Mr. Bache replied that in the military, when a senior officer gives an order, it must be carried out, and he was commanding me to accept his orders. That was it. I told him that it was with great regret that I could not take advantage of his wonderful offer. Actually with tears in his eyes, he said how much he respected my decision. We shook hands.

Later that morning his senior partner, Charles Schwartz (more about him later), asked me to lunch, privately, at the Wall Street Club. I knew

Daughter Cathy steers the first Lady Del *with her dad (left).*

Cathy and Rich skiing with their father (top).

Ed and Eleanor at Lake Placid.

what was coming. He asked me to reconsider, that nobody rejects the managing partner (he used the word "ultimatum") and that he, Schwartz, was confident that I could handle the job. Doing otherwise would hurt my career. I explained my reasons for turning the job down, but to no avail.

Late that afternoon, I was called back to Mr. Bache's office. He was tense as he told me he was relieving me of my job as head of the Branch Division, that I would now be his assistant. Eleanor and I were in complete agreement that my decision was correct. **I would rather be a kingmaker than a dead king.** For five years I would serve my prison time. The irony of it was that Mr. Bache offered the job of running both the Branch AND the Sales Divisions to the young and ambitious Detroit manager who had absolutely no idea of the politics of the home office. Mr. Bache also promoted Tom Lynch to run the F&C Division. At least he confirmed my choices. However, I felt so strongly that this young manager from Detroit would eventually fail trying to run the two divisions, that I conveyed this to Mr. Bache who said he would invite the manager to his Park Avenue home where I could give him my thoughts after which he could accept or reject my ideas. We met for dinner, after which I recommended to my replacement that he should consider coming to New York and become the head of the Branch Division, that I would help him if he wanted. I strongly urged him to let Bob Hall continue to run the Sales Division where they could work together. Too ambitious, he said he could do both jobs. He accepted the "bear hug." Five years later, our young friend was burned out and departed for Francis I. du Pont, a major firm that eventually failed. Tom Lynch eventually left to join E. F. Hutton & Co.

At that time Harold asked me to again take over the Branch Division which I did, on the condition that I would not also be given the Sales Division.

Without Eleanor's full support I could not have survived those five long years in the deep freeze as Assistant to the Managing Partner. The other saving feature was that I raced my sailboat more aggressively, winning well over 100 trophies including the DeCoursey Fales Trophy for top boat on Long Island Sound. Many years later, when Richard was at Harvard Business School, I explained the above course of events. He said it had the makings of a Harvard Business School case study.

Rich steers the first Lady Del *while Ed holds Peter, Babe's son, 1954 (note the period life jacket).*

A. CHARLES SCHWARTZ

A. Charles Schwartz (ACS) was a commanding personality and a noted sportsman with friends worldwide. One of these was Bernard Gimbel (founder of Gimbel's). They would box together, and with former heavyweight champion Gene Tunney. ACS was close to the Duke and Duchess of Windsor and many top movie stars. In the 1920s, when he was a partner of the investment banking house, Eastman Dillon, he closed the deal that created Chrysler Motors for which he received a substantial finder's fee. That was the tie-in with Jules Bache who, you may recall, owned Maxwell Motors that merged with Dodge to become Chrysler. ACS later became a major partner of J.S. Bache & Co.

ACS loved sports of all kinds, including thoroughbred racing. Over his desk was a beautiful painting of his favorite horse, Blue Peter. In World War I, ACS had been an officer in the U.S. Army in France. Assigned to him was a young British orderly. In one of the trench warfare battles, ACS was wounded in the no man's land between the lines, and the orderly saved his life. After the conflict ended, ACS hired the orderly to run his household in New York. Several years later, ACS's horse, Blue Peter, was doing so well on American tracks that ACS decided to try his luck in the English Grand National, a very difficult event. ACS, the orderly, and many of ACS's friends headed to England to watch the race. ACS and many of his friends wanted to bet on Blue Peter, so ACS arranged for his orderly to place the bets. The orderly tried to convince ACS to bet less heavily but ACS would not hear of it. When Blue Peter won, ACS and his friends began the big celebration. The orderly asked to talk privately with ACS, informing him that he felt terribly ashamed and sorry, but to prevent ACS from losing so much money, he had never placed the bets. ACS laughed when he heard, paid all his friends their rightful winnings, and told the orderly not to worry, that he never would have left France alive if the orderly had not saved his life.

The story of Blue Peter did not end there. Many years later, the old orderly died, leaving ACS a life insurance policy that equaled the amount of money that Mr. Schwartz had laid out. ACS was extremely wealthy, and did not want the money, so he had his staff find the orderly's relatives in England and gave them the money. I first learned of this story when I read it in <u>Readers Digest</u>.

Sailing again (1950) after the war. Ed steers,
Tommy O'Sullivan enjoys the fast ride.

Ed, in the top hat he often wore to get the morning newspaper, posing with Cathy before she left for a dance.

WESTCHESTER SEMINAR

Bache hired the management consultant firm Cresap, McCormick & Paget to organize a five-day seminar for our senior management at the Westchester Country Club. One day, three of my partners were looking for a fourth to play a round of golf. Scraping the bottom of the barrel, they insisted I be the fourth. I explained that I had never played golf except as a young lad when I worked on a miniature golf course. I agreed to play, and did manage to hit long drives, but to left or right field. It was quite lonely following my ball as my three partners drove straight up the fairways. On the south course, the 18th hole was a dogleg, passing in front of a large cement-based veranda. They explained to me I needed to drive straight ahead to a point just past the veranda -- the hole would be to the right. I hit a long, high drive. The ball landed on the veranda, bounced at least 20 feet high, landing within a few inches of the hole. It was a hole in two. That was the last time I played golf. **Quit while you are ahead**.

At one of the sessions, we were asked to describe some of our management philosophies. I explained that I was challenged when I learned that someone in the branches had domestic, financial, or any other type of problems. They laughed. I explained that it gave me the opportunity to be helpful, and the end result would be a happier and more appreciative manager, salesperson, or clerk. Another philosophy was to learn both the strong and weak points of my associates.

I avoided upstaging the many service sections of the firm with which I had to work. I did not like it when a department head would simply tell me what they thought I would like to hear. I wanted to know the facts, and did not encourage "yes" men. I wanted to get both sides of a question. In running a meeting, I would make every effort to give each one attending the chance to express his/her opinion. As diplomatically as possible, I would keep the meeting moving along, avoiding long speeches and non-pertinent remarks. Where there might be strong differences of opinion, I would make every effort to bring the parties together. If a meeting was going on too long or too late, I might suggest we reconvene in the morning. Meanwhile, I would summarize the discussion and when we reconvened I would present solutions for agreement that were usually accepted.

The higher you rise, the more you are susceptible to criticism, jealousies, political backstabbing. After all, you are in an ivory tower. I always was quite alert to such actions, but did not let it distract me from my job. I was pretty critical of the ass-kissers. I was active in the Quarter Century Club (employees having served for 25 years), as that would bring me into close contact with all the different levels of employees.

As the years went by, I became Chairman of the Executive Committee and finally Vice-Chairman of the Board. I never aimed to become Managing Partner or Chief Executive Officer. To aspire to such roles you must be willing to give it your absolute all. My wife and our growing children were my prime concerns.

INCORPORATION

On February 1, 1965, the Bache partnership became a corporation and went public as a listed company on the New York Stock Exchange. Merrill Lynch had set the pace. It was a most difficult and intriguing challenge. The prime problem was that the partners with the most capital often had the key managerial responsibilities and higher salaries, even though they might be lacking in management skills. Their earnings were primarily based on their personal capital investments in the partnership. In the corporate world, executives would be rewarded on the basis of management skills and their results. At Bache, each partner would be given his proportionate share of the corporation's stock based on his capital interest in the partnership. In other words, money talked and management skill was secondary.

Having been chairman of the partnership's Compensation Committee, I was asked to serve as chairman of the corporation's Salary and Options Committee. The partners trusted me, although often we didn't agree on various matters. I had plenty of professional help in arriving at the appropriate salaries for our corporate executives. Nevertheless, so many senior partners were unhappy that right after the incorporation, under pressure from the malcontents, Mr. Bache unceremoniously had the Board of Directors remove me as Chairman of the Salary Committee. One year later, I was reappointed.

Even after the incorporation, for the years I was there, I felt Bache was still a partnership in corporate clothing.

*U*se "ultimatums"
only as a last
resort, and after
discussion with those
you trust.

SALARY COMMITTEE STANDOFF

A dramatic face-off occurred during a very difficult period on the Street when some of the large firms were going out of business. Many Bache employees had been released and salaries were shaved or frozen. The Salary Committee was meeting and I was once again the chairman. This committee consisted of the most senior members of the Executive Committee. I was surprised when members of the Salary Committee proposed that the Executive Committee receive raises. I strongly objected and said (another ultimatum) that I would resign as chairman if that action were approved. I firmly believed it would create havoc if word were to get out that we took care of ourselves while employees were being released and salaries reduced. I was over-ruled. I recommended that we all sleep on it and meet again in the morning, to which they agreed. That night I related the event to Eleanor and she approved my stand. I then called my wonderful friend and advisor, Stan Rich, who also said I was doing the right thing. Next morning, the committee unanimously decided not to approve the proposed raises.

I should inject here that my reason for bringing up some of my management experiences is not to boast but to present situations as episodes that might be valuable to my grandchildren and their children, or others coming up in the world. I do caution them about the use of ultimatums. Use them only as a last resort and after discussions with those you trust. **Keep cool.**

When reading this I had to laugh. I must have absorbed this technique from Dad, because it is the way I have tried to run meetings in business, sailing, and my charitable work. I work especially hard to encourage everyone to participate, and I often schedule large or important meetings to span two days so people can sleep on divisive or important issues, perhaps resolving them privately before the meeting reconvenes. – **R. du M**.

PRE-RETIREMENT

As one of the key inducements for the partners to approve incorporating the firm, a Former General Partners (FGP) Pension Plan was established. The purpose of this plan was to reward the partners for their years of service. The employees had a pension plan that was protected by the laws of the land. In the case of the FGP plan, if the company went out of business, so would that pension program. A partner could retire based on a formula that included years of service and age. On February 1, 1975, I was eligible to retire. I was sixty years old, and had 42 years of service (they counted the years of service in World War II). I knew that based on the formula, I would receive the same income from the FGP pension that I was receiving as an officer.

RETIREMENT

For several years, I made it known that I planned on retiring at age 60. I don't think many people believed me since voluntary retirement was not often practiced! On my official retirement in 1975, I was asked to remain on the board and be chairman of the Audit Committee, advisor on Personnel and Compensation Matters, and be chairman of the Employee Benefit Committee. I would retain my director's fees and be paid under contract for the other duties. Not too bad. I had my own office and use of a secretary. I planned to go to my office only on meeting days, and no more than once a week. Since I had learned typing at NYU, I would draft my Audit Committee and other reports at home.

It was at this juncture of my life that Richard du Moulin and Andy MacGowan, in a case of reversed nepotism, pushed Eleanor and me into the most exciting years of our lives, involving the America's Cup. I will not go into those twenty-five wonderful years. They are well chronicled in The America's Cup and Me published by the Herreshoff Marine Museum of Bristol, Rhode Island.

My official retirement was effective February 1, 1975. In 1976, I became heavily involved with the America's Cup, but my Bache responsibilities were carried out without complication until the end of March 1980. Back in the 1970s and 1980s, most corporate directors did not attribute much value to Audit Committees. Nevertheless I took my job seriously, and had warned the board to better monitor the company's risk position with commodity and margin loans to customers.

THE SILVER CRISIS

In 1980, I was in California with our two America's Cup boats, *Freedom* & *Enterprise*, when I received a call to return to a special Bache board

*T*he Hunts had tried to corner the silver market through aggressive buying of silver futures.

meeting the next day in New York. Eleanor and I flew back to our home in Sands Point, where we had moved in 1967 after Richard and Cathy had both graduated from Hewlett High School. The board meeting was a shocker. Our largest commodity customers, the Hunt brothers from Texas, were unable to meet a large margin call on loans from Bache. This began the well-publicized Silver Crisis of 1980. Also known as Crisis at Bache.

The Hunts were major commodity speculators. Bache Halsey Stuart, a subsidiary of the Bache Group, was their prime broker. Merrill Lynch and others were also involved. The Hunts had tried to corner the silver market through aggressive buying of silver futures. They managed to run the price of silver from under $10 per ounce in 1979 to $50 per ounce the following year. (As of 2006 it is still under $10.) The silver was purchased on margin. In other words, the Hunts would put up as little cash as required with the brokers providing the balance. The collateral we received, instead of cash, was silver. Our exposure was $122 million, representing 84 percent of our capital. The Hunts could not keep the price of silver up forever, and finally the silver price fell to the point that they could not meet the margin calls (additional deposits of cash or collateral) from Bache, Merrill, and other firms.

The failure of Bache became imminent. Through a horrendous period of less than two weeks, the 106-year-old firm, which survived all the panics of the twentieth century, almost collapsed. After some complicated transactions in New York and London, at the very last minute our banks agreed not to call our loans. Appeals were made at high government levels and the Street worked cooperatively for mutual survival. Bache managed to narrowly avert disaster. We also successfully pressured the commodity exchanges to lower the margin requirements. Now, how did this affect my family and me?

The Saturday before the miraculous escape, Eleanor and I gathered our family at Cathy and Jerry Morea's home at 10 Winthrop Road in Port Washington. Richard and Ann, along with Stanley Rich, met us there. I explained that if they read in <u>The New York Times</u> on Monday that Bache had failed, they should not worry. I had started 47 years before with nothing, and that all of our capital was invested in Bache (what happened to the **don't put all your eggs in one basket** theory?). I pointed out that if I lost all my investment and pension at Bache, that Richard and Cathy and their families would still be OK. I added that our home in Sands Point was mortgage free, and we could move to a more modest home. As for our boat, we could be happy with a much smaller one. No one slept Saturday or Sunday nights. It was over that weekend that the miracle happened.

The U.S. Securities and Exchange Commission issued a treatise called *The Silver Crisis of 1980* several years later. It is in my possession. It would be exciting reading for my family and a wonderful lesson about reckless business management, over-extension of credit, and unsubstantiated faith in the ability of wealthy people or organizations to meet their commitments.

END OF BACHE AS AN INDEPENDENT COMPANY

Circa June 1981, Prudential Insurance Company made an offer to buy the Bache organization. I was still on the Bache Board of Directors. To me, this was an amazing development and I believed Bache needed to be part of a larger, better-managed organization. It led to the end of my career with Bache and an important financial windfall for all the stockholders of Bache. Prior to Prudential's surprise offer, Eleanor understandably felt I should sell some of my Bache stock at its market price of $7 for reasons of diversification. As always, I kept in close touch with Stan Rich who urged me and my friends Arnold Green and George Meyer to hold all our shares. To satisfy Eleanor, I sold a token number of shares. Arnold, the most conservative, sold all of his, but George stood fast. When the Prudential deal was finally consummated the stockholders received $32 per share instead of $7. Stan was correct again. This is why it is always good to get an honest, thoughtful professional opinion before making important commitments. **The final decision is yours to make, but you should first seek ideas and suggestions from those you trust.**

MY LAST EXECUTIVE COMMITTEE STANDOFF

Many important resolutions had to be approved by our board leading up to the actual takeover by Prudential. The Former General Partners (FGP) Pension Plan was up for discussion. Our chairman was given a special pension arrangement. Much to my surprise, the board was presented with a proposal to change the FGP Pension. In it was a provision demanded by

Prudential that, in the event the firm lost over $250,000 in a particular year, pension payments for that year would be reduced by 50 percent. If in the following year the firm lost money, the pension reduction would stand. If however, in the following year after the initial loss, the firm made a profit, the reduction would be restored. I would not sign it. The chairman objected to this, stating that all directors must sign it so the negotiations with Prudential could go smoothly. I pointed out that the chairman had improved his own pension arrangement and had no such loss provision. Why should the other former general partners, most of them already in retirement and without any representation in the transaction, be treated differently? I was told not to worry, that it could be changed after the takeover. That, of course, was unsatisfactory. I told the board that they would have to pass the new provision over my dissenting vote, but they were afraid to have any recorded dissent. The board meeting ended without resolution, but would meet again. That evening I spoke with Stan Rich who wisely pointed out that once Prudential took over, there would be no way to check the books of a subsidiary company, when the parent company could easily allocate charges to the subsidiary, resulting in losses.

When the board reconvened, the chairman had the contract revised to meet my objections. I sensed deep resentment by the chairman. I told Eleanor and Stan that I should resign but they urged me not to do so on the practical basis that, as a director, I was still being paid. For once they were wrong. I was informed, shortly after, that I would no longer be a director. However, for years after, I would receive phone calls from some of my brother directors and FGPs, thanking me for my one-man stand. For several years after the acquisition, the Bache subsidiary did show losses!

MY TIES ARE CUT

During my active days at Bache, when retired partners would pay an office visit, they often wanted to know what was going on. I would be very patient and polite, but at the same time, I couldn't wait until they moved on so I could go back to work. My mind was made up that when I retired, I would not call on my old colleagues. I never did, nor did it ever bother me not to. You would think it would have, after 47 years.

Through all the near disasters, wars and Depression, the firm did survive. The Silver Crisis and the Prudential deal were the final chapters of an exciting history. Although I had my many differences with the firm's leaders, they did lead us to the promised land.

To review my years at Bache:

1. It was the only real job I ever had.
2. I met Eleanor there.
3. It was a great experience.
4. It gave my family financial security.
5. It proved Sam Lauterbach's theory that **"a sticker never gets stuck."**

PART IV
LIFETIME INTERESTS
& FAMILY

My main interests in life, always and still, revolve around my family and friends, with sailing my primary sport. I have never been interested in security trading. My portfolio is half invested in equities, half in cash and bonds, mainly treasuries. Stan Rich would never recommend that I buy municipals or mutual funds. Rolling over short-term treasury bills or notes was more satisfactory than leaving it in lower paying money market funds. Paying bills quickly is a fetish, and paying off my mortgage was a high priority. Setting up college funds for my grandchildren was a prime objective for Eleanor and me; particularly so, as we never graduated from college. I read The New York Times cover to cover and, up to 2000, The Wall Street Journal. I like to clip articles and pass them along (few magazines or newspapers leave my hands intact). I am a happy reader of most sailing magazines. Politically, I am a conservative Democrat and normally vote Democratic. As a Depression baby and learning of the excesses of Wall Street, I supported Franklin Delano Roosevelt. His strong leadership and New Deal legislation impressed me, both during my early Wall Street days and World War II.

I am an avid follower of American history, as are Richard and grandsons Chris and Edward. I consider Winston Churchill the outstanding statesman of the twentieth century. A close second would be FDR. I am an Abraham Lincoln buff. On March 4, 1865, Abe gave his second inaugural address, my favorite:

"With malice toward none, with charity for all, with firmness in the right as God gives us to see the right, let us strive on to finish the work we are in, to bind up the nation's wounds, to care for him who shall have borne the battle and for his widow and his orphan, to do all which may achieve and cherish a just and lasting peace among ourselves and with all nations."

PIANO PLAYING

I have always enjoyed listening to someone playing the piano. Eleanor was a fine player. Today with Eleanor and Cathy gone, unfortunately the only one who touches our piano is the piano tuner. Some day maybe Carrie

Ed in team colors, aboard XANADU *in Newport prior to the start of the Bermuda Race in 1966.*

The family that sails together....Ed, Eleanor, Cathy, and Rich.

will return to the piano just for relaxation, as did her mother, Cathy, who often played late at night when something was on her mind. We enjoyed the theatre, some of the more popular operas, a good movie. Eleanor was an avid reader of good books, often reading well into the morning hours. At times, I felt some jealousy toward the books she read at night. Eleanor was an unusually graceful dancer and suffered my conservative style. She walked and looked like a fine athlete but never rode a bike or roller skated. She tried skiing once but twisted her ankle. Eleanor did manage to swim across a small pool knowing she could stand up, if necessary. But on the water she was wonderfully at home, even when pregnant with Richard. She could read a book while cooking a meatloaf in the oven with the boat

If I fell overboard, I would be dead of a heart attack before I hit the water.

bouncing along without getting seasick. When people would find out she could not swim, they questioned why she didn't wear a life jacket when on our boat. Her answer was: "If I fell overboard, I would be dead of a heart attack before I hit the water." She had great confidence in me and rarely would sail with others.

THE BOSTON DU MOULINS

Brother Babe (Ted) is going strong at 87 along with his faithful wife Edith. They married in 1946 and live in Wareham, Massachusetts, at the base of Cape Cod. Babe was a strong oarsman and is still a good swimmer. He belongs to the Cambridge Boat Club, world-famous for the Head-of-The-Charles Annual Regatta, where the entry gate is named for him and his wife, who have been dedicated volunteers. For many years after WWII, Edith worked at the Veteran's Hospital serving quadriplegics. When she retired, the governor of Massachusetts honored her.

Babe and his wife Edith have three boys. Their first was Gary who loved the military and graduated in 1969 from Norwich University, the oldest private military school in the U.S. He spent 38 years in the Army Reserves, retiring as Chief of Staff, 804th Medical Brigade. Gary received various degrees including a PhD in microbiology. Today he is in charge of quality control at the Genzyme Corporation and travels around the world giving presentations. He has published over 150 original works on microbiology and other subjects relating to his field of study. During his military career he has received ten service ribbons including the Legion of Merit. Among his various assignments, he commanded the 399th Combat Support Hospital. Gary has also caught the sailing bug and is active with Community Boating in Boston, a great organization. Gary is happily married to Barbara, and they have two wonderful sons, Andrew and David.

Unlike Gary, Edith and Babe's son Peter did not take to military life. He also went to Norwich University, but when my mother Adele and I visited him there, he seemed unhappy. Peter dropped out of Norwich, and did not return home. When Eleanor learned that he was on the road, she tracked him down and convinced him to visit us, with no questions asked. I met him at the Long Island Railroad information booth in Penn Station. On the train ride home, Peter happened to open his wallet and I noticed a photo of President Kennedy. He said he loved President Kennedy, adding that he hated the Vietnam War.

At that point in time, I had the more conservative view common with my generation, so was happy to turn him over to Eleanor. Both were active smokers. Late at night, after I turned in, Eleanor sat up with him, smoking and talking. Eleanor kept in touch with Babe and Edith, who were very happy Peter was with us. But Peter was not yet ready to discuss any plans or problems with them. Peter eventually got a job as a teller in a local bank and continued to live at our house. Eventually Peter found a sense of direction and was ready to leave. It was an emotional goodbye for all three of us. We came to really love him. Our fingers were crossed. When he left us, Peter wasn't ready to connect with his parents but eventually, with Eleanor's guidance, slowly built up a closer relationship with his parents that is strong today.

Peter went back to Vermont and found a job in a Catholic hospital. He wanted to work the late night shift with terminally ill patients. Peter and a priest served these patients. His second job was tending bar. On his own, Peter enrolled in the University of Vermont, receiving a Master's Degree in Human Services. Hired by the State of Vermont as head guidance counselor for the local junior and senior high schools, Peter worked with students who had drug problems. He was in his element and dressed in a most informal manner. The school board tried to make him dress in a tie and jacket when attending meetings. He refused to do this, and was finally permitted to dress in the style he adopted when working with his students. For his work, he has received awards and recognition. Peter met a wonderful girl Kay, and together they raised two great children – Daniel and Brittany. He loves baseball and is a frequent visitor to the Cooperstown Hall of Fame. A plaque Peter gave us is proudly hung on our wall. It reads:

> A Child Reached Into The Darkness
> You Took His Hand
> He Became A Man

Barry du Moulin is the youngest son of Edith and Babe. He has always been independent. Barry has been involved with the U.S. Coast Guard at various times, inspecting LNG tankers and other ships entering Boston

Harbor. He has received a Letter of Commendation from the Commandant of the U.S. Coast Guard. Between Coast Guard assignments, he was the harbormaster of Onset, Massachusetts. In 2005 he became Security Officer on a large new cruise ship. He has maintained, in Bristol fashion, various powerboats of his own. Neighbors of Edith and Babe were the Maleskas. He was the famous (or infamous) individual who wrote the New York Times crossword puzzles. When Eleanor first met Eugene Maleska, she said, "How I hate you." After Eugene passed away, Barry developed a wonderful, long-term relationship with Carol Maleska. Barry continues to receive special assignments with the U. S. Coast Guard.

THEODORE WEISBERG

My nephew, Ted Weisberg, has had a most interesting Wall Street career. At the University of Denver, he was a fine skier (even though he never wore any ski socks). When he injured his leg, he continued to ski – on one leg. In his summers Ted worked for Bache. Whatever job they gave him, he did it with a smile. In his early days, Ted worked the chalkboard, on which he would mark the changing stock market prices. Later, male board markers were replaced by girls in tight slacks, who were replaced by electric teleregister boards. After graduation, Ted was hired by Bache and studied to be a salesman. Although he had difficulty passing a newly established New York Stock Exchange (NYSE) test (I think the results indicated Ted should look for another line of work) I had every confidence in his ability to be a successful salesman, which he was, and is.

As the years went by, Ted said he wanted to represent the firm on the NYSE floor. I explained that there were a number of people ahead of him, who were awaiting that opportunity. However, if he wanted to become a Bache floor broker on the American Stock Exchange, I might be able to arrange it. He served several years there, was well liked and did a good job. Even so, he still wished to be a broker on the floor of the New York Stock Exchange. At that point, he left Bache and became a floor broker for a fine old carriage firm in Cleveland. After a few years, he was determined to have his own seat and decided to leave.

Ted came to me for advice, asking if he should buy a NYSE seat at that time. I told him the story of our Greensboro branch manager who had bought his NYSE seat in 1929 just before the Crash for over $600,000. At the time Ted was asking me, a seat on the NYSE then sold for less than a New York City taxi medallion. I posed the question, "If you bought a seat at that big price and it went to zero, would it change your lifestyle?" He said, "No." So I advised him to go ahead. He bought it, and created a fine, family-run brokerage firm, Seaport Securities, in which his two children Rebecca and Jason are important associates and business partners, and Richard and his family all keep accounts. Ted recently reminded me that I was the only one who encouraged him to buy the seat.

Ed at the helm.

Ted is a fine sailor, a former commodore of the Knickerbocker Yacht Club and member of the New York Yacht Club and the Royal Bermuda Yacht Club. He has a Peterson 34 sloop that he maintains in top shape. She is named *Thora* after Sam Lauterbach's yawl. He is a fine helmsman, particularly upwind, as when he served as race crew for me. For many years, he was Arthur Knapp's partner in a Shields class sloop. Ted met Arthur on the floor of the NYSE where they both worked.

When Dad was ill during his last six months, Ted visited him frequently, and was of great help to our family. Ted gave a very moving eulogy at the memorial service held at Knickerbocker Yacht Club. — **R. du M**.

Modern Sailcloth

In 1954, Richard, age eight, accompanied me while I visited Louis Larsen Sailmakers in Port Washington to order a new jib for the old gaff-rigged *Lady Del*. I intended to have it built of the best Egyptian cotton, but Louis, a big beefy Norwegian, suggested I consider the new "miracle" fabric called Dacron. I said I preferred the time-tested cotton, but he insisted that Dacron was far stronger. To demonstrate, he picked up a piece and tried to pull it apart. Then he handed it to me, challenging me to test its strength.

I reluctantly picked it up and pulled it. With a ripping sound, I tore it into two pieces. Louis turned pale, and I was quite embarrassed. Feeling bad for Louis, I ordered a new jib out of Dacron. It turned out to be a fine sail.

RICHARD'S ACCIDENT

We then headed home. I was driving our two-tone blue Desoto and Richard was sitting in the front seat, and as this was 1954, the car had no seat belts. It was in the dead of winter, with snow banks along the sides of the wet streets. As I proceeded down a main avenue, a car came from a side street and hit us on the right rear door. It spun us around and sprung open the front right door. I made a futile grab for Richard but centrifugal force carried him out. Fortunately, he was wearing a heavy coat and hat. He skidded across the road, landing in a snow pile, miraculously missing oncoming cars. One shoe was knocked off and he suffered some lacerations and broke some bones in his foot. We were right in front of a dentist's office. The dentist helped give first aid, and then we went to a local hospital where Richard was treated. I do not remember any details. Although shaken up, I was able to bring him home the same day. The next week I had seat belts installed in the car, and you can be sure that our family always puts them on.

OUR TRAVELS

As far as non-sailing travel, throughout our married life Eleanor and I would attend business meetings in various parts of the United States, Puerto Rico and Bermuda. Starting when Cathy and Richard were five and seven, we would go to various Eastern ski areas, including the eight Christmas and New Years vacations we spent at the Manoir St. Castin, a warm and friendly small hotel north of Quebec City. They had superb French cooking and owned their own small ski mountain. The old head ski instructor, Fritz Loosli, was one of the pioneers of teaching parallel skiing in North America. The children learned some French and made many local friends.

A little farther afield, with the Greens we visited London, Sweden, and Denmark. We had a fun trip to France with our America's Cup friends, Frances and Mort Bloom. Frances spoke fluent French. Later, we traveled with Ann and Bob Conner to Italy, leading to our Corsica cruise with Malin and Roberta Burnham aboard their great yacht *Bert and I*. Of course, the

America's Cup campaigns took us to Newport, California, and Australia. For my 80th birthday, we had a wonderful family vacation in St. Thomas, along with the Riches and their family.

In 2000, I went with my nephew Ted Weisberg, then president of World Match Racing, to New Zealand for the Cup. Now, I am ready to give up chasing the Holy Grail of Yachting. My 67 years of following the Cup are well covered in <u>The America's Cup and Me</u>.

Eleanor and I had made plans to be with Ann and Bob Conner, Bertie and Andy MacGowan, and others in Cowes, England, for the fantastic 150th Anniversary of the America's Cup in September, 2001. But as Eleanor had died just months earlier, deciding whether to go was a difficult decision for me. I am glad I went; Eleanor would not have minded--in spirit she was with me. While in Cowes, the greatest yacht designer of our time, 93-year-old Olin Stephens, and I (at age 86) walked the docks together, getting invited on board almost every boat we passed.

BACK TO HEWLETT

Shifting the scene back to 1960: When Richard was ready to enter Hewlett High School, we moved to a larger home in Hewlett Harbor about one mile from our first house in Woodmere. Later, Cathy also attended Hewlett High. In Woodmere, early each morning, winter or summer, I would dash out in my underwear to bring in the newspaper that had been dropped on the lawn. When we moved to Hewlett Harbor, a more elite area, Eleanor asked me to be properly attired when I retrieved the paper. The first morning, Eleanor and the children were surprised to see me run out for the paper wearing my underwear – and a formal top hat. Almost 30 years later in 1987, with our America's Cup team in Australia and living next to the Burnhams, I would also pick up the newspaper in my briefs. One early morning Roberta was waiting with a camera. At my 90th Birthday party, Roberta provided a blowup of that candid camera photo, and many of her birthday cards to me refer to me having performed that morning chore.

Our new neighbors in Hewlett Harbor were Rita and Herb Gold. Herb had built our house. They had a son Ricky who was a classmate of Cathy, and a very warm and nice individual. The Golds are most unusual folks. Rita is very talented and has worked miracles with the children of Head Start.

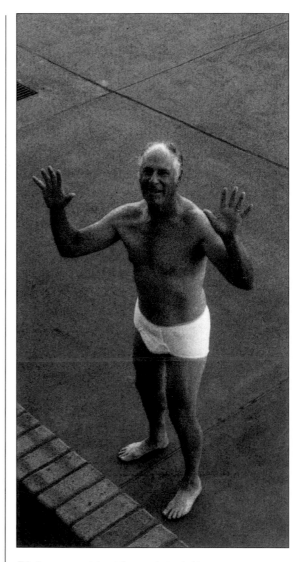

Ed always ran out to get the newspaper in his briefs during the 1987 campaign in Fremantle. One day, Roberta Burnham caught the moment on film.

Over many years, they have sponsored aspiring young opera singers. Many have performed at the Metropolitan Opera. Their foundation supporting this program is in memory of Ricky who died of AIDS at an early age.

One day the Golds were going to an auction at one of the Gold Coast (North Shore) mansions and asked us to join them. Herb was interested in bidding for a truck with a snowplow which was to be auctioned off at 1:00 pm. Herb and I walked to the driveway to look at the truck, leaving the women at the auction. A short time before the truck was to be auctioned, Herb and I returned, whereupon Rita and Eleanor explained to us that they had spent all the cash ($2600) so we could not bid on the truck. They would not tell us what they had purchased, so we drove home somewhat confused and chagrinned. During the next week, Herb was angry with Rita as she continued to stonewall him. Saturday morning, on his birthday, Herb woke up and when he walked through the garage found a shiny Rolls Royce Silver Dawn wrapped in a bow with a birthday card on the windshield from Rita! Rita had spontaneously bought the car when it came up for auction, and a few minutes later turned down a dealer who was late to the auction and had offered her $8000. A few days after the auction, she had Richard drive the car home, wash it, and hide it in our garage until Herb's birthday. Herb was very happy with the surprise, and even managed to laugh when we suggested that since he failed to get the truck with the snowplow, maybe he could put a snowplow on the front of the Rolls. The Golds kept the car for several years, but Herb was afraid to drive it to work. Ricky and his friends had real fun with it, particularly at prom time. I suggested that a sign be placed in the back window, explaining that it only cost $2,600.

From our kitchen, you could look across the yard to our enclosed patio. One morning I happened to see Cathy sneaking a cigarette. I shall never forget her startled look when she spotted me staring at her. Fortunately, she gave up smoking in her early twenties. Sadly, Eleanor didn't stop until she was in her late fifties. She tried every advertised method including hypnotism. When several of her friends, over a short period of time, died from lung cancer, she stopped "cold turkey." I know smoking affected her later in life.

One Sunday, I was reading The Times in our backyard. It was about lunchtime. Eleanor opened the back door and in a commanding voice yelled, "Come in, stupid!" I quietly put the paper down and started for the door. Eleanor looked at me and laughed, saying she was calling the cat, not me. This was quite embarrassing for a young executive. The cat and I had a nice lunch inside.

FATHER DE LATTRE & KURT LEWIN

It was while living in Hewlett Harbor that the story of a Vatican priest, Father Michel de Lattre, unfolded. The name of the Bache economist who earlier in this book advised Richard to go to business school was Kurt Lewin. Kurt was a sensitive but tough individual, who had a distinguished record as an officer in the Irgun, the Jewish freedom fighters who helped create the modern state of Israel. In the 1960s, Father de Lattre was sent by the Vatican to contact Kurt in New York. His mission was to research the history of a Lithuanian Catholic metropolitan who had been recommended for sainthood. Kurt's father had been the chief rabbi and a close friend of the metropolitan. When the Nazis entered Lithuania, the metropolitan told the chief rabbi that he would give sanctuary to what turned out to be more than 100 Jewish children. For the balance of the war, the children, including Kurt, lived and were educated in the convent. Kurt's father refused to go into hiding and was killed by the Nazis.

Kurt and Michel became close lifelong friends. Quite a contrast. Kurt was short and serious; Father de Lattre was tall and always had a twinkle in his eye. His beautiful French accent reminded us of Maurice Chevalier. Kurt wanted to introduce Michel to my family, and over the years they visited us a number of times. Michel was very impressed with Cathy who was about 16, and who had a boyfriend named Lance. Michel told Cathy that she would grow up to be a beautiful person, inside and outside – he could tell by her eyes. On one visit Eleanor and I took Michel and Kurt to a local restaurant. Each would jokingly accuse the other of trying to convert him. Michel asked how Cathy was doing. Kurt said that there was a problem - she was going out with a non-Jewish lad. Father de Lattre said, "Oy, Oy."

Later, Michel phoned Kurt and invited him to come to the Vatican as the Council, which reviewed those recommended for sainthood, wanted to interview him. Kurt objected since the full story was already in their hands. Michel said that the Council wished to hear the story directly from Kurt, and be able to further question him. Kurt finally went. Our last visit

Portrait of Cathy du Moulin in her early twenties.

with Michel was on his return from a Canadian trip. He was sent there to explain the new Church doctrines, such as conducting Mass in English. He was exhausted and told us it was the most difficult assignment he ever had; he never had met more stubborn people. He passed away a few years later. During his life, we received beautiful notes from Father de Lattre each Christmas, always inquiring about Cathy. Kurt Lewin later married a very attractive Italian countess, and moved to Italy.

SAILING AND SAILBOATS

Around 1950, we joined the Knickerbocker Yacht Club in Port Washington where I moored my second boat, a malachy green handsome 32-foot Pilot designed by Sparkman & Stephens and built by Knutson's of Huntington, Long Island. She was 10 years old and in excellent condition. I had sold the first *Lady Del* for $500 to my Bache friend Tom Lawrence, whom I had taught to sail.

Sam Lauterbach's private yacht signal was registered with Lloyds. In memory of Sam, who had passed away in 1974, I designed my burgee using his swallowtail design with blue background with a white circle on which appeared his initial "L." My design replaced the "L" with a double "E" for Eleanor and Edward, and in opposite corners, two white stars, representing Richard and Cathy.

It was this second *Lady Del* that won the DeCoursey Fales Trophy in 1964, emblematic of the Long Island Sound Distance Racing Championship. At 14, Richard was my foredeck man. This was the boat used in a program I organized to train young sailors. In September, 1960, hurricane Donna passed through Manhasset Bay. A powerboat broke its mooring and drifted into *Lady Del*, severely damaging her starboard side. She was restored by Knutson's Shipyard where she was built. This was my only insurance claim in over 70 years of sailing.

In the 1960s, the Handicap Yacht Racing Club was formed with Dick Wagner of the Port Washington Yacht Club as commodore. For a number of years it was very active. In addition to some wonderful day races, we enjoyed the weekend events. We would race to Price's Bend, Great Captains Island, or Morris Cove, where the first boat to arrive would drop anchor, and the rest of the fleet would tie alongside, with an occasional boat throwing out another anchor. These "raft-ups" often became circular as each end of the raft sagged back. The crews would eat, drink, and often sing while Harold Oldak played his guitar. If bad weather threatened, we would break up the raft, and often reconstruct it when the weather cleared. The next day we would race home. One particular day it was blowing over 50 knots from the northwest. Racing was cancelled, and the race committee ordered the fleet to proceed to Lloyds Harbor in a safe manner. This was the first time our 32-foot Pilot and our crew had sailed in such a strong breeze. In no time, we entered the harbor for the night. The raft-up was safe from the weather, and we had drinks for all hands, followed by music, revelry, and dinner. Each boat anchored on its own hook for the night. Next day was a fine race back to Manhasset Bay.

I had won first in class in a Bayside Yacht Club race in which our Handicap Class participated. At the awards presentation, I walked up the center aisle to receive my trophy when Bill Borst, very drunk, confronted me. He looked up at me and in a loud voice said: "For years, I have been looking up du Moulin's ass, and now I want to see what he looks like." After about ten years, we phased out our Handicap (%) Class Club. Participation in our "family" events had dwindled, as so many other racing events were scheduled by the established clubs on Long Island Sound.

LADY DEL II, *an S&S Pilot 32 built by Knutson. She was the family boat from 1956 to 1968.*

These overnight raft-up weekend events are missed by many of us. Adam Loory has recreated this style of event with his "Expressly Yours" overnighter to Northport. — **R. du M**.

FAMILY CRUISES

When Richard was about nine and Cathy seven, Eleanor and I cruised to Nantucket on *Lady Del*. Over the two-week cruise, Eleanor knitted a scarf that grew to nine feet long. We moored at the New Bedford Yacht Club,

Eleanor, Rich, and Cathy in the cockpit of Lady Del II.

where the children swam off the boat. Suddenly, Cathy screamed. I dived in and brought her on board to find out that the turk's head rope bracelet I had given her had shrunk and her hand was turning blue. Out came the knife. It was scary. No more rope bracelets!

On another cruise, there was a distant threat of hurricane Brenda. As we cruised near Cuttyhunk, we decided to proceed to Block Island where we were happy to pick up a mooring not too far from the marina. That afternoon the entire New York Yacht Club (NYYC) cruise arrived. The storm was rapidly moving up the coast. I removed everything I could from the deck, put an extra line to the mooring buoy, and chafing gear around the mooring lines. While Eleanor and the children slept, I kept tuned to the radio. About 0400, still dark, I woke Eleanor. I decided that we were going ashore as soon as we could gather some clothing and the kids. Not surprisingly, Eleanor also thought to gather up the dirty laundry to take with us. We put on life jackets. I first took Richard ashore in the dinghy, then came back for Eleanor and Cathy. We called a cab and about 0600 arrived at the Surf Hotel which faced east.

Our room was not ready yet, so we sat on the porch in the rockers. Soon we saw the fishing boats coming from the east returning to the harbor. The wind was building, and the empty rocking chairs were beginning to rock in the gusts. The eye of the storm was predicted to pass through around 1100. We grabbed breakfast and went into our room. At 1030, Richard and I took a cab back to the dock to watch *Lady Del*. Meanwhile, the NYYC yachts were moving around to anchor at the windward end of the harbor. I am sure they all had hangovers, and probably returned to their bunks after re-anchoring. The storm hit with winds up to 70 knots, and a few boats were beached, but our little vessel was just fine. The eye of Brenda actually passed directly over the island, providing the NYYC fleet a good opportunity to shift their anchors to the opposite end of the harbor, the new windward end as the breeze filled in from the west after the eye passed.

The next day, we decided to head for Shelter Island. There was a clear northwesterly blowing. However, there were very large swells left over from the hurricane, about which I wasn't too happy. I didn't want to scare the family. To amuse them, I sang "On The Road To Mandalay" as loudly as I could with my arms swinging. I have absolutely no singing talent but it sure took their minds off the swells.

Ironically, in 1991, Ann and I were vacationing on Block Island when Class 5 hurricane Bob struck. John Storck and his family left Jonrob *on a mooring and took shelter with us in our heavily-built rented Old Barn. Similar to hurricane Brenda, the eye of hurricane Bob passed directly over the island, however Bob had gusts to 150 kts. that pushed more than 60 yachts ashore.* — **R. du M**.

Eleanor, Julie (Ed's sister) and Ed sailing on LADY DEL II.

RACING *SPRINKHAAN*

In 1968, we decided to build a larger boat that eventually became the Hinckley 38. Our trusty Pilot 32 *Lady Del* was quickly sold with great regret and wonderful memories. That fall, I received a phone call from Dolf Le Compte, a Dutch boat builder and well-known racer, who owned a marina/ shipyard in New Rochelle, where Richard now keeps his Express 37 *Lora Ann*. Dolf also owned and raced his Medalist 33 *Sprinkhaan*, which means "grasshopper" in Dutch. Dolf said he would be spending the next summer in Holland supervising the construction of some boats for the Dutch navy. He asked if I would race *Sprinkhaan* while I was waiting for my new boat to be built. I declined as I didn't feel comfortable taking on the responsibility of racing someone else's boat. He asked me to keep an open mind and discuss it in the spring.

In March, Dolf phoned and invited me to meet him in New Rochelle. Eleanor and I met with him, and he was very persuasive. I asked if the boat was insured. He said no and quickly said he would insure her. We then inspected the boat. I had noticed the waterline seemed high. I soon found out that he sailed the boat with minimum equipment. There were no anchor, anchor line, flares; not even a yacht ensign; and no water in his tanks. When I asked him what he would do, should the Coast Guard board *Sprinkhaan* for a surprise inspection, Dolf ran below and came up holding his Dutch flag. I said that if I did race her, I would load her down to the waterline. When he said he would put all the required equipment on board, I finally agreed. He did provide all the equipment I requested. Before departing to bring the boat over to my Knickerbocker Yacht Club mooring, I asked him about fuel. He said there was plenty. We started the motor, cast off our lines, waved our goodbyes, and headed out under the nearby drawbridge. We had not moved 100 yards when the engine coughed and stopped. A red-faced Dolf towed us to a nearby fuel dock to fill up our empty tank. We finally had an uneventful sail to Manhasset Bay.

One week later, in May 1968, we entered the New York Athletic Club's Stratford Shoal Overnight Race, the first distance race of the season, which would start at 8:00 p.m. Saturday. Richard and a classmate, Rick Pabst, drove down Friday night from Dartmouth. Andy MacGowan, about to do his first race with me, and Rick were the newcomers to our crew of seven.

We decided to practice the afternoon before the start and then eat dinner at the NYAC, next to the Le Compte yard. The weather was ominous – rain with 20 to 25 knots of wind from the northeast, and lumpy seas. It would be a nasty night. We raised sails and she seemed fine going upwind. When we went downwind, we noticed the mast leaned too far forward and the boom extended at too wide an angle. Richard also noticed that there were no aft lower shrouds. We worked our way back to Dolf's yard, even though it was closed. I phoned him at home and explained about the missing shrouds. He told us how to locate them in the storeroom, and instructed Andy MacGowan how to use the crane. By the time we finished the rigging job, it was too late to eat dinner. We did start the race on schedule, and it wasn't too long before our Dartmouth friend became seasick. (Rick got revenge on Richard a week later when they capsized while whitewater canoeing in Vermont). However, Andy MacGowan was outstanding as crew. It was the beginning of a lifelong friendship with Andy. He has had a wonderful sailing career, including ten years with Sparkman & Stephens, ocean racing, and America's Cup involvement. The Stratford Shoal Race was not easy – 87 boats started and only 33 finished. We won our division, the first of many prizes that season. We entered nineteen races scoring 6 first places, 10 second places and 3 thirds. *Sprinkhaan* was a wonderful boat, even loaded to her waterline.

The weather was ominous – rain with 25-30 knots from the northeast, and lumpy seas.

MARVIN CARTON

In the early 1970s, Marvin Carton, a member of the Knickerbocker Yacht Club and an ardent bluewater sailor, often raced with me on *Lady Del.* Marv was a successful investment banker with Allen & Company. One year, Marv entered his Bermuda 40 *Tiare* in the TransPac Race, shipping her to Los Angelos by rail. On a Sunday just prior to Marv's departure, we were chatting with Tom Lawrence on the porch of Knickerbocker. Marv showed us a range finder he had purchased. It would permit him to judge how far a competitor was from him. I tried it and, while doing so, asked where he bought it and the cost. He answered, "Manhattan Supply for $25." While I was playing with the range finder, Tom was asking Marv if he should buy stock in Syntex, a company that Marvin had discovered in Mexico which produced a plant that provided the key ingredient in birth control pills.

Richard takes his mom for a sail on the Blue Jay.

Allen & Co. had invested heavily in this company for which Marvin received a large bonus. Marvin told Tom that by the time he would return from the TransPac Race, the stock should triple and pay a dividend. The next morning upon the opening of the Stock Exchange, Tom eagerly purchased a good number of shares, while I could hardly wait until lunchtime so I could run up to Manhattan Supply to buy the range finder. By the time Marvin's *Tiare* crossed the finish line in second place in the TransPac, Syntex had tripled and Tom had a nice profit. The price of the range finder has been marked down to $17.00. At least my poor choice cost me no capital gains tax.

RICHARD – JUNIOR SAILING

Richard has sailed with me since he was two-and-a-half years old. At age 11, Richard joined the Knickerbocker Yacht Club Junior Sailing program. Each weekday morning, Eleanor would drive him 45 minutes from Hewlett to Port Washington and bring him home in the late afternoon. He loved the sailing program, starting off in 14-foot Blue Jays. After he'd sailed the "club tubs" for a few years, we bought Richard a second-hand Blue Jay in excellent condition. This was number 529, *Lucky Shackle*. In those days, the KYC program was excellent. Richard looked up to Elliott Oldak who was in the program, two years older. About 30 years later Richard would be Elliot's best man. He learned from Elliot how to maintain a boat in Bristol (perfect) condition. Also in the program were several other excellent sailors, including Ricky Farmer. Eleanor and I took Richard and his crew (Carol Seeger and Russell Palmer, later Didi Rosen) to all the leading regattas on Long Island Sound, either trailed behind the car or towed by *Lady Del*. They won many trophies. The competition was intense, particularly from his main rival, Steve Moore and crew Peter Rugg, from Manhasset Yacht Club. In one

Manhasset Bay Race Week, Steve was first and Richard second for five straight days. On the sixth day, *Lucky Shackle* took the lead from the start. Richard was so busy covering Steve, he failed to see Gail Rundquist slip down the center of the Bay. She won – Richard was second again, completing the week with six seconds and no firsts.

The Junior Sailing Program had a major influence on Richard's life. He learned to be independent and met young boys and girls at the various regattas, often staying in their homes. Friendships were made that have lasted almost 50 years. Many of his young friends crewed with me, and many went

Rich (sporting Buddy Holly glasses), and Ed with some of the silver they had won over the years.

on to worldwide sailing. Some, like Richard, crewed on various America's Cup contenders. It is particularly gratifying to me that Richard's four children enjoy sailing. Cathy and Jerry Morea's Doug and Carrie have also attended the KYC Junior Sailing program. Carrie, at age 17, is a sailing instructor at the Manhasset Bay Yacht Club where Richard once taught. All of us were thrilled when Carrie crewed in 2004 with Danielle Powers to win the Dennis Conner/Ed du Moulin Cow Bay Junior Match Racing Trophy in 420s.

Dad's observation is very accurate – many of my present crew on Lora Ann *are my competitors from the 1960s-- Elliot Oldak, Steve Moore, Peter Rugg, George Huntington, John Browning, Chris Reyling. Nowadays, we Junior Program stalwarts are called Team AARP.* – **R. du M**.

HONESTY

One of the important junior regattas, Eastern Junior Race Week, was held at the Riverside Yacht Club in 1960. Richard's great rival in the Blue Jay class that season was George Huntington. In the first day's race, the finish occurred in the rain with lots of boats coming across the line together. George finished a few boat lengths in front of Richard. The next morning, at his host's home, Richard read in the newspaper that he was first and George was listed as DNF (Did Not Finish). Richard asked to be driven to the Club early. When the Race Committee arrived, Richard said he would like to talk to them. He explained that he was second, that the Race Committee might not have seen George in the rain, and that George Huntington had won. They thanked him. A great reporter of the era, Everitt B. Morris, was in the Race Committee room, and heard the discussion. The following day the sports page's lead article was about the "honest skipper." At the end of the regatta, the Riverside Yacht Club gave both George and Richard first place trophies.

Unknown to us, the article found its way into Richard's Dartmouth application file through his high school counselor, and during freshman week, the Dean called Richard in, showed him the article, and said that it was an important part of his early decision acceptance. In 2003, I was asked to tell this story to a large group of parents of the juniors at the Manhasset Bay Yacht Club during a forum about sportsmanship and honesty. George Huntington was there – 44 years later. George, by the way, is one of Richard's crew on *Lora Ann*.

LIGHTNINGS, ROTC, NAVY

Continuing Richard's sailing days, in 1964 he graduated from his Blue Jay (sold for more than we paid for her). He wanted to next race a 19-foot Lightning, a popular international class. We drove him to Buffalo to see Tom Allen, the class champion and builder of fine boats. We trailed a spanking new Lightning back to Manhasset Bay. Of course, all this time he continued to race

Ensign Rich du Moulin says goodbye to his mother as he goes off to the Navy in 1969.

with me when there was no conflict with his own racing.

43 years after Dad bought my Lightning from Tom Allen, my son Mark is college roommates at Hobart with Tom's grandson Rob Crane, son of Brenda Allen and Jim Crane, my friend and rival from junior sailing. It is a small world. – **R. du M**.

While at Dartmouth, Richard raced on the school's sailing team, and was Honorable Mention All-American in his senior year. In 1967, for his first America's Cup experience, he accepted an invitation by Bus Mosbacher and Bob McCullough to sail on the *Intrepid* and *Constellation* America's Cup team. He became a sail trimmer on *Constellation* with his friend John Browning cranking the winch as grinder.

As a member of Navy ROTC, upon graduation from a five-year engineering program, Richard received his commission as an ensign in the U.S. Navy in 1969. After sea duty, he was transferred to the Naval Academy where he ran the shipyard and worked as Ocean Racing Coach. A number of the Navy midshipmen crew had come from landlocked areas of the country but were fast learners. Several of these young men developed into great sailors, including Tom O'Brien and Tom Ternes, who crewed on *Courageous* during their America's Cup win in 1974.

In 1971, as a lieutenant j.g., Richard was Officer-in-Charge of the 54-foot *Rage*, and was authorized to train a racing crew to enter the Southern Ocean Racing Circuit (SORC), then a truly world-class series of ocean races with 120 yachts from all over the world competing. With help from coaches like Tony Parker, Scott Allan, and Carl van Duyne, along with talented midshipmen, *Rage* finished fourth in A Division where she was the smallest boat. Bob Bavier, editor of Yachting, wrote that had they been rated one point lower, they would have been in B Division and won five out of six races.

Eleanor and I met *Rage* in Nassau, the final port of the SORC. On the Miami-Nassau Race, *Rage* lost a big bet with rival *Yankee Girl*. With the two boats tied together in Nassau, *Rage* was the host vessel for the party to be paid for by Richard, the loser. Eleanor was given a double-grip winch handle to mix the rum in a large plastic garbage can. At one point a well-endowed girl standing by the rail stripped naked (not helped by Richard) and dove off the boat with a bunch of sailors after her. She swam across the basin to the

*E*m sat at the table
and ordered
a large and varied
breakfast that had to
be cooked by a very
queasy sailor.

biggest boat in the fleet, *Windward Passage*. Since the boat was high-sided, a bosun's chair on a halyard was lowered into the water. She climbed in, and the crew hoisted her up, but instead of stopping at deck level, she was hoisted to the top of the mast to the cheers of the party crowd, and the crowd of onlookers ashore. At that point, Eleanor and I decided to depart. The next day, we all went to a beach party. More mayhem, including driving a rental car, fully loaded with sailors, into the water. Not to be outdone, young John Potter drove a rented speedboat at high speed over the beach and into the woods. All this led to the banning of such parties in future SORCs.

I was invited to sail back to Florida on board *Rage*. It was a rough night, crossing the Gulf Stream with a strong northerly blowing. In the morning, few of us were particularly anxious to eat much, if any, breakfast. Nevertheless, Emrys (Em) Black, the enlisted seaman (the boat keeper) was hungry, and quoting from Navy Regs, instructed the officers on board that it was their responsibility to feed the enlisted crew. Richard, the skipper, delegated this job to the most junior ensign. Em sat at the table and ordered an especially large and varied breakfast that had to be cooked by a very queasy officer. Em later sailed with Richard on the America's Cup contenders *Intrepid* in 1974 and *Enterprise* in 1977.

TRANSATLANTIC

In 1968, when Richard was 21, he and his closest friend John Browning, an outstanding bluewater sailor and a welcome crew, were invited to race on Huey Long's maxi-yacht (72 feet) *Ondine* from Newport to Bermuda and then transatlantic to Travemunde, Germany. Eleanor and I didn't worry a bit. John, Rich, and Rich's college roommate Lee Reichart (who had sailed on another boat) toured Europe, team-raced in Norway, and had a great time.

Four years later after his navy service, Richard sailed on Jesse Philip's 57-foot *Charisma*. Andy MacGowan skippered the Bermuda Race, with Richard and Andy Radel navigating. Loran was not allowed, and GPS did not yet exist – sextant and dead reckoning were required. That was the year a passing hurricane obscured the finish line for most of the fleet, at the height of the storm. *Charisma* did find the finish line, winning class and missing first overall by a few minutes to a well-sailed British boat.

After the Bermuda Race, Rich skippered *Charisma* from Bermuda to

Spain, with a number of his and my former crew on board, including John Browning, Chris Reyling, Rick Farmer, and John's father Don, a great sailor who had crewed for Bus Mosbacher on *Weatherly* in the 1962 America's Cup. Don and another crew, Steve Lirakis, were full of tricks. On one occasion while the boat was sailing downwind under spinnaker, Richard's watch came on deck at midnight. Ten minutes later the jib miraculously hoisted itself and filled. Upon close examination, Rich's watch traced the jib halyard from the mast through a porthole into the cabin where Don and his watch had hoisted it from below. On another occasion, when Rich's watch came on deck, Don's entire watch was missing...not onboard...disappeared. After a search, Rich's men heard laughter behind the jib, and there, standing on rope slung over the side of the boat, were Don and his four mates.

BUSINESS SCHOOL AND WORK

Following Richard's naval service, temporary work at North Sails with John Marshall, and year racing *Charisma*, the question of whether to go to work or business school finally got resolved when he was accepted into both Stanford and Harvard business schools. He selected Harvard and had two very enjoyable years, during which he made lifelong friends, including his investor/partner Ken Jones.

During the summer between first and second terms, he was hired by Jim Barker and Paul Tregurtha at Moore McCormack, a well-known shipping company primarily running U.S. flag vessels to South America and Africa, plus ore carriers on the Great Lakes. At the end of his summer employment, he asked Jim for a bonus. Jim stated that summer employees didn't get a bonus, and asked if Richard had spent all his summer earnings on booze and women. Richard said he had some leftover, so Jim recommended that Richard buy company shares if he thought he had added value to the company. Richard reluctantly bought $500 worth of shares; two years later they were worth over $10,000.

When Richard graduated from HBS, he was offered a permanent position with Moore-McCormack, but chose to join an international tanker company. This led him to Ogden Marine, founded by a wonderful gentleman, Mike Klebanoff, who was born in China and grew up in Shanghai. Richard eventually became Chief Operating Officer and second-in-command there. In 1989 the opportunity to purchase and run a shipping company arose. Richard and his group acquired Marine Transport Lines, the oldest American-flag shipping company. It was formerly the Mallory Line founded in 1816. Twelve years later he sold MTL to Crowley Maritime Corp. After a one-year transition, Richard and his partner Mark Filanowski left Crowley to re-activate Intrepid Shipping in Stamford, Connecticut. With the support of investors like his Harvard friend Ken Jones, Intrepid is in the process of building up another fleet of modern ocean-going ships. They already have five vessels under their control.

Richard, today, is a director of Tidewater, the world's largest offshore supply boat operator. He is also a trustee of the Seamen's Church Institute, of the New York Yacht Club, and has just rotated off the board of the American Bureau of Shipping. He served three years as the chairman of Intertanko, the worldwide organization of tanker owners. Among his various awards, he holds the U.S. Coast Guard Distinguished Service Medal.

He is a member of the New York and Larchmont Yacht Clubs, the Royal Ocean Racing Club, the Cruising Club of America and, in 2005, he was elected Commodore of the Storm Trysail Club, a club of blue-water sailors to which I also belong. He conducts Safety-at-Sea programs for juniors and continues to campaign his *Lora Ann*.

Mistaken Identity – One night, in the early 1970s, Eleanor handed me the mail to read. Upon opening one of the envelopes, under a U.S. Navy letterhead, I read, "Dear Mr. du Moulin." Intrigued, I blushed when it described my reputation as a sailor and leader. On page two, it ended with an invitation to become a member of the distinguished Naval Academy Fales Committee, which advises the Superintendent of the Academy on sail training and leadership development. With an expanded chest, I turned to Eleanor and told her how pleased I was to be so recognized. She asked if I had looked at the envelope's addressee. Much to my chagrin, it was addressed to Richard T. du Moulin. As Richard's father, I was quite proud.

BERMUDA RACING

Our first Bermuda Race in 1966 was with my longtime Bache partner and friend, E. Bates McKee on his 49-foot varnished yawl, *Xanadu II*. She had a clipper bow and great cabin aft – a world traveler. She was a slow boat with a great crew of nine. This was 19-year-old Richard's first Bermuda Race. We had two watches. Richard was part of the "Filthy Four." I was part of the "Holy Trinity" (we didn't drink or curse). One early morning, I woke up and came on deck, where the on-watch was having breakfast. My mouth was dry. I reached out of the hatch and grabbed Richard's orange juice. To my surprise it was a screwdriver. His watch was living up to its name. When we arrived in Bermuda close to the tail end of about 150 boats, Bates congratulated me. He explained he had doubts about having a father and son on the same boat. He complimented me for not seeming to worry about Richard. My true answer was that I was more concerned about my own ass than Richard's.

Xanadu *crew, Bermuda Race 1966.*
Owner Bates McKee is at the helm.

The du Moulins sporting vertical and horizontal stripes for an evening out in Bermuda after a race from Newport.

Bottom at Amagansett

Prior to another Bermuda Race with Bates McKee on *Xanadu II*, I sailed with him on the feeder race from Annapolis to Newport. There were light headwinds and fog. Approaching Long Island, around 0300, we felt a strange surge. I had been watching the fathometer looking for the 10 fathom curve but the fathometer failed us and we were almost into the surf before we realized it. Bates immediately spun the boat around while several of us frantically cranked up the centerboard. We did touch bottom. It was off Amagansett, Long Island. When we arrived in Newport, Bill Rosen dove overboard and removed a piece of copper sheathing that had been partially ripped from the bottom of the centerboard. I hid it in my seabag and had it mounted on a mahogany base with a brass plate, "Landing at Amagansett, L.I." Bates had been skipper of an LST which landed on beaches in WWII. It was presented to him at *Xanadu II*'s 10th anniversary at Nonquitt, Massachusetts. We had promised not to say anything to Bates' wife Katie about the grounding, as she would have berated him. However, it showed up in the local papers. We called McKee's old summer home in Nonquitt, and had the housekeeper discard the paper before Katie could get to it.

On that Bermuda Race, in the late afternoon the day before the race, I checked the sail locker. Unbelievably, the sail bags holding the spinnakers had been eaten away by a rat that had also eaten holes in the nylon spinnakers. We lugged the spinnakers to a local and temporary Hood loft where they were patched, just in time for our late morning departure to the starting line. In our bunks at night we could hear the rat moving around, still on board! It eventually ate through some plywood and got into the cereal boxes. It wasn't until the boat returned home that the exterminators were finally successful in getting rid of the unwelcome stowaway. Never dull sailing with Bates, and always a great pleasure.

New York Yacht Club

It was Bates McKee who, in 1967, sponsored me for membership in the New York Yacht Club. Seconders were Past Commodore Macrae Sykes of the Manhasset Bay Yacht Club, Everett Morris of the Port Washington Yacht Club and James Roe. Richard joined the club in 1972 after completing his time in the Navy, and currently is a Trustee. When I learned that Bates had proposed me for the New York Yacht Club, I was concerned that if I were turned down (there were few Jewish members) I probably would not want to visit 37 West 44th Street again. I was pleased to become a member, as was my nephew Ted, several years later.

NEW YORK YACHT CLUB CRUISES

For over twenty years, I raced in the New York Yacht Club Annual Cruise. I've mentioned several such cruises earlier. We won a few fine trophies, including one in a windy race from Edgartown to Marion. My 32-foot Pilot, with an 18-year-old Louis Larsen wire luff spinnaker, won overall against over 90 other vessels. That week, one of our competitors, *Hotfoot*, designed by Alan Gurney, won every race in my division but one. The advertisements run later by the designer read "1, 1, 1, OOPS, 1, 1." My *Lady Del* had provided the OOPS.

In all the years of racing, I only recall one protest: in 1972 at a NYYC start on the south side of Woods Hole. I was protested and lost to Commodore John Nicholas Brown in his *Mazurka*. It was his beautiful home in Newport, Harbour Court, which the New York Yacht Club purchased in 1983 after our loss of the America's Cup. That facility has tremendously expanded the racing activities of the club.

For many years the NYYC sailing instructions called for racing through Woods Hole, one of the scariest passages to negotiate by sail. Currents run to six knots, past rocks, through twisting channels. After a number of accidents, the decision was made to power through the Hole. Hadley's Harbor, a most wonderful harbor opposite Woods Hole, was the usual overnight anchorage and lay day.

Later in the cruise, we were to race for the Astor Cup off Marblehead on *Lady Del*. It was blowing about 25 knots. A few minutes before the start, I noticed Tom O'Sullivan was not on deck. As I called for him to come to help, the genoa sheet parted. Tom came scrambling through the hatch trying to close the zipper on his pants. Once we got things organized and were on our way, I asked why he was late coming on deck.

He sheepishly replied that he had a tick, acquired in Edgartown, affixed to his private part(s) and was trying to get it off with alcohol and a cigarette. When I called him, he quickly tried to remove the alcohol that was burning

NYYC Race Instructions called for racing through Woods Hole, one of the scariest passages negotiated by sail.

him. He pleaded to go below and finish the job. The crew was convulsed. We ended up in the middle of our division. My entry in our log was: "O'Sullivan brined his balls in alcohol."

KNICKERBOCKER YACHT CLUB CENTENNIAL

In 1974 the Knickerbocker Yacht Club celebrated its 100th Anniversary. My last year as commodore was 1973; I was followed in 1974 by Stanley Swaback. I knew Stanley would do a first rate job, which he did. I kept the fund raising responsibility for the centennial event, and today there is an attractive plaque at Knickerbocker on which several hundred contributors are listed. Shortly before the centennial, the club's three launches were lost in a fire in the neighboring shipyard. This fire was attributed to arson and also destroyed Manhasset Bay Yacht Club's beautiful fleet of wooden Resolutes that had been built in Norway.

My idea was to use the centennial dollars for permanent and practical use. We purchased a centennial launch that is still in use. Contributions were made to the U.S. Naval Academy, U.S. Merchant Marine Academy, and the Maritime College at Ft. Schuyler, so that each year the income from these invested contributions would support a KYC Centennial prize to be awarded to a worthy midshipman or cadet. Also, a contribution was made to the Mystic Seaport to finance a sailing dinghy for young sailors. Every six or so years, we give them a new dinghy. In my library is a copy of the "100 Years of the Knickerbocker Yacht Club."

ARTHUR KNAPP AND THE KNICKERBOCKER CUP

Arthur Knapp was a special friend of ours. He was a world-famous sailor, America's Cup veteran (*Ranger* 1937 and later various twelve meters), America's Cup Hall of Famer, and writer of the very popular book, Sail Your Boat Right, which is still considered the bible for racing sailors. We were together at the Congressional Cup in Long Beach, California, in 1977. This 40-year-old event was the forerunner of today's major match racing regattas around the world, and the only one in the United States at that time. Today, match racing is a major sailing activity in many parts of the world, usually with significant monetary prizes. The Congressional Cup and other such events are proving grounds for America's Cup skippers.

After we returned home, I asked if Arthur would join me in establishing a similar event here on the East Coast to be organized by the Knickerbocker Yacht Club. He agreed and in 1982 the Knickerbocker Cup was established. This year, 2006, will be the 24th annual K Cup. It is one of only two big-boat match race series in the U.S., the other being the Congressional Cup. Chris Pollack with Dave Dellenbaugh as tactician won the first K Cup, and Dave also won the second. Richard and his regular crew won the third, the only time a "local hero" has won. Over the years, the competing skippers have become more professional, with stars like Paul Cayard, Ed Baird, and Peter Gilmour making successful appearances.

Ed presenting the Knickerbocker Cup to World Match Racing Champion Peter Gilmour of Australia.

Working with Scott MacLeod, who developed the Swedish Match Racing Tour (now, in 2006, the World Match Racing Tour) into a powerhouse event with my nephew Ted Weisberg's help, we attracted sponsors like Brut and Cigna Insurance. They were interested in the event primarily because Gary Jobson filmed the racing, with worldwide distribution. The event has brought most of the world's top match racers and America's Cup skippers to our area.

As an added attraction for the sponsors, we changed the venue to New York City and raced off the Statue of Liberty. After several years there, the Board of Governors decided to bring the K Cup back to Manhasset Bay where the Club could better extend its hospitality to the contestants from so many parts of the world. Members valued welcoming the sailors into their homes, and the sailors enjoyed that warmth and hospitality. Thus, we lost our sponsors, but the K Cup continued to thrive. Remarkably, a yacht club of less than 175 members managed to fund the event itself.

Ted Weisberg, as Commodore of KYC, was active helping to organize many K Cups, and was a close friend and crew for Arthur Knapp. Ted became active in the promotion of match racing events throughout the world, ultimately serving three years as the president of World Match Racing, and as a director of the Swedish Match Tour.

At the 2004 Knickerbocker Cup dinner, I was surprised to be especially honored for my many years of involvement in the K Cup. It was quite an evening. My closing words, aimed particularly at the visiting twelve crews were **Sail Fair, Sail Safe, Sail Fast**.

I missed attending the 2005 K Cup due to my present illness. I did submit

Dennis Conner flew in on the red eye from San Diego and gave a thrilling pep talk to the young sailors.

some remarks that included:

"…Arthur Knapp and I, when we created this competition in 1982, enjoyed having rock stars like Cayard, Baird, Coutts, Gilmour but most of all we were interested in the younger match racers who would become the future America's Cup helmsmen such as Jim Spithill, Ken Read, Peter Holmberg, Francesco de Angelis…for those who didn't win this week, take heart as neither did they."

ISRAEL – MACCABIAH GAMES

On April 17, 1985, I was asked to serve as honorary chairman of the U.S. Sailing Team that was to participate in the 12th Maccabiah Games in Israel. Much like our Olympics, this event takes place every four years. It brings together Jewish athletes from around the world. I agreed, as it would give Eleanor and me the chance to visit Israel. One of my responsibilities was to raise funds for the sailing team. We arranged an evening at the New York Yacht Club. I was pleased with the large turnout. The entire sailing team was there and to my pleasant surprise Dennis Conner flew in on the red-eye from San Diego and gave a thrilling pep talk to the young sailors. Dennis flew back to California the next morning.

Sightseeing the many historic places in Israel was a wonderful experience. The racing took place in Nahariyya about ten miles from Lebanon. Security was tight. Patrol boats were plentiful, and soldiers were stationed on rooftops. The actual games themselves were exciting, as were the attending spectacular flying, parades, and music. Later we toured the Golan Heights where I found a metal ammunition container (like the ones the U.S. Army had) with bullet holes. To everyone's surprise, I managed to bring it home. It is now in the possession of the Moreas along with an empty 3-inch 50 caliber WWII shell from the *Ingham*.

CATHY

Cathy enjoyed sailing but not racing, although she did do some night races with us. One of her self-appointed jobs was to spread spray deodorant around the cabin. Funny, none of the men seemed to notice the need to improve the atmosphere.

Cathy was a delightful handful. As a baby, she could spot the tiniest bug in the most distant corner of the ceiling. Eleanor and I might have had a hard job locating it, but we had to destroy it or no sleep for any of us. When she was no more than three, Cathy somehow found a rubber circular object, like a small frisbee, and threw it over the balcony leading to her Grandma Adele's apartment below. When Mom picked it up, she had absolutely no idea what it was (Eleanor's diaphragm). Meantime, Richard until age three had a habit of dropping flashlight batteries into the toilet – he liked the sound of the splash. Each time the plumber had to be called, and each time he would have to unbolt the toilet to remove the missile(s).

In Woodmere, our neighbor called Eleanor to say that Cathy (also at about three) was walking down the street with high heel shoes but no clothes. Fortunately no one had camera phones or the like. At mealtimes, Cathy frustrated Eleanor by not wanting to eat. At the same time Muriel Green was going through the same problem with her Ellen. To maintain their sanity, Eleanor and Muriel would toast each other as they drank a scotch.

LAKE PLACID

Cathy always wanted to do what her older brother did. In Lake Placid, Richard and I walked to the top of the Olympic ski jump. Cathy insisted on doing it too. Up we went, and when we got to the top, the view made her too scared to make the descent. I had to carry her down. Then I took Richard to the Olympic bobsled run. Cathy was too young to be allowed that ride.

The four-man bobsled was crewed by two German-speaking Austrian professionals, the driver in the front and the brakeman in the rear, with Richard and me in between. The handholds were short pieces of leather with a large ball at the end. I told Richard to hold the ball tight and not let go. I did not know that we were supposed to hold the leather in front of the ball, which was there to keep our hands from slipping off. We started down and rapidly accelerated. Between the speed and sharp turns, the centrifugal force made it feel like your head was going to come out your ass. By our not having correct handholds, Richard and I slipped back against the brakeman. As we hurtled down the mountain, at first the brakeman started to scream in German. It was so exciting that we joined him as we thought he would have wished. Finally we reached the outrun and as the sled slowed down, the brakeman jumped off and in a panic started to run around holding his ass in his two

Ed and Richard on the Olympic bobsled run,
Lake Placid, 1957.

Ed, Eleanor, Cathy, and Rich skiing in Canada.

hands. Then we noticed his ripped pants and realized that by not holding the grips correctly, we had pushed his rear end off the sled so he was dragging his ass on the ice at 60 miles an hour. The driver and brakeman were less than friendly when I asked if we could take a second run (we did not). We were all happy to depart the scene.

No, Cathy never got to ride the bobsled. Richard, Ann, with their kids and friends, in January 2006, were in their ski house in Minerva when they decided to visit Lake Placid and do the bobsled run again. This time the ride went smoothly.

SKIING IN CANADA

I hadn't skied since before World War II. When Richard and Cathy were six and four we went to Lake Placid with Sam and Mom and stayed at an inn owned by the Ryans. Eleanor tried skiing one day, twisted her ankle, and decided she would rather stay with the women non-skiers and talk, knit, or read. In the mornings, the children were taught by the son of the Ryans. I wanted Richard and Cathy to learn to ski, as it is a wonderful family and lifetime sport. Today, all of my seven grandchildren ski.

As related before, we spent the Christmas-New Year's holiday at the wonderful Manoir St. Castin, ten miles north of Quebec City. Each morning, we skied under the direction of the Austrian parallel ski pioneer Fritz Loosli. I was in a more advanced class and found it somewhat challenging as I had learned to ski by the seat of my pants. The young ones developed beautiful form from the start. The time came when they advanced faster than I did. I would go down slower than they would, and could do a telemark that would make them laugh. The day they moved ahead of me, Richard cried because he thought I would be upset. I assured him that I couldn't be happier that he and Cathy had passed me by.

In 1959, Eleanor, Cathy, Richard, and I went to Mont Tremblant north of Montreal. This was quite elegant and social compared to other areas. We had rented a cottage at the foot of the mountain. One night, we were awakened by noises from Richard's room. Apparently, a broken thermostat had permitted the room to become intensely hot. Richard was delirious. We received medical help promptly and by morning he was ready to ski. The main slope was great. You could take the lift to the mountaintop, and ski down either side of the mountain. If you chose the far side, a bus would meet you at the bottom and return you to the Lodge. One morning, I had urged Cathy to use the bathroom before we took the tow. She insisted she didn't have to go. Halfway down the mountain, with no other skiers in sight, she finally did have to go, and with no time to spare. She left a very bright yellow stain on the virgin white snow. We left our "mark" on Mont Tremblant and never did return.

Richard and Ann have taken their four children, Lora Ann, Ed, Matt, and Mark, skiing all over the world. Ann is a conservative solid parallel skier, while the others are aggressive skiers and have now mastered snowboards as well, including Richard. Mark suffered a broken collarbone from snowboarding. Lora Ann continued her skiing in the Andes while living in Chile. For the winters of 2004 through 2006 she has been a ski instructor at Jackson Hole, Wyoming. In April 2006 she goes to work for the World Health Organization in Geneva, Switzerland, where I am sure she will ski the Alps.

Since Dad passed away, grandson Edward also became a ski instructor at Jackson Hole.
— **R. du M**.

CATHY AT CAMP

With Richard actively involved in junior sailing, we thought it would be nice for Cathy to go to camp. Eleanor selected Camp Allegro near Pittsfield, Massachusetts. As the day approached for Cathy to be driven to the camp, she began to have second thoughts. We were confident that once she got there, she would be fine. At the parting, we kissed her goodbye and left her crying. For about ten days we would get daily calls from her, asking that we bring her home, backed up by various threats of bodily damage. We were miserable and consulted with her pediatrician who urged us to stand strong.

*W*hen I explained the plan was worked out sitting in the bathroom, they referred to it as the Toilet Loan.

Finally, after several weeks, she adjusted. We, of course, would visit her at every opportunity. She became active in plays (including playing a stripper in "Gypsy"), team sports, and developed warm friendships.

MOVE TO SANDS POINT

After Cathy graduated from Hewlett High in 1966, we finally moved to Sands Point on the North Shore near Knickerbocker Yacht Club and the boat. Eleanor was shown several houses by Evelyn Caro who became a good friend. The 12-year-old house we purchased was all on one floor and situated on two and three-quarters acres. The house at 15 Tibbits Lane, diagonally across from the Sands Point Town Hall and Police Station, appealed to Eleanor from a security point of view. After all, I was traveling a good deal. Over the almost 40 years the local police have been very helpful. When Eleanor would call to advise them we would be away, they would ask, "Do you have a burglar alarm?" Eleanor's answer was always, "Yes, you." When the first New Year's Eve approached after settling into our new home, I asked Eleanor if we should send over sandwiches and refreshments to the police on duty that night. After determining that no other neighbor had been doing this, every New Year's Eve since we arrange to do so.

GREEN MOUNTAIN COLLEGE

Cathy wasn't sure what she wanted to study or where she wanted to go to college. Richard, in his second year at Dartmouth, suggested Green Mountain College in Poultney, Vermont, a Methodist college founded in 1834. It was near enough to Dartmouth that Richard could keep an eye on her, and it was a two-year program. As expected, when we drove her there with all her equipment, she was quite unhappy. We left her on the steps of her dorm crying (just like Camp Allegro). It was hard on us, too. Cathy quickly adapted. Two years later she graduated and then enrolled in Boston University to obtain a four-year degree. She studied education and spent a great deal of time working with schoolchildren in a slum area of Boston.

Reverend Raymond Withey, the President of Green Mountain College, later invited me to join their Board of Trustees. I served for 25 years, meeting some wonderful people, particularly Steele Griswold, an alumnus, WWII flier, and ocean sailor. He served as chairman of the board for a number of years. There was a time when Green Mountain was having a financial problem and needed cash for a short period. The board discussed various solutions but could not come to a practical conclusion. The meeting was adjourned until the following morning. There were some festivities that evening. After Eleanor and I returned to our room, and not to disturb her, I sat in the bathroom for an hour and half with a legal pad on my lap, and outlined a method of getting the needed $200,000. Why not ask each of twenty-plus trustees to lend $10,000 for up to three months, with interest at 6%? At the next day's meeting, Steele passed a slip of paper to each trustee so they could, in private, agree or not. It worked perfectly. When I explained the plan had been worked out while sitting in the bathroom, they referred to it as the Toilet Loan. When the slips were totaled, we had gone over the required amount. Three months later, the loans were paid off.

During my days at Green Mountain, the school adopted a four-year college program and went co-ed. In 1987, after Dennis Conner recaptured the America's Cup from Australia, President Pollock asked if I would arrange for him to receive an honorary degree at the May graduation. Dennis gave a great talk to the students (details in my America's Cup book).

Eleanor and I met a wonderful couple, Connie and Charles Brewer (not the boat designer Ted Brewer) in Ft. Myers, Florida. We both were outfitting our new 42-foot long Brewer 12.8s. Mine became my last *Lady Del* (number four). Charles was the former head of architecture at Ohio State University, with numerous awards in his field. Both he and his wife were highly educated. After sailing their Brewer around the world they planned to settle in Vermont. I asked Charles if he might be interested in joining the board of Green Mountain. He did join the board and later became chairman. What a fine job the two Brewers did in planning and executing major physical changes to the college. I also introduced Stanley Rich to the board where he did fine work in recruitment and financial guidance.

HINCKLEY 38

In 1967, Eleanor and I visited Eastbourne Lodge in Newport where the America's Cup crews of *Constellation* (Richard included) and *Intrepid* were housed. The great designer Olin Stephens was present tending his two creations. His firm had also designed my 32' Pilot *Lady Del* back in the

US Naval Academy yacht RAGE, *skippered by Rich du Moulin, tied up next to* LADY DEL III *while visiting Port Washington.*

1940s. I asked Olin if he would be interested in designing a 38-foot sloop, with the famous *Intrepid* underbody, which had a trim tab attached to the keel and a skeg-mounted rudder. Olin agreed to do the design. I interested Harold Oldak, who had previously organized several successful class syndicates, the best known of which was the Bermuda 40, to help form a new syndicate. He agreed and we gathered a group of eight members of the Knickerbocker and Manhasset Bay Yacht Clubs.

We wanted Hinckley, who had built the Bermuda 40s, to construct what became the Hinckley 38. Olin Stephens objected. I set up a meeting at the New York Yacht Club with Harold, Henry Hinckley, and Olin. Olin's objection was that, in the past, Hinckley would change his design without consulting the Sparkman & Stephens design firm. After a frank discussion, we all shook hands.

Everything went smoothly primarily because Gil Segal, an engineer and boat surveyor, agreed to represent the syndicate members in dealing with the designer and builder. Gil would periodically visit the shipyard, film the progress, and then meet with the prospective owners to bring them up-to-date. The eight of us would chip in to pay Gil for his time and expenses.

The smooth operation of our H-38 syndicate resulted from several guiding principles:

1. Any equipment that had to be installed by the yard (winches, instruments, for example) would be purchased through the shipyard, so that the yard would make a profit. However, items like sails, life jackets, and the rubber dinghy, Gil would buy at a discount for us.

2. We would agree on one sailmaker and one instrument package. If any one of us had a faulty instrument, we could always check it out

LADY DEL III, *the Hinckley 38, starting a rough Block Island race. The* LADY DEL III *regulars, standing, from left: Gene Miller, Jerry Farmer, Tom O'Sullivan. Bottom (left to right), Elliott Oldak, Ted Weisberg, Andy MacGowan.*

against one of the other syndicate boats.

    3. We would not individually pester the shipyard but operate through our project coordinator.

We had agreed on having a Westerbeke diesel engine installed. To keep the weight low and centered, it was to be placed amidships, under the main cabin sole. Henry Hinckley said there would be no problem, but to fit it in, and without consulting our designer or Gil, Hinckley expanded the hull where the keel met the hull. The shape of the bottom was supposed to be like a wine glass, but instead had a wide vee section where the hull and keel met. Olin was upset when he discovered the *fait accompli*. However, the boat was beautiful, comfortable, and very competitive for two years.

Henry Hinckley took the first boat finished and I received the second, my new *Lady Del*. Eleanor, my nephew Barry, and Roger Lowlicht (later a member of the *Intrepid* America's Cup support crew) had an interesting (and cold) initial cruise from Southwest Harbor, Maine, to Manhasset Bay. En route, we joined a New York Yacht Club annual cruise and raced a few races. Unfortunately, the NYYC commodore passed away, canceling the cruise. Exiting the west end of the Cape Cod Canal, we ran into terribly rough water. I was aware of the rough conditions when a late afternoon sou'westerly blows against the fast moving ebb out of the Canal, but I had had a lapse of memory. As we exited the Canal, waves were breaking into the cockpit and we were hardly making headway under power. We were very happy to anchor in Onset Harbor at dusk.

Several years later the racing measurement rules were changed to IOR. Those of us who were serious racers decided to sell our H-38s, and look for a boat that would measure up more competitively vis-à-vis the new IOR Rule.

DOVE TO MAINE

While wondering what my next boat might be, I chartered for $1.00 Stewart Greene's Swan 43, *Dove*, for the 1972 New York Yacht Club cruise to Maine. Stew came with us along with a fine diverse crew. Chuck Stetson had been a Blue Jay National Champ as a kid. Andy Radel our navigator had raced *Charisma* to Bermuda with Richard, and was a retired Army Air Force colonel, having been in charge of Air Force One for three presidents.

Robbie Lager ran the foredeck with a young John Devine on his first ocean run. From the east end of the Cape Cod Canal, we were to race to Rockport, Maine. The start was late afternoon with winds 25 to 30 knots from the southeast and a dense fog. We raised the spinnaker and blooper, and were off and flying.

We had no radar, so our hand-held radio direction finder was invaluable. Normally conservative, I just hoped we would not hit anything as we sped along. Visibility was so bad that Robbie was checking the spinnaker with the spreader lights. From the cockpit it was hard to make Robbie out. Straining our eyes, there was just enough light to see Robbie "mooning" the afterguard. I had the midnight to four watch. With me in the cockpit was young John. *Dove* was rolling from side to side when I offered the wheel to him. He said no. I insisted, assuring him I would be right behind him. After a short while, the boat broached. There was a loud crash below – the drawer with the silverware had come loose. I took the wheel back as Stew yelled from his bunk, "Put someone on the wheel who can handle her." I answered that everything was under control. Like the rider on a horse who has fallen off, I ordered John to take the wheel again and he did, reluctantly. I explained this was his chance to learn the ways of the sea – take advantage of it. Today, he is a professional with the experience of several transatlantic crossings.

While approaching Rockport, still in the heavy fog, Andy Radel was taking RDF bearings. We could hear the surf. Over the radio we learned that two famous sailors, Bus Mosbacher and Bob McCullough, had apparently got dangerously close to the rocks. We felt our way into Rockport Harbor in the early morning. Almost immediately, a Coast Guard boat came alongside and told me that I was to fly home as my mother was failing. A few days later, Mom passed away. What a sensational lady she was. Meanwhile, *Dove* and crew continued the cruise to Maine. The following year, Chuck Stetson and I did one other New York Yacht Club cruise on *Dove*, and won the Royal Sydney Yacht Squadron Bowl.

YOUNG RACING CREWS

A major accomplishment in my years of yacht racing was my program to invite, each year, two young, promising sailors to race with me. Each January, I would circulate my racing schedule to about 25 friends, asking

Straining our eyes, there was just enough light to see Robbie "mooning" the afterguard.

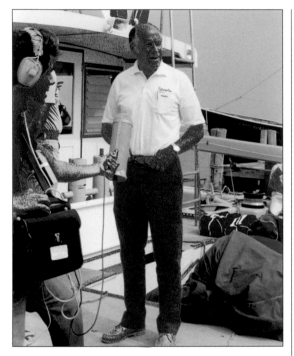

Ed (top) faces the media as head of the Enterprise Snydicate in 1977. The Enterprise crew: front row from left— Dave Pedrick, the late Fritz Jewett, Ed, and Olin Stephens.

them to check off the races on which they would like to be crew. Although some you might call regulars, there always were the newcomers. Those with the right attitude and potential ability, who wanted to spread their wings, I would recommend to my old friend and business partner, E. Bates McKee, for an invitation to sail on his *Xanadu II* (the previously mentioned 49-foot, varnished hull, Tripp-designed yawl) on a return trip from Bermuda. I would receive a report on their performance at sea. If warranted, I would then recommend them as crew on a race to Bermuda. Later, many would become crew on popular yachts like *Ondine*, *La Forza del Destino*, *Charisma*, and many other fine blue-water racers. Some would wind up on ocean races like Capetown to Rio, the Transatlantic or Transpacific races, and even on America's Cup contenders. Today, many of my "young" crew race with Richard on *Lora Ann*. They are now in their fifties and sixties – on *Lora Ann*'s transom it says it all: "Team AARP."

At Bache, my first boss insisted that I keep notes. He claimed that this would relieve my mind, and avoid overlooking important chores or events. Richard has always maintained such notes, as does Chris. I keep meticulous check lists including winterizing the boat, spring commissioning, etc. This habit served me well in business, sailing, and America's Cup management.

Here is an example of involving the crew. In a downwind run to the finish line of an important overnighter, I wasn't sure of the proper tactic. When I asked Elliott Oldak and Gene Miller, two fine crew who knew a great deal more than I did about tacking downwind, they told me as captain I should make the decision. Sure I could, but I wanted their opinions. One said tack downwind and the other go dead downwind. I asked them to go forward to the shrouds and come to an agreement. They did and we tacked downwind to win the race. Gene became a naval architect after graduating from Webb Institute, and Elliott has been in charge of the Naval Academy yacht maintenance program for almost 25 years.

Joseph Cooper wrote the book <u>Lands End and Waters Edge</u>. In it, he described racing with *Lady Del*, and Eleanor's cooking that contributed to our fun and success. The most popular meal of all was Eleanor's pot roast with gravy, which Andy MacGowan particularly enjoyed. It always seemed we were heeled over, sailing through a choppy Plum Gut or the Race when it was served, but no one missed his portion.

BLAZE *sailing on Long Island Sound*

BLAZE

Realizing our Hinckley 38s were no longer competitive, Harold Oldak and I together searched for our next boat as partners. We learned that a new Carter 39, built in Greece, was at a shipyard in Mamaroneck, New York. It was a Dick Carter design, patterned after his Admiral's Cup winner *Frigate* in England. At first sight, we both liked the bright red, powerful hull, deep rudder and skeg. The boat had minor damage on deck from hitting an overpass that reduced her price, so in 1974 we purchased her as partners, and named her *Blaze*. Tom O'Sullivan drafted a flashy name for the transom in yellow incorporating lightning bolts, and Richard and Harold repaired and modified the deck arrangement.

BLAZE *, Ed's Carter 39, racing Block Island Race Week.*

We were in a state of confusion regarding sails. Richard had just completed an America's Cup summer sailing on *Mariner* with Ted Turner, then *Intrepid* with Gerry Driscoll, Bill Buchan, Andy MacGowan, and John Marshall. Richard was convinced that North Sails was the way to go, but our friend and tactician Steve Moore worked at Hard Sails and had made us an offer too good to refuse: a full inventory for the price of materials. Richard was a close friend of John Marshall of North Sails who wanted the order, anticipating that the Oldak/du Moulin combination would be competitive and help his sales. John finally solved our dilemma by hiring Steve and giving us an exceptional discount.

Our first major event in 1975 was Block Island Race Week. I had hurt my back and was unable to be on board, so Richard took over for me. With Harold, Steve and crew they won class (four firsts and a third), and were awarded the Everett Morris Trophy as the outstanding boat of the week.

BLAZE *flying downwind under spinnaker and blooper.*
This shot appeared in the 1975 North Sails calendar.

A great photo of *Blaze* running in heavy air with spinnaker and blooper pulling powerfully became the calendar photo for North Sails in 1975, so everyone was happy.

Our toughest competitor in 1975 was Tom Whidden on Dick Hokin's *Love Machine*. At Block Island they lost their mast, but in the Vineyard Race we had a great boat-for-boat race in heavy conditions, only passing them the final night by flying our starcut spinnaker in 30-35 knots of wind when no one else could carry a chute. Tom was to become a wonderful friend in my years of America's Cup management.

Our next Block Island Race Week was not until four years later in 1979, due to our family's involvement with the 1977 *Enterprise* Campaign. Back at Block Island defending our Everett Morris Trophy, as usual we had a great crew that included Tony Parker, Chip Whipple, Tom Gallagher, Chris Reyling, and John Browning. Also along for the ride was Richard's fiancée Ann (Capelli) for her first ever big-boat race (she had been Richard's frostbite crew). Richard was the tactician with Tony advising, and I was at the helm. Rich was always aggressive at the start of a race while I was usually more conservative. Early at the committee boat end of the starting line, we managed to hook the Race Committee's anchor chain, allowing their bowsprit to pierce our new jib. It took us nearly ten minutes to disengage while our division sailed away. We finally freed ourselves and started with the next class, which promptly rolled over us. As we sailed off, Ann calmly enquired of Rich and Tony, "Are all your starts like this one?" Eventually we salvaged a fifth place for the day.

The next day as we arrived at the starting area, our crew placed brown paper grocery bags fitted with peepholes over their heads. The fleet greatly enjoyed the sight, and later at the Storm Trysail awards affair we were given the Blockhead Trophy. Quite a contrast to the overall prize four years before. No one has accomplished that feat, before or since.

Years later, in 2001, my Lora Ann, *having won the prior Race Week, once again earned the Blockhead for further deeds of glory. In the recent 2007 Race Week, historical photos of previous Race Weeks were published, and of course the paper bag crew was featured prominently.* — **R. du M**.

Ed and Rich on board the tender, CHAPERONE, *during the Enterprse America's Cup campaign in 1977.*

BLAZE & BERMUDA

In 1978, *Blaze* won the Malabar Trophy for MHS division D in the Bermuda Race and came in second overall. We had a great crew: Richard, John Browning, and Tony Parker were experienced celestial navigators but John Storck, who had asked if he could be the navigator on his first Bermuda Race, became the official navigator. I had taken a refresher course but never got the chance to use my sextant. John Storck had plenty of sextant experts looking over his shoulders. Others on board were Lee Reichart, John de Regt, and Tom Ternes. Four of the crew were America's Cup veterans, and all had extensive ocean experience. When we tied up to the dock, the boys collected their liquor winnings from our Bermuda-owned sistership, the aptly named *Climax* (in recognition of the crews' sexual exploits), who finished behind us (too much sex?).

Several crew slept aboard in St. George's near the finish line, while those with wives in Bermuda headed for the hotels. Tony's wife was in a bed & breakfast waiting for him. Near midnight, having consumed some of our liquor winnings, Tony arrived in front of the house where he thought she was staying. The doors were locked and lights were out, so Tony called for his wife in a loud voice and then proceeded to throw stones at the upper window. A man's head appeared:

> Tony: You've got my wife. Give her to me!
> The Head: I do not have your wife. Leave or I shall call the police.
> Tony: I am a Washington lawyer!
> The Head: I am the Chief Justice of Bermuda.

A few minutes later, the constables arrived and they kindly offered Tony

*D*uring the night the curtain caught fire from a faulty air conditioner. Cathy managed to escape.

a bed in jail for the remainder of the night, while his bride slept soundly elsewhere. The next morning he was released in her custody. Meantime, Richard's new girlfriend, Ann, also joined us in Bermuda.

After another Bermuda Race, Eleanor and Cathy met us in Bermuda. Cathy had a room at the Waterloo Hotel. During the night, the curtain caught fire from a faulty air conditioner. Somehow, Cathy managed to escape and alert the manager and the other guests. She singed her throat, however, and also lost all of her clothes to smoke damage. Despite her heroics, the hotel tried to charge her for the night. Richard intervened and the hotel cancelled the charges, and paid for new clothes. It was a miracle she survived.

In our three Bermuda Races with *Blaze*, Eleanor and I rented a cottage on the beach where crew and friends would barbecue and hold crew parties. All three return trips, bringing *Blaze* home, were skippered and crewed by Rich Feeley and his friends.

Blaze was Richard's favorite boat. After several years, I bought Harold's interest. We continued to build up a fine record. Once I became actively engaged in the America's Cup, my time on *Blaze* was limited. During the Cup races of 1977 and 1980, she became a guest hotel at our Newport base. In 1981, I donated her to the Maritime College at Ft. Schuyler Foundation, through which our Cup campaigns were conducted.

A CRUISING BOAT

Eleanor and I enjoyed an exceptional 1983. Early in the year, we decided that this would be our last year involved with the management of an America's Cup campaign. We would spend more time with the growing grandchildren, and get back to our own sailing. In July, from Newport, I contacted Harold Oldak and told him of our goal. I suggested that we form a new syndicate to build a cruising sailboat that would not look like a houseboat.

Harold agreed to look around and eventually located a Brewer 42 in Florida. (This boat was later destroyed in the 2005 hurricane, Katrina). She was a ketch with a cockpit amidships, and a lovely sheer line. She did not look like a houseboat, and was the American version of the famous Canadian Whitby 42. Harold and I agreed, that with certain modifications, she would be just fine. Ft. Myers Yacht & Shipbuilding Co. had built the Brewer 42, and once again Harold was able to secure the services of Gil Segal who would serve as project manager. When the word got out that we were forming a new syndicate, seven others from the Knickerbocker and Manhasset Bay Yacht Clubs signed on.

Harold and I made up a list of over 100 specifications/changes. He contacted Ted Brewer, the designer, on the major changes, such as: a cutter rig; a five-foot taller mast (for light winds of Long Island Sound); air-foil shaped keel and centerboard; a 90HP Lehman-Ford engine; skeg-rudder; and cockpit changes. Other items we worked out with the builder included: electric winches; ability to pump the bilge through the engine water pump; automatic changing engine oil; backup engine starter in engine room; davits; Hood roller furling for headsails; and rod rigging for shrouds. One of the key attractions was the ability to walk from main cabin to the aft cabin below deck. We also were able to enter/exit the aft cabin on a ladder similar to the one in the main cabin. We followed the same principles as we did when we built the Hinckley 38s - all equipment installed in the boat would be handled through the shipyard; other items such as Avon dinghies, sails, and tools Gil could purchase for us at discount.

I was to get delivery of the ninth boat that would become available about January 1, 1984 after I finished managing the *Liberty* campaign in Newport. One day, Dick Leather of Manhasset Bay Yacht Club visited our compound in Newport and mentioned he was looking to buy a boat about 42 feet long. I told him about our program and said, if interested, he could take my number nine hull, and I would take delivery of number ten. He arranged to join the group. Gil did a fine job of coordinating the ten-boat program. All of us were completely happy with our new Brewer 12.8s (42 feet), and particularly pleased were our wives, with the double bedroom aft, complete with private head/shower/hot & cold water. They also appreciated the refrigerator and freezer. Twenty-two years later, four of the original owners still are sailing their Brewer 12.8s.

Eleanor and I had a great time in Ft. Myers commissioning our new *Lady Del*. We enjoyed the trip to Manhasset Bay assisted by Andy Radel, the Chesebroughs, and Greens. Over the years we had wonderful cruises to Block Island, Maine, Martha's Vineyard, and ports in between.

A favorite sport was to hoist the young ones, one at a time, and and lower them at a fast clip into the water

CRUISING *LADY DEL*

One of the great advantages of our Brewer 12.8 was that we could accommodate our seven grandkids, and their parents. The children would sleep in the cockpit and on the after cabin roof. On occasion, we would anchor overnight in New York Harbor, near the Statue of Liberty or in a ship docking area. A favorite sport was to hoist the young ones, one at a time, in the bos'n chair and lower them, at a fast clip, into the water. We even provided some spinnaker flying. I would never do these exercises unless Richard was with us. All the grandchildren enjoyed many nights aboard, including our annual raft-up in Oyster Bay or elsewhere with *Lora Ann*.

We cruised for almost fifty years on our various boats with Arnold and Muriel Green and, after Arnold died, with Dot and Dick Chesebrough. We would often troll a fishing line astern. Through those years, Eleanor would not permit anyone to bring a bluefish aboard. I guess she was afraid of the smell or blood on deck. However, they could catch and release. This frustrated Harold Oldak and Dick Chesebrough, in particular, as both were ardent fishermen. Dick's family was one of the original settlers of Stonington, Connecticut, in the early 1600s. His family, from early on, were fishermen. After Eleanor passed away, Dick hooked a blue and promised me that not a drop of blood would land on the deck. With a look skyward, I figured Eleanor would approve giving him a chance. After the fish was carefully cleaned, Dick wanted to put it in the refrigerator – that, I know, Eleanor would not have approved, so we packed it in ice.

One year in the early 1990s, Eleanor and I were cruising with the Chesebroughs, heading for Block Island to visit Richard, Ann, and their four children in the house they had rented. They planned to be on the Coast Guard beach near the narrow cut into Salt Pond to watch us enter the harbor. Dick and I were busy below as Eleanor and Dotty navigated *Lady Del* through the narrow cut. As we passed Richard and his family, Eleanor yelled and Dick and I popped our heads on deck to wave. Richard noted our big grins and sweaty faces and commented to Ann, "I bet they have been repairing a broken head (toilet)." He was correct; Dick and I always enjoyed repairing things together, even the head.

Casting Bread Upon the Waters

Dad was always training young sailors and then helping them move on to bigger ocean racing yachts or America's Cup programs. He and Mom also helped others with more serious challenges. Both my parents were compassionate and highly skilled at helping others. They believed in "paying it forward," where their good turn would be multiplied by the recipient sometime later in that person's life. Like the story of Dad and Mom's relationship with my cousin Peter du Moulin, here are four other nice stories. — **R. du M**.

Helping Hand to Kevin

Eleanor and I took great pleasure in helping others as best we could, we liked to do good deeds, and we took a special interest in people with various problems.

Kevin was a big (6 foot 5 inch), strong, handsome (looked like Clint Eastwood) sailing friend of Richard's. He also sailed with me at various times. He was an alcoholic at 14, and, probably due to that problem, lost his berth on the America's Cup contender *American Eagle*. But Kevin was warm and intelligent, and Eleanor and I liked him.

Despite some negative advice, I invited Kevin to crew for me, particularly on night races. In the late afternoon, he would come aboard with a tall cup of black coffee and sleep for hours. He would be up for the midnight watch, refreshed, and do a great job the rest of the night. We were on a Vineyard race one night, riding the tail of a hurricane. Off Montauk, I sent young Chuck Karo forward with the strong and experienced Gerry Silverman to change the headsail. They both had harnesses on. The sail change was slow and Kevin was very upset because I would not let him go forward and help. I wanted young Chuck to get the experience under difficult conditions.

During a day race, Richard and Kevin were racing with me. Richard called for me to tack for the mark; Kevin disagreed and said there was too much current. Richard insisted so I tacked; we missed the mark. Kevin was so angry he kicked the side of the cabin and broke his toe. Richard thanked Kevin for taking his anger out on the cabin!

In later years, we learned Kevin's marriage was in jeopardy. Eleanor and I tried to counsel them. Kevin spent one night at our house talking with us till dawn. We later invited the young couple for a weekend cruise, hoping the close quarters would bring them together. It only worked for a while.

Kevin later joined Alcoholics Anonymous, after which I got him a job in Bache's Municipal Bond Department. He worked hard and well. After two years, he left. The problem was that he had little patience for lack of efficiency in his department. Several times, to cool off, he went to a house for recovering alcoholics. The miracle was that not too long afterwards, he met a wonderful girl, moved away from the city, and raised a family. I retained the moving letter he sent to Eleanor and to me thanking us.

A Special Call for Help

This is another story of extending a helping hand. Richard spoke to me about his friend Chuck, who at the time was living in the same New York apartment building as Elliott Oldak, George "Jory" Hinman, and Andy MacGowan. Richard explained that this bright talented individual needed some guidance that he thought Eleanor and I could supply. Richard had raced against Chuck as a junior, with Chuck winning the National Blue Jay Championship.

I invited Chuck to race with me in an important regatta in waters with which he was familiar. In a strong northwesterly breeze, we were beating toward Connecticut. I asked my newest crew to tell me when to tack (usually there is a header as you approach shore). The time came and I waited for his "Tack now," but there was no response. Finally I said: "If you were in your Blue Jay, what would you do?" Chuck immediately said, "I would tack." That broke the ice. He raced with me many times, usually serving as navigator. I learned Chuck had been a naval officer in Vietnam involved with river fighting. He had been educated in a fine prep school, graduated from Yale, and had studied in Europe. He was an excellent skier and tennis player. Eleanor and I had many conversations with Chuck in our home. His parents apparently had pressured him so much that he didn't want to visit them. We were not sure whether his lack of confidence came from Vietnam or family pressure – possibly both.

At one point, Chuck told us that he thought all families were constantly fighting, and was surprised that Eleanor and I were so compatible. After sailing with me on a number of New York Yacht Club cruises, he asked if I would sponsor him for membership. I suggested he do it through his uncle, already a member. He insisted that I sponsor him, which I did. After a number of months, Eleanor suggested that he visit his parents before he went back to the city. Chuck was hesitant. Eleanor pointed out that he well knew what his parents would say and how they would act, and just ignore it. Finally, he made the visit home and survived. From that time, the relationship with his parents improved. He became particularly close to his father, before he passed away in 2003.

Meanwhile, Chuck was unable to find a job on Wall Street. To me, he had the background (his grandfather had been chairman of the Guaranty Trust Co.), intelligence, and manners to be a successful investment banker in a prestigious banking firm. His lack of confidence and stuttering were his main obstacles. I explained that my firm was a wire house – a brokerage firm with minimum investment banking capabilities. However, if he was hired, he could learn a great deal, as we were unstructured in that field. I arranged for an interview with our Personnel Department who informed me that they did not recommend that he be hired. They explained that he made a fine initial impression, but soon broke into a sweat and began to stutter. I spoke to a close associate, Tom Lawrence, and asked if he would take this young man under his wing. With Tom's agreement, I exerted pressure and Bache had a new employee. Several years later, Chuck was transferred to our San Francisco office representing our Investment Banking Department.

After ten successful years with the firm, Chuck accepted an excellent offer from a fine local banking house in San Francisco. He met an attractive young woman in his office. He asked if they could join Eleanor and me on *Lady Del* when we were sailing in the Vineyard. Chuck wanted Eleanor's opinion of his lady friend. We had a good time and Eleanor approved his choice. They were married in St. Mary's Church in San Francisco. I was to be best man although I was old enough to be his father. I suggested he ask Andy MacGowan. We compromised. Andy and I were his "best men." Eventually, the couple moved back to New York. They have three beautiful daughters and during their vacations they charter cruising sailboats all over the world.

Over the years Chuck has written articles for the Harvard Business

Review – a most sophisticated publication. At times he would call to ask my opinion on a particular piece he was writing. I would listen, take notes, and then tell him I would call him the next day. That night I would phone Richard who had just graduated from Harvard Business School and ask him what our friend was talking about. Rich would explain it to me and the next day I would call and give Chuck "my" comments.

As an independent venture capitalist, Chuck has been a huge success. In recent years, he has spent much time and his own money to promote a program to prisons and school systems called "The Bible and Its Influence," covering all religions. It has been approved by every major religious group, and has been adopted in several states. The major political parties are also showing an interest in it. In spite of the separation of church and state, I believe he can succeed in this private endeavor.

PETER HYERS

This is the story of Eve (Hyers) Kelley. Eleanor and I met Eve through Tom Lawrence. Eve struggled hard to raise her two children, Nancy and Peter. We were close friends and were happy to help in various ways. Peter was a cute young redhead who wanted to sail. Tom arranged for him to join the junior sailing program at the Centerport Yacht Club and eventually bought him a Blue Jay. Eleanor and I would take him sailing with us on *Lady Del*. Peter was a good sailor, and while in high school decided he wanted to go to the Naval Academy. Richard, who was at that time the Naval Academy's ocean racing coach, invited him to the Academy for a weekend with the sailing team. Thereafter Peter's mind and heart were set on the Academy.

However, Peter was just a bit under the minimum height limitation. The Navy suggested he go to Bainbridge, the Navy prep school, as an enlisted man for one year, and then reapply. While at Bainbridge he worked hard to stretch himself. He chinned, ate special foods and finally was admitted to the Academy, having made the minimum height requirement. At the Academy he earned All American on the sailing team, and after graduating became a distinguished helicopter pilot and served on aircraft carriers all over the world, including service during the first Gulf War. In Japan, he was commanding officer of the finest helicopter squadron in the

Navy (Helicopter Anti-Submarine Squadron 14) and retired after 20 years as a captain.

A few years ago Peter helped my grandson, Doug Morea, get into the Naval Academy. Eleanor and I believed good deeds lead to other good deeds, I often call it **Bread Cast Upon The Waters**. We keep in close touch with Peter, who with his wife Jane and two children live in Hilton Head, where he is local ferry boat captain and skipper of the old America's Cup yacht *Stars & Stripes*.

LEE REICHART

About 25 years ago, Horace Hagedorn (my friend who founded Miracle-Gro) called to ask me to recommend someone to him from among my young sailing friends who might be interested in a sales position at Miracle-Gro. I made a list of about 20 names, listing them in order, based upon what I thought their capabilities might be. Richard reviewed them. His close friend and ex-roommate from Dartmouth, Lee Reichart, was on the top. Lee, when about 18, raced across the Atlantic and distinguished himself when he had to go up the rig and repair a bent mast in rough going. Richard was his best man when he married Gaye. Lee has a great personality and was working at the time in the Midwest with a major pharmaceutical corporation. I phoned and asked if he might like to come back to his home area. He was interested, and flew east to meet Horace. It was love at first sight. He has had a most successful career with Miracle-Gro.

My son-in-law Jerry Morea was between jobs. One morning I drove him to the Long Island Railroad in Port Washington. Just before he was to board the train, Lee Reichart saw us. He asked Jerry what he was doing and Jerry replied, "Looking for a job." Jerry is a graduate of Manhattan College, a CPA, and has his Masters. Lee said, "Forget the train, come meet Horace. He's looking for a chief financial officer." Jerry was immediately hired. Miracle-Gro's office was one mile from Jerry's home. For ten years (until the company relocated to Ohio), Jerry was a happy part of this close, family-oriented "gold mine." Another case of **Bread Cast Upon The Waters**.

Eleanor and I believed good deeds lead to other good deeds. I often call it, "Bread Cast upon the Waters."

CATHY AND RICHARD MARRIED

Our daughter Cathy married Jerome Morea, and son Richard married Ann Capelli, both in the beautiful chapel at the U.S. Merchant Marine Academy, on March 14, 1976 and November 4, 1979, respectively. To use the chapel, each had to have some connection with the Academy or a Naval service. Richard and I met the requirements, me through U.S. Coast Guard service, and Richard through Naval service and, of all things, navigating the ill-fated America's Cup yacht *Mariner*, which was owned by the Kings Point Foundation. Both weddings were memorable events, with the services performed by the dynamic duo of Father Peter Jacobs, a Woody Allen look-alike, and Cantor David Benedict, who had a fabulous singing voice. March 14, 1976 was a sunny day and we were able to watch the Academy's small boats sail with New York City in the background. November 4, 1979, was the same, and as we later learned, the day the hostages were captured in Iran.

Rich and Ann's family wedding portrait. Ed and Eleanor are at left. Cathy and Jerry Morea are at right.

Cathy met Jerry Morea at a special course given by the Marine Midland Bank where they both worked. Cathy's previous job had been working in Bache's Research Department. Ann Capelli and Richard were introduced by a wonderful friend, Judy Fitzgerald (Fager) on a dinner date. Ann was a nurse for many years at New York Hospital, in charge of the cardiac care units. Today she works as staff nurse at the Metropolitan Museum of Art as well as the Tiffany jewelry plant, normally two days a week at each. On winter weekends she helps as nurse for the ski patrol at Gore Mountain, in upstate New York. She also tends to many of her neighbors and their children when they have accidents or illnesses, and was a big help organizing medical care for both Cathy and Eleanor, and now for me.

BARBARA AND DOUG MOREA

Doug is Jerry's younger brother. He is a lawyer and his wonderful wife, Barbara, is an accountant and tax advisor. They share offices in the Equitable Building, live in Manhattan, and have a beautiful home in East Hampton, Long Island, where we often go for dinner on Christmas Day. Their son Alec is eight at this writing. He is a delightful young man with great athletic promise. His older cousins all love him. During our Thanksgiving dinners at Ann and Richard's house, you will find all cousins up on the third floor running the electric trains with Alec.

JOINT HONORS FOR RICHARD AND ME

Richard and I were surprised and pleased to learn we were to be the 1997 honorees at the Tenth Annual Admiral's Ball of the SUNY Maritime College at Ft. Schuyler on November 8, 1997. Admiral Brown and his staff arranged for an outstanding evening. The co-chairmen were Halsey Herreshoff and Reverend Peter Larom of the Seamen's Church Institute. Besides our extended family, Dorothy and Richard Chesebrough, Ann and Robert Conner, Captain USN and Mrs. Peter Hyers and many others were there.

I was recognized for my close association with the Maritime College, the cadets, and its Foundation, through which we financed three America's Cup campaigns and endowed it with about $2,000,000. Richard was honored as chairman and CEO, Marine Transport Lines, and chairman of Intertanko (The International Association of Independent Tanker Owners). This was the only joint father-son award event that either of us had experienced, and was very gratifying. We both gave short speeches!

BIRTHDAY AND ANNIVERSARY PARTIES

On August 30, 1990, Richard and Cathy organized a surprise 70th birthday party for Eleanor. It truly was a surprise, and quite difficult to pull off with

Ed and Eleanor surrounded by their grandchildren at his 80th birthday, celebrated in St. Thomas.

Eleanor, who knew everything and could almost read minds. About sixty family and close friends assembled in the Commodore's Room at the Knickerbocker Yacht Club. The room overlooked the harbor and it was a beautiful day. Mel Greenberg made a special album covering the occasion. We must have five or six of his superb albums covering various parties and sailing trips.

Eleanor's cousin Paul Hyams was one of Eleanor's favorites and was in attendance. I kidded him about purchasing a dress owned by his favorite singer, Barbara Streisand. The joke turns out to be on me; the dress has recently been appraised for over $100,000. I should own a few. Years later while celebrating Chris Morea's 25th birthday in January 2005, I took the occasion to return to Paul a beautiful eulogy he had written for Eleanor's memorial service.

For our 50th wedding anniversary in August 1992, Dennis Conner surprised us with a special gift commemorating the 50th anniversary of our wartime marriage. What wonderful years they were. Dennis had reserved a special room at the St. Regis Hotel in Manhattan that included wonderful meals and fine champagnes. In addition, Cathy and Jerry arranged for a special dinner party celebration at one of Port Washington's top eating places – La Piccola Luguria.

On December 31, 1994, I was 80 years old. Eleanor and I decided to take our growing family to St. Thomas to celebrate. The Stanley Riches joined us. Our seven grandchildren and the three Rich grandchildren had a wonderful time, as did the chaperones. I was very happy with that very special birthday celebration. Water sports such as windsurfing and snorkeling were enjoyed by all. At the time, I was concerned about all of us flying in the same plane, and since 9/11, would not do it again.

A few weeks earlier on December 5th, Eleanor and I were invited to the New York Yacht Club for a private dinner in the Afterguard Room to celebrate Bob Conner's birthday. Not so. Mary Ann and J. Patrick Moran had organized a special group of close friends as their surprise treat for me on my 80th birthday. It was a heart-warming evening. I was soon to find out that the partying wasn't over yet.

Richard, who was a trustee of the Seamen's Church Institute (SCI) and master of ceremonies at their annual fund raising dinner, informed Eleanor and me that the board of the SCI wanted to meet us on January 7th to thank me for directing the pilot boat to the Museum. Eleanor and I familiarized ourselves with the names of the trustees. Richard met us at the entrance and accompanied us up to the top floor. We were completely taken aback by the crowd of 120 friends and relatives we encountered who greeted me with a "Happy 80th Birthday!" It was another surprise party, this time engineered by Richard, Ann, Cathy, and Jerry. I had tried to call my sister in Florida and brother in Massachusetts the previous day but didn't reach them -- they were already in New York for the surprise. My crew of many years was out in full force, my yacht club friends, tennis partners, my Friday bar mates from Louie's Bar & Grill, and especially my seven grandchildren. It was quite over-whelming to Eleanor and me.

There was a stage set up with a small (actually pretty low quality and somewhat dilapidated) model of the schooner yacht *America*, first winner of the Cup, on a table. A few years earlier, when the SCI moved to their present impressive building near the Fulton Fish Market, they established a program called Adopt-A-Ship, the purpose of which was to restore many of their very old ship models. At that time, I asked Richard to pick out an interesting historical model and I would pay for its restoration. Richard normally would follow through quickly on my suggestions, but for several years I pushed him to no avail. Each time he told me he hadn't found a satisfactory model. During the presentation part of the evening, Richard and Rev. Larom asked me to approach the stage. Each said nice things about me and then mentioned my desire to sponsor one of the old ship models. At this point, they presented me with the small sad little model of the America. My heart sank, but I hid my disappointment. I had not noticed a curtain behind the platform. Suddenly, Peter and Richard opened

Model of the clipper ship Great Republic, *now at Seamen's Church Institute.*

the curtain and there was a seven-foot-long, gorgeous model of *The Great Republic*, the largest clipper ship ever built. I had tears in my eyes as Richard read the plaque:

The Great Republic

Part of the Seamen's Church Institute's
Permanent collection on display at 241 Water Street
Was restored by the friends and family of
Edward I. du Moulin on the occasion of his
80th Birthday, December 31, 1994

Richard had sent a letter to my family and friends inviting them to the party, suggesting no gifts, but if they wanted, to send a tax deductible check made out to the SCI toward the model restoration program that would be appreciated. They more than paid for it. My old combat artist friend from World War II, Tom O'Sullivan, then presented me with a magnificent framed watercolor of *The Great Republic* under sail.

We then were served a wonderful meal from the dining room with an outstanding view of the Brooklyn Bridge and East River. A very special and warm telegram from Dennis Conner was read. The special birthday cake, with icing in the form of our *Lady Del*, was catered by Dave Aldrich. Looking back from today to my 80th Birthday, too many of my most beloved people are no longer with us – Eleanor, Cathy, Dorothy, Gen and Jerry Morea Sr. I shall always recall that wonderful "Night to Remember." So ended my 80th birthday celebrations. How lucky I have been.

Burnhams and Conners

During my America's Cup days, Eleanor and I became very close friends with Roberta and Malin Burnham of San Diego, and Ann and Bob Conner of Newport, Rhode Island. We met in Newport in 1977 when I was manager of the *Enterprise* campaign. Skipper Lowell North selected Malin as the upwind helmsman and second in command. Bob was with Raytheon and secured (as donations) our radios, navigation instruments, and set up our weather stations. Roberta and Eleanor helped run our crew quarters, while

Ann helped on the social front. Malin was one of the business leaders in San Diego. He was the youngest winner of the World Star Championship at the age of 17 with Lowell as his crew. His years involved with the America's Cup are fully described in "The America's Cup and Me."

After we were no longer active in the Cup, the Conners, Eleanor and I had a wonderful vacation together in Europe in 1989. Bob liked to drive and that was fine with me. We combined this trip with a most exciting cruise with Roberta and Malin who owned a handsome 95-foot motor yacht named *Bert & I.* We joined the Burnhams in Sardinia at the Yacht Club Costa Smeralda. It was the Aga Khan's club and required a 100 mile cab ride from the airport over mountainous roads. Every intersection was an adventure. The scenery was magnificent. We lunched with Gianfranco Alberini who had been involved with the Italian America's Cup challenges and was the club's commodore.

From there we cruised to ports like Ajaccio, Bonafaccio, and later Nice. Bonafaccio was spectacular. Entering the harbor you passed through a narrow channel dominated by high cliffs. The dizzying heights were important to the training of the French Foreign Legion. As usual, Malin, the most relaxed person I ever met, did not have a reservation for his 95-foot yacht. He managed to tie up to the main street in the only space available (about 100 feet long for our 95-foot yacht). We were immediately given a pamphlet that said that if we were witness to an accident or a shooting, we were to ignore it, as the Corsicans will take care of it themselves. We climbed to outlooks with stunning views. Malin took us in his whaler on a trip around the island, in and out of amazing caves in the rocks. On the other side of the island, I asked Malin what he would do if the whaler's engine stalled, since the handheld radio couldn't transmit to *Bert & I.* He said the captain would

Stars&Stripes chorus line, Fremantle 1987.
From Left: Betsy Whidden, Roberta Burnham,
Judy Conner, Frances Bloom, Dotty Chesebrough,
Lynn Soares, Eleanor du Moulin.

come after us in the other whaler if we hadn't returned within a reasonable amount of time.

Some of the larger homes were accessible only by whaler and known to be occupied by Mafia. Nevertheless, Malin approached the dock of one of the big homes. A guard in a car, with a rifle, immediately warned us off. Malin smooth-talked him into allowing us to walk the property as the "boss" was in France. After our return home, I cut out various articles on recent Corsican bombings and arson.

Malin wanted to buy some good native wines. He rented a van and we drove to visit friends who lived on the far side of the island. It was a frightening journey as Malin drove through torrential rain along muddy, narrow roads in the mountains. We spent a short time at our friends' home and on the return trip stopped at a winery near the edge of a cliff where we purchased several cases of fine wine. Muddy, washed out roads continued to challenge our driver, but eventually we all sighed with relief upon our safe return to *Bert & I*. A few days later in Ajaccio we visited the birthplace of Napoleon and paid respects to his statue. We all had a great time.

The six of us were again together on *Bert & I* on the 1997 New York Yacht Club Cruise, starting and ending in Newport. I raced with Ann Conner's sister Jane and brother-in-law Bruce Berriman from Newport to Edgartown. We had a great sail on his 47-foot Jeanneau, finishing in the middle of our division. The Berrimans are a fun couple who later sailed across the Atlantic and are now cruising the Mediterranean. Bruce comes by it naturally as a Kiwi (New Zealander). Andrea Watson and I remember having a great time celebrating Anzac Day with jovial Aussies and Kiwis in Newport. There were serious speeches commemorating the tragic losses at Gallipoli where they fought the Turks in 1915-1916.

In 2001, with Eleanor gone, Roberta and Malin invited the Conners and me to visit them at their beautiful vacation home in San Jose del Cabo in Mexico. It is ten miles from Cabo St. Lucas, a fishing and yachting mecca. It was pleasant for me to have a change of scenery with close friends.

In 2002, Malin was inducted into the America's Cup Hall of Fame. I made one of the introductory speeches, as Malin did for me in 2000.

Malin and Roberta flew to Bristol, Rhode Island, for Dad's memorial service at the

Herreshoff Museum in June 2006. Once again Malin was a keynote speaker along with Halsey Herreshoff, Tom Whidden, Gary Jobson, and myself. Bob and Ann Conner were also there. — **R. du M**.

SEPTEMBER 11, 2001

The Trade Center tragedy was a great shock to all of us. For days after the collapse of the Twin Towers, we could see the smoke as we sailed *Lady Del* on Western Long Island Sound. Jerry Morea drove us all to Brooklyn Heights to view the disaster from there.

During the early weeks following 9/11, the Seamen's Church Institute opened a food service in front of St. Paul's Cathedral where the rescuers were able to recover and eat. The facility was manned 24 hours a day by volunteers including Ann, Richard, and young Ed du Moulin. What an experience for Ed in particular. For the first two weeks of the rescue operations, the Seamen's Church building across lower Manhattan became the logistical support center for Ground Zero operations until the Javits Center took over.

September 15, 2002, was a memorable day on the water. To commemorate the first anniversary of the 9/11/01 attack, SAIL AMERICA was organized by Michael Fortenbaugh of the Manhattan Yacht Club that was located at North Cove Marina adjacent to the disaster. It was through this marina that all forms of boats rescued many thousands fleeing the fire. The anniversary flotilla of 1200 yachts, mostly sail, came down the East River, the Hudson River, and from under the Verrazano Bridge. The fleet included all kinds of rescue boats and tall ships. The Around The World Alone racers departed that day. More than 3,000 memorial pennants were displayed by the armada. Each pennant had the name of a victim of 9/11. The fees paid for the privilege of flying them from the boats went to a disaster relief fund. It was a beautiful day with a light breeze. Joining us on *Lady Del* were Ann, Richard, and Mark du Moulin, Jamie Merolla, Andrea Watson, Jerry and Carrie Morea, Danielle Powers, and Marcia Konrad. The Long Island Sound flotilla of several hundred boats proceeded down the East River led by the *Kings Pointer*, a U. S. Merchant Marine Academy vessel. At noon, the entire armada filed by Battery Park City, paying homage to the victims and heroes. It was a day to remember.

The Seaman's Church Institute opened a food service in front of St. Paul's Cathedral where rescuers were able to recover and eat.

GREAT AMERICAN II *gets a New York welcome after breaking the Hong Kong-New York record set by* SEA WITCH *in 1849. The crew: Rich Wilson and Rich du Moulin.*

Ed welcoming Rich after he crossed the finish line on GREAT AMERICAN II.

HONG KONG TO NEW YORK

In 2002 Richard told me about an invitation he received from Richard Wilson of Boston who owned the 53-foot trimaran *Great American II.* Wilson asked Richard to join him on a 15,000 mile non-stop voyage to break the clipper ship *Sea Witch*'s record run of 74 days, 14 hours, set in 1849. I advised him not to do it in view of his family and business responsibilities. But Richard had great confidence in Wilson's experience, preparations, and in the trimaran. Ann du Moulin supported the idea based on her husband's determination to go for it, and her confidence in his sailing ability. She joked that it also would give her a chance to clean out his closet and do a little redecorating.

Piracy along the 2,000 miles of the South China Sea was rampant. Using Richard's worldwide shipping contacts, they established a so-called safety route and contacts with local authorities. They were advised how far offshore to sail as they passed island groups in the South China Sea and parts of Indonesia. No firearms were carried; often at night they sailed with no running lights. Another major danger was collision – with ships, debris such as containers, and whales. They departed Hong Kong on March 16,

2003, sailed through the Sunda Strait into the Indian Ocean March 29, rounded Cape Aghulas and Cape of Good Hope almost a month later, and finally, after 72 days, they passed Ambrose Tower off New York to beat the *Sea Witch*'s record. During the voyage, they were in daily touch with 250,000 school children following Rich Wilson's SitesAlive program.

To welcome them to New York Harbor, across the emotional finish line at the Statue of Liberty, a group of us including close friends John Browning and Stretch Ryder joined John Thomson on board his powerboat that sped us down the East River to New York Harbor. It was most exciting as *Great American II* sailed by the statue. The spectator boats blew their horns and tugs shot towering streams of water through their fire hoses. When the trimaran docked near Pier 66 on the Hudson River, we joined the intrepid sailors at a reception and media session. Richard had lost 17 pounds but he and his skipper looked well. The record-breaking trip is well-documented on a beautiful DVD.

FROSTBITING

There is one fun sailing activity that I have not yet discussed. For all my many years, I have kept close to the water. It is my great escape and, I am sure, has contributed to my relatively good health. On January 1, 1932, the Frostbite Yacht Club was started at the Knickerbocker Yacht Club. Over the club's fireplace is a plaque commemorating the 30 stalwarts who organized this crazy form of sport, to race little eleven-foot dinghies on weekends throughout the winter. The Manhasset Bay Yacht Club has carried that tradition forward for over 75 years. They provide the race committee and an ugly raft-like committee boat, *Worry Wart*, along with a sufficient number of small crash boats, manned by folks like me, for rescue work.

Today, many of the skippers (from 17 to over 80) and crews (10 years and older) have dry suits. Those without dry suits, who end up in the drink, get soaked and cold despite many layers of clothing. Water temperature ranges between 30 and the low 40s. The crash boats first rescue those in the water, and rush them to the clubhouse, while another crash boat retrieves the dinghy and its equipment. For the race committee and the crash boaters, there would be hot dogs, hamburgers, or more interesting fare. Each Sunday, a different individual supplies the food. Drinks of all kinds were supplied by the MBYC. Four of my grandchildren as well as Richard and Jerry have all participated in frostbiting, some across the Sound at Larchmont. One of the main reasons it attracts many racing sailors is that from five to ten races are run each racing day. This is great practice for their summer racing, particularly for starts. Before Richard married Ann, she crewed for him when they won the Manhasset Fleet Championship in 1978. After getting married in 1979, they capsized and soon decided that Rich had to find another crew. The winter of 2005-06 is the first time I missed riding a crash boat, due to my MDS affliction. I do miss the whole scene.

After Dad passed away, we donated one of his America's Cup half-models of Stars and Stripes *to MBYC. They have kindly dedicated it as an award to the person who does exemplary service promoting frostbiting at MBYC. The first winner was Andrea Watson who has done wonderful publicity and photography for the fleet.* – **R. du M**.

NEWPORT WITH FRIENDS

In July of 2004, my friend Andrea Watson and I went to Newport to watch and photograph the match races between *Alinghi* (Switzerland) and *Oracle* (U.S.) off Fort Adams. The viewing was outstanding with good winds. Andy MacGowan took us out one day on his fast powerboat to follow the racing. We were within yards of the contestants in quite rough seas. It was a great thrill. Later that week we were guests on board the 12-meter *Courageous*. Our wonderful hosts in Newport were Ann and Bob Conner. Ann, her friend Carol O'Malley, and Andrea steered and helped with the grinding. I sat on the transom, quite content. For the start of the Bermuda Race, we were guests of Adrienne and John Thomson on their beautiful 150-foot *Affinity*. We watched Richard and Chris Reyling depart on *Lora Ann*'s second two-handed Bermuda race, which they won, repeating their victory two years before when Richard double-handed with Peter Rugg. All in all, Richard has raced in 18 Bermuda Races.

In 2006, three months after Dad's passing, Chris and I again double-handed Lora Ann *winning for the third time under one handicapping system, second under another. We often thought of Dad, and also our friend Jim Mertz who, at age 94, passed away having raced a record-breaking 30 Newport-Bermuda Races. We spread some of Jim's ashes in the Gulf Stream during a beautiful sunset. My goal is to equal Jim's Bermuda record.* – **R. du M**.

Ed and his grandchildren on board LADY DEL IV.

THE GRANDCHILDREN

Six of my grandchildren sail – the seventh and oldest, **Christopher Morea (born 1/4/81)**, preferred contact sports, but is still at home on a boat. He had four great years at Cornell where he played lacrosse and was co-captain of his team. He belonged to and was a leader of his fraternity that was a pig pen. After an interview held at Cornell, Chris was hired by Cintas, the largest uniform supplier in the U.S. He went through an intensive two-year training program. Now, he is in sales and doing very well. This may not be his permanent employment. He is a very strong personality, a hard worker, with great integrity and very serious. Ultimately, he may wind up associated with a sports company. In May of 2004 he moved to Long Beach, New York, where he roomed with two college friends. They enjoyed surfing in the Atlantic. He is a strong leader and an avid reader of history books. Injuries from college lacrosse, for which he still receives treatment, will keep him out of military service. Were it not for this problem, he would likely have joined the Marines with his close friend, Lieut. John O'Brien who will soon return to Iraq for the second time.

Ed with grandson Chris, Captain of Cornell Lacrosse team 2002, and Jerry and Carrie Morea.

Ed with granddaughter Lora, looking through Ed's first book – The America's Cup and Me– *on board* Lady Del IV.

Grandson Doug Morea graduates from the United States Naval Academy in 2004.

In 2007, Chris joined STX, the leading manufacturer of lacrosse equipment! Dad knew best. – **R. du M**.

Lora Ann du Moulin (born 6/25/82) graduated from Boston College on May 24, 2004. She is a fine sailor and skier. Having spent 2003 living with a wonderful Santiago, Chilean family, she is fluent in Spanish. After graduation, she spent the summer of 2004 in Brazil working in an orphanage and surfing. She is now also fluent in Portuguese. Just after Thanksgiving 2004, Lora, and several of her Boston College friends drove to Jackson Hole, Wyoming, where Lora became a ski instructor. In 2005-06 she once again is a ski instructor there. Lora is a free spirit and beautiful inside and out. In April, 2006 she reports for work with the World Health Organization in Geneva.

Lora is still in Geneva, working for a consulting company in micro-finance, helping poor families in the developing world. She now speaks French as her fourth language. – **R. du M**.

Douglas Michael Morea (born 8/8/82), after four whirlwind years at the Naval Academy where he majored in aerospace engineering, is well into his training to become a Navy jet fighter pilot. He is now in Texas. On January 14, 2006, he flew solo, making eleven landings and performing a number of loops. Doug is extremely bright, but in his last year at Schreiber High School (Port Washington), Doug rebelled against study, cut classes, and risked having the Academy revoke his appointment. Cathy, while suffering from cancer, kept after him until he signed the necessary papers. We wondered if Doug would ever make it, however he scored very high SATs and the Academy wanted him! The Academy also knew he had leadership potential from a one-week intensive summer program he attended at the Academy while in high school. When Doug finally started at Annapolis, our concern for his work attitude evaporated as we followed Doug's academic and military success. Chris was always confident Doug would do just fine.

Doug is now assigned to the air wing attached to the nuclear carrier Theodore Roosevelt *in Norfolk, Virginia. –* **R. du M**.

Edward Samuel du Moulin (born 2/9/84) is in his last year at Georgetown University. He is a very good student and a co-captain of the sailing team. In summers, he has been a sailing instructor at the American Yacht Club in Rye, New York, and on the Vineyard. In 2003, 2004, and 2005, he skippered *Lora Ann* for the Georgetown sailing team in the Intercollegiate Offshore Championships. For three years in a row, they have won their division. Starting early January 2006, after visiting Lora in Wyoming, Ed started a two-day a week internship in Senator Edward Kennedy's office. Should be exciting. He got the job on his own.

Ed finished Georgetown leading the sailing team to the National Championship, and followed in Lora's footsteps as a ski instructor at Jackson Hole. In the summer of 2007, Ed headed up the Block Island Maritime Institute's program, teaching inner city children sailing. This winter he will again teach skiing at Jackson Hole. – **R. du M**.

Ed and Richard, in full sailing gear, visiting young Ed at Georgetown.

Matthew Richard du Moulin (born 4/18/86) is attending Johnson & Wales College in Providence where he is studying criminal justice. He is a lively young man. When he was younger he attended Trinity-Pawling, a private school where I was invited to talk to his small class about my WWII experiences. With me, I brought the 3-inch 50 caliber shell from the *Ingham*. After the talk, each of the students sent me a letter thanking me and saying that the most important part of the talk was the shell. On another occasion, when he was at Trinity-Pawling, Andrea Watson and I went to see Matt wrestle. Andrea was getting the camera set. When we looked up he had already won the match – in a matter of seconds.

Matthew transferred this year to Lynn University in Florida where he is majoring in business and doing well. This past summer he taught sailing at Horseshoe Harbor Yacht Club and next summer will be head instructor. – **R. du M**.

Ed and grandson Matthew.

Mark Andrew du Moulin (born December 31, 1987) shares the same birthday as my brother and I. Mark will graduate from high school in 2006. Mark plays lacrosse, sails and skis, and is the only one of four still home with Ann and Richard. Carrie is quite close to Mark. She and Mark remember when Mark was about four years old, and in an adventurous

Ed and Cathy tripping the
light fantastic.

moment, stuck his finger in one of my boat's electric fans. At first, it sounded like machine gun fire (rat-tat-tat), then a loud scream brought us all to the cabin. Neither the fan nor the finger were damaged. Mark has been accepted, on early decision, by Hobart College whose sailing team won the Nationals in 2005. His sailing certainly helped him.

Mark successfully finished his freshman year and is on the sailing team. In the summer he teaches sailing at Noroton Yacht Club, where he will be head instructor next year. — **R. du M.**

Carrie Adele Morea (born October 17, 1988) is doing well at Schreiber High School. She is an exciting and beautiful girl with a wonderful puppy named Snickers. Several years ago when the Moreas were considering purchasing a puppy, everyone gave them advice that they did not follow. In spite of this, Snickers turned out to be just perfect. For the past several summers, Carrie was in the junior sailing program at the Knickerbocker Yacht Club. In 2004, she and her friend Danielle Powers raced a 420 with Carrie riding the trapeze. They won the Dennis Conner-Ed du Moulin Junior Match Racing Trophy and had a great time. Carrie is popular and loving. She and Lora Ann are particularly close. Cathy's best friend, Barbara Sternberger, keeps in close touch with Carrie, including shopping excursions. Barbara is the niece of the late actor (a favorite of mine) Burt Lancaster. She and Cathy were great roommates years earlier. Ellen Williams, also a close friend of Cathy's, is another important influence for Carrie. Other local friends of Cathy's who have helped Carrie in her studies are Rita Marcus and Joan Lager. Although Carrie is a natural athlete, she doesn't take to high school sports other than gymnastics. I remember when she was about 11, watching her in a lacrosse practice. Across the field I heard her say to her friend Vickie, "If you get the ball, don't throw it to me." Shortly after, Carrie gave up lacrosse.

Carrie is a freshman at University of Rhode Island, and a member of the sailing team. — **R. du M.**

Ed and grandson Mark.

Ed at the wheel of Lady Del IV *with Carrie.*

Millenium

Our Millennium 2000 was celebrated in Florida. Eleanor, Ann, Richard, Cathy, Jerry, and I, with all the grandchildren, went to Miami Beach to be with my sister Julia. That same week, Richard, Lora, Ed, Matt, Mark, and cousin Doug Morea all raced in the Orange Bowl Regatta in Coconut Grove. Having already celebrated my and Mark's birthdays (and phoned Babe for his) at Julia's apartment, one minute before midnight December 31, 1999, found all of us at Miami Beach. Precisely to the second of the first minute of the new millenium, all of the kids jumped into the ocean for the first American swim of the millenium. We then watched the Miami fireworks. Little did we realize the family tragedies that would soon follow.

Losing Friends and Relatives

Eleanor and I were very fortunate that Ann du Moulin's parents, Ann and John Capelli, and Jerry Morea's parents, Gen and Jerome Morea, Sr., all became close friends of ours. We celebrated all the major holidays together. Jerry's Aunt Mary, an important influence in his life, was the first to pass away, followed by Jerry Sr., Gen Morea, and Ann's father, John Capelli. In the millenium year 2000, on August 1st, my wife of 58 perfect years died, followed on December 20th by our beautiful daughter Cathy, after a long and losing fight against breast cancer. Cathy and Jerry had kept Eleanor and me in the dark for many months about her condition, and fortunately Eleanor went before Cathy.

Dorothy Garbowitz, Eleanor's younger sister, was a very sweet, unselfish person who lived a modest life in New Jersey. She married Sam, a kind and humble man. They had two wonderful children, Robert and Edith. Robert married Lynn and produced two bright youngsters, Zach and Annie. After Sam passed on, Dorothy moved to Port Washington to be near Eleanor. Shortly after Eleanor's death, I drove Dorothy to the hospital as she had felt faint. Shortly after arriving, she recovered. However, the doctor had recommended an angioplasty procedure, suggesting I pick her up late afternoon. There was a delay. I was told to pick her up the next morning. Something went wrong during the procedure and Dorothy was gone. Another shock to all. They say things happen in threes. It was like

Ed and Eleanor with Halsey Herreshoff at Ed's America's Cup Hall of Fame pre-induction party in Manhattan. Herreshoff is president of the Herreshoff Marine Museum.

weathering three bad storms – Eleanor, Cathy, and Dorothy.

It didn't end there. Kevin Sheehy, husband of Elaine, Ann's sister, and a role model for the du Moulin children, suddenly died on Valentine's Day from a heart attack while playing charity basketball against his students at Tottenville High School. Kevin was an outstanding citizen of Staten Island and highly respected. Every flag on Staten Island was at half-mast.

The grandchildren had a most difficult period, particularly Chris, Doug, and Carrie Morea with the loss of their mother and three of their grandparents. The surviving seniors and cousins formed a strong circle of support. My foremost objective was to show strength and character. Ann and Richard were of great comfort to me.

THE CELEBRATION OF ELEANOR'S LIFE

Eleanor's memorial service was held at the Knickerbocker Yacht Club and was something I shall never forget. The club was packed with family and friends (young and old), covering the long span of our lives. Richard did a fine job organizing and conducting the ceremony. Among those who gave beautiful eulogies were Ann Conner, Babe, Donna Wenger, Paul Hyams, and Hank Green. Dennis Conner and Bill Trenkle flew in from San Diego on the red eye, and Dennis gave a warm eulogy. Rev. Peter Larom gave the invocation while Cantor Herb Strauss performed a memorial service. Grand-niece Jamie Weisberg sang some of Eleanor's favorite songs including *"Don't Rain On My Parade."* and '*The Music That Makes Me Dance*." Rose and Stan Rich's son Jonathan accompanied Jamie on the piano. Marla Freeman produced an attractive A Celebration of Life program.

Only four months later we would have a Celebration of Life for Cathy, with help once again from Rev. Peter Larom and many of Cathy and Jerry's loyal friends.

HERRESHOFF AND ELEANOR

In the commemorative program of my induction into the America's Cup Hall of Fame on September 17, 2000, was included the following tribute to Eleanor:

Eleanor C. du Moulin (1921-2000), in memoriam

by Halsey Herreshoff

An Induction Ceremony, with all its surrounding pomp and circumstance, is an occasion to reflect upon the remarkable achievements of individuals. Such is the case this year with the induction of Ed du Moulin. Yet it is hard to think of Ed without his closest of friends, his companion, and wife of 58 years, Eleanor. Eleanor was a very special person, beloved by a whole generation of America's Cup crew members. Her "joie de vivre" lit up every occasion, and her great charm had an infectious effect on all who met her.

Many an America's Cup sailor will recount the warm and nurturing role Eleanor played in so many of those long and hard fought Cup efforts. Then, elation was often mixed with years of deflation but always Eleanor was present to support and give strength, not only to Ed, but to all involved.

I last saw Eleanor at the announcement of this year's inductees at a function in New York City in June. She was, as always, radiant. Proud of her husband's achievements yet totally selfless in her demeanor, Eleanor graced that occasion. This celebration today, is in part a tribute to Eleanor du Moulin.

YACHT CLUB RELATIONSHIPS

My first yacht club involvement was before World War II, when I belonged to the Rockaway Park Yacht Club. When Richard and Cathy were reaching the age where they could benefit from a junior sailing program, I joined the Knickerbocker Yacht Club in 1956.

As Knickerbocker's race committee chairman in 1965, I worked with two wonderful friends from our neighboring clubs, Manhasset Bay Yacht Club (MBYC) and Port Washington Yacht Club (PWYC). Together we

Ed at the helm of Lady Del IV, *as featured*

in Yachting Magazine.

formed the Cow Bay Committee to alternate running the weekend racing series. Up to that time MBYC ran the races exclusively, and inter-club relationships were shallow at best.

Walter "Duke" Dayton, Jr. (PWYC) and Harman Hawkins (MBYC) and I rose in the ranks and became commodores at the same time. Harman played a key part in my America's Cup activities. He sadly passed away in 2002. Duke and I maintain an extremely close relationship. In December 2005, I attended the 100th Anniversary of the Port Washington Yacht Club and shortly thereafter the 75th Chamber of Commerce dinner, where Duke and my long time friend Ginger Martus were honored.

After Dad passed away, in addition to the America's Cup model that I donated to Manhasset Bay YC, I also donated one to Port Washington YC. Duke Dayton had it transformed into a beautiful trophy that he and I awarded to the PWYC member who did the most for junior sailing. Duke was a very warm and true friend of our family. – **R. du M**.

For 37 years, I have been a member of the Storm Trysail Club of which Richard became commodore in 2005. For about forty years, I have been a member of the New York Yacht Club. I was especially pleased to become an honorary member of the Manhasset Bay Yacht Club where I help their Frostbite Racing. Olin Stephens is the other honorary member. Olin's firm's very first design in 1929 was the Manhasset Bay One Design (MBO) that is still active here in Manhasset Bay. It is a privilege also to be an honorary member of the Port Washington Yacht Club. In 1983, the Manhasset Bay YC presented me with the George Hinman Award for contributions to yachting.

I also enjoy other volunteer work and am a founding member of the Port Washington Public Library's Nautical Center and a trustee of the Manhasset Bay Sailing Foundation through which I hope to see the establishment of a Community Boating Center. Meanwhile, the foundation has supported a high school sailing program and in 2005 ran a very gratifying pilot project for underprivileged children.

With George "Jory" Hinman and Gary Jobson, I serve as an advisor to the Waterfront Committee of the Maritime College. I am also very much involved with the Herreshoff Marine Museum and America's Cup Hall of Fame.

Andrea Watson

I share my on-going nautical interest with my friend Andrea Watson, a long-time member of the Manhasset Bay Yacht Club. She writes a sailing column for several local papers and <u>WindCheck</u> magazine. She is press officer for the Knickerbocker Cup and other Long Island Sound regattas, and is always busy with her camera. She does all this, in addition to her regular job involving childcare.

In the summer of 2005, working with a special sub-committee of the Manhasset Bay Sailing Foundation consisting of Debbie Greco, Art Donavan, and myself, Andrea established a wonderful program for 40 underprivileged children selected through a local school project. The hope is that in 2006 it will be expanded. Andrea has a 90-pound magnificent and extremely friendly Golden Retriever named Bentley. He often keeps me company, and vice versa.

Family Cars

Eleanor and I each had our own car. For years she liked the Buick LeSabre, while I usually owned a Jeep. We would keep the cars for at least seven years. As the grandchildren came of age, we would pass along our old cars to them. One car stood out. In 1983 my friend, John Storck, donated an American Motors Eagle to our America's Cup team for my use in Newport. After the campaign, I bought the car from the Maritime College Foundation. It is still alive and running. It must have been passed to at least three grandchildren and, finally, Richard gave it to my good friend Stretch Ryder's son. It was one of a kind, adorned with dozens of bumper and other stickers (which I think hold it together). Stretch calls it a zip code car, that is, the car cannot be allowed to be driven outside the residential zip code.

Carrie now has her learner's permit and probably will get my current 1999 Jeep. Eleanor's Eagle Vision was acquired by Doug Morea, who took it with him to Annapolis and on to Pensacola, disposing of it before going to Corpus Christi, Texas, where he bought a new and sporty car – suitable for a jet pilot, officer, and a gentleman.

America's Cup Hall of Fame

The America's Cup Hall of Fame was established in 1992 by Halsey Herreshoff at his Marine Museum in Bristol, Rhode Island. The first induction ceremony was held at the Marble House in Newport, where eighteen members were inducted at that time. Halsey asked if I would be its first chairman and help draw up its by-laws. After study of other sporting halls of fame, I produced a draft set of rules that were adopted by the Museum's board of trustees. I served for three years as chairman and thereafter we instituted a policy of two-year terms.

A Selection Committee of up to 22 members plus the chair was organized. It consisted of well-known, experienced America's Cup participants – managers, designers, committee veterans, journalists, historians, and sailors. We normally select only three new inductees each year from the thousands of worldwide participants of this oldest sporting event that began in 1851. We hold annual Selection Committee meetings, usually in Bristol. Formal induction ceremonies bring out dignitaries and guests numbering in the hundreds, and have been held in varied locations such as Cowes, England; Auckland, New Zealand; and New York. In 2006 it was held at the St. Francis Yacht Club in San Francisco. Poor health prevented me from attending.

I was fortunate in the year 2000 to be inducted into the Hall of Fame with many friends and family present. Sadly Eleanor had passed away a few months earlier, but fortunately Cathy was strong enough to attend.

With the help of funds from John Thomson, Horace Hagedorn, and myself, a data bank was established which lists the thousands of Cup participants. The idea came to me after encountering such a system at the Navy Memorial in Washington, D.C. If you know Navy, Marine, or Coast Guard veterans of World War II and wish to review their service records, they can be easily retrieved. Since the vast majority of Cup participants will not enter the Hall, at least their children and children's children can review their roles through this data bank. Check out both these sites: Herreshoff. org, and, via Google, Navy War Memorial in Washington, and then Navy Log. Use "du Moulin" as an example.

Ed delivering his acceptance speech at his America's Cup Hall of Fame induction ceremony.

Ed with Cathy and Olin Stephens at Ed's Hall of Fame induction.

Jack Sutphen (left), Dennis Conner, and Ed, on the occasion of Ed's 90th birthday.

Ed with sister Julia and brother Babe at Ed's 90th Birthday.

PHYSICAL FITNESS

Over the years I have managed to keep physically active. In my younger days, sandlot baseball, school gym, shoveling snow, swimming, sailing, delivering groceries, odd neighborhood jobs, and working the beaches kept me trim. Skiing, of course, was a great activity from the early 1930s to 1964. In summer months, working on the boat and sailing filled the time. I also enjoyed chopping wood (the neighborhood gardeners left their cut-down trees in our backyard).

I played tennis, mostly on my neighbor and good friend Dan Kurshan's tennis court, until I hurt my back around 2000. Although I didn't take up tennis until my sixties, I chased every ball and managed a good game. I did 70 pushups each morning until the back injury. This habit of exercise, good genes, and good luck allowed me to enjoy more activities, especially sailing, as I got older.

MY 90TH BIRTHDAY PARTY

Ann and Richard planned my 90th Birthday party, held on December 19, 2004, at the Knickerbocker Yacht Club. What a wonderful effort on their part. About 170 old and young friends and relatives from all over the country were there. I missed others who were ill, including the Hagedorns and Vaughans. To my surprise, the Club was beautifully decorated with large photographs of my life. My niece, Jamie Weisberg, contributed her wonderful singing group. Jean Toomey, Don Fanning's friend, also performed. Stan and Rose Rich's son Jonathan (a professional) played the piano for the singers.

Reverend Peter Larom, formerly executive director of the Seamen's Church Institute and a family friend, gave the benediction. Richard was Master of Ceremonies and introduced, as speakers, Halsey Herreshoff, Andy MacGowan, and Tom Whidden. There were many gifts and donations made in my honor, which were much appreciated but unnecessary. Adding to the fun, Richard showed carefully selected slides. Several days after the party, Dr. Mel Greenberg who had been taking photographs surprised me with three gorgeous, well-planned, photo albums of the affair. Each album contained 100 photos.

Dave Aldrich arranged for a large birthday cake with accurate

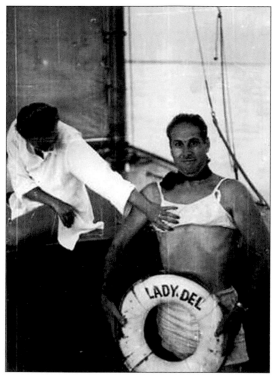

Anything for a laugh: Ed as sexy sailor, vampire pilot, jockey shorts model, tourista, and merman.

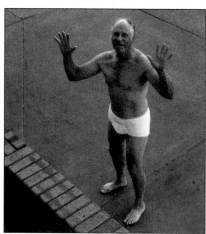

pictures of every boat I owned artistically formed in the icing. In addition, Dave arranged for a special photographer to set up a website, eds90th. com, so friends who weren't able to make the party could view it on the internet. It was wonderful to have my seven grandchildren, sister Julia (91) and brother Babe (86) together and in good health.

THE DU MOULIN SKI HOUSE

During Christmas week following my 90th birthday party, Ann and Richard drove me, along with Ed, Matt, and Mark (Lora was a student in Chile), to their recently acquired ski house in Minerva, New York, close to Gore Mountain in the Adirondacks. It was a welcome chance to relax.

We visited the local museum at the North Creek railroad station where Theodore Roosevelt was sworn in upon being informed that President McKinley had been killed. It was of particular interest to me as it contained memorabilia from the days I skied at Gore Mountain in the time before uphill ski lifts. We climbed using skins on our skis, and then at high speed, and with marginal control, skied down through the woods.

Richard particularly enjoys cross-country skiing at the Garnet Hill trails where I had skied many years earlier. Back in 1938 at the opening of the Garnet Trail, along with other skiers, I was given a garnet stone which I kept for many years.

DAY SAILING

Over the past several years, I talked about selling *Lady Del* and replacing her with a smaller vessel. Since I did not do much cruising anymore, it seemed like a waste to daysail a 42-foot cutter that was capable of sailing around the world, as a number of her sister ships have. My family said, "Don't sell her as long as it she is not too much for you to handle."

I particularly enjoyed sailing to various regattas to watch Richard or the grandchildren compete. Three or four times a week, I would sail for five hours or so with a diverse crew of friends, most of whom are retired. My guests usually sail the boat while I tinker. However, I always keep my eyes open, as some crew are less observant than others, particularly in situations where they feel they have the right of way.

My crew was quite diverse, running in age from the sixties into the nineties. One frequent crew was Howard Seymour, one of Manhasset Bay's finest, who moved to Florida where he passed away. There were also Al Kohn, my most frequent crew, and George Asher, Don Fanning, Bill Mavrogiannis, Dr. George Wisoff (who has his own Brewer 12.8), and Bo Sweeney. The average age increased at an alarming rate. They had various backgrounds, were mostly retired, all with sailing experience. I supplied the cookies and soft drinks, while each crew supplied his own sandwich. Sometimes we would head in and have lunch at Louie's with Dave James and the Louie's gang.

My weekend overnights and raft-ups with other boats became less frequent as did my longer cruise to my favorite town – Newport, Rhode Island. Now, of course, having sold *Lady Del*, I look forward to being a guest.

Ed du Moulin the younger, Ed's grandson, photographed in front of Ed's old cutter INGHAM, *now retired in Charleston, S.C. Ed and his Georgetown sailing team had just won the intercollegiate team racing championship in June, 2006, two months after his grandfather had died. The final race finished in the shadow of* INGHAM's *stern.*

SURVIVING LOVED ONES

With the great support of family and friends, I have managed to survive the deaths of Eleanor and Cathy. After all, I was indeed fortunate to have Eleanor for 58 years and Cathy for 50 years.

As for my life with Eleanor, our marriage was made in heaven. We shared much together and without argument. An example of fair play: as long as I could race sailboats during the sailing season, I would agree to go with her to Florida for one winter month.

I live alone in our comfortable home in Sands Point but am only seven minutes from Carrie and Jerry, and 45 minutes from Ann and Rich in Larchmont. Cooking is not my favorite pastime. I can make jello, toasted cheese sandwiches, scrambled ham and eggs, peanut butter and jelly, or ham and swiss cheese sandwiches. Yes, even spaghetti. I am always welcome to eat at the Moreas. Andrea Watson is a great friend and we eat out once or twice a week, depending on how strong I feel. Most every week, Chris and Carrie join me for dinner. Life is not too complicated but my check lists are still pretty long. I often wonder what retirement would be like.

Last August, for the first time in my life, I felt run down, without the normal get-up-and-go. One day while walking down the Knickerbocker dock, I had to stop to catch my breath. At that time I knew something was wrong, so on August 4, 2005, I visited my doctor of 46 years, Marvin Gross, who suggested I check in to North Shore Hospital. I called my daughter-in-law, Ann, a nurse of many years. It turned out I immediately needed a

Ed, at 90, watching the latest America's Cup boats sailing.

transfusion (my first ever), and received two pints of blood. In fact, my red blood cell count was so low that the doctors could not figure out how I was still alive. It was probably due to being in good physical shape. For the first time in my life I had to spend time in the hospital to receive treatment. I sure cannot complain. At 90-and-a-half years of age and being of sound mind, I finally had my first real hospital experience.

After four days, I was back at home, and after several visits to specialists, I was eventually diagnosed with Myelodysplastic Syndrome, commonly called MDS, where the bone marrow stops producing healthy red blood cells. I was warned that this usually progresses into leukemia.

At this writing I have had another twelve pints of blood. I have donated blood over 25 times in my life, the first time being in 1939, in the "Blood for Britain" drive. This kind of evens things out. At this writing, the transfusions are helping, and my hemoglobin, which was under eight, is now over ten, probably a reaction to watching Bo Derek in "*10*" and listening to Ravel's "Bolero." I am taking pills galore, and getting enough steroid shots once a week to qualify me for the New York Yankees next season.

My first line of support is the ever-concerned Ann, more a daughter than a daughter-in-law. With a world of nursing experience, she has been in constant touch with all the doctors coordinating my treatments. Richard and Jerry have kept a close watch over me, for which I am forever grateful. Jerry, who (like Ann) is more of a son than a son-in-law, has taken care of me as he did Cathy. I speak to him by phone every morning.

Andrea drives me to and from the doctors' offices, and is a great cook, preparing the finest meals, which I consume like grandson Chris, who with his sister Carrie, is one of my regular visitors. The other grandchildren keep in touch from various corners of the world. Sister Julia, who will be 93 in March, flew in from Florida for a delightful week with me. Ted Weisberg frequently visits and takes me out to lunch, and my sailing friends are always dropping by.

During this healing period, as people like to call it, I am busy with the America's Cup Hall of Fame Selection Committee nominations, and am following the 23rd Knickerbocker Cup, now underway. This is the first one I will have missed. I am working out of my office at home, often dubbed the "Black Hole of Calcutta."

My *Lady Del* is in great shape and, throughout her 22 years, has given all of those who have sailed on her wonderful experiences, both cruising and day-sailing. With all my recent "excitement," I decided to sell her to my friend Dick Gumprecht and his partner Gary Lash from Newport. Dick is an experienced blue-water sailor, and told me several years ago, when I took him sailing off Newport, that I should call him when the boat was placed on the market. Richard, Robbie, and Joan Lager helped with the paper work. In preparation for Dick and Gary to take delivery of the boat, Andrea drove me to the Town Dock where Richard and the Knickerbocker launch picked me up for the ride to *Lady Del.* This eliminated the long walk down the Knickerbocker dock that I could not accomplish. On board, I worked hard to prepare the boat, and we even did a few quick sails, which did not help my MDS. When Dick and Gary came down for the boat, she was ready, and I was pleased she was in such good hands.

I still enjoy chatting with Ted, Richard, and others about new boat plans, maybe a lovely Alerion 28, or Herreshoff 12-and-a-half. We are thinking ahead. In all my years of boating, I have loved each boat I owned, but never regretted moving on.

The internet has made it simple to keep in close touch with friends, and particularly the grandchildren. The typing expertise I acquired in the 1930s has enabled me to be a very effective communicator by email, despite not being a part of Generation X. My typing has also helped me write this book, and my first book <u>The America's Cup and Me</u>, whose proceeds (like this book) go to the Herreshoff Marine Museum and America's Cup Hall of Fame.

Whenever my time comes, I will be prepared as usual with my various checklists. To all I wish you the life I have had, am having, and plan to have. No regrets and, "no worries, mate."

Each night I count my blessings, remember to say my prayers in which I include family and many friends. Life will go on. I will have left my mark. God Bless.

Ed du Moulin

January 14, 2006

-The End-

Dad passed away March 29, 2006. — **R. du M**.

POSTSCRIPT

D ad passed away at home in Sands Point on March 29, 2006. During Dad's illness, Ann and Jerry treated Dad like their own father, and were ceaseless in their help. I had been in Houston, and had rushed back in time to be with Dad at the end. As I flew home, brother-in-law Jerry, son Mark, friend Andrea, and sailing friends John Browning and Stretch Ryder were of great help to Ann.

A huge crowd attended the Memorial Service at Knickerbocker Yacht Club. Family friend Reverend Peter Larom, retired Director of the Seamen's Church Institute, led the service. Touching and often humorous eulogies were presented by grandchildren Chris Morea, Lora du Moulin and Ed du Moulin, and son-in-law Jerry Morea, America's Cup Hall of Fame Chairman John Burnham, nephew Ted Weisberg, friend Chuck Stetson, and finally me. Ralf Steitz, the offshore sailing coach of Kings Point Merchant Marine Academy, brought over a flotilla of motor launches and three fully manned Farr 40s to escort cousin Jason Weisberg's powerboat for the spreading of Dad's, Mom's and Cathy's ashes all together in Manhasset Bay.

Many of Dad's sailing friends from all over the world could not make the first service, so Halsey Herreshoff organized a special celebration at the Herreshoff Marine Museum and America's Cup Hall of Fame in Bristol in early June. This wonderful event included eulogies by Halsey, Gary Jobson, Tom Whidden, and Malin Burnham. We concluded with my narration of a photographic history of Dad's life (many of those photos are in this book).

From the eulogies and many letters the family received, I have selected several excerpts to close this book. We thank all of you for your friendship with Dad and our family all these years.

FROM TED WEISBERG

"For Uncle Ed, life was a rhumb line. Whether sailing or living life, Ed never lost sight of the rhumb line. It is true that many of us who loved Ed would on occasion take a "flier" in life, and tack away from the rhumb line. But when this happened, Ed was never judgmental. He never said "I told you so," but he would encourage and applaud us if we were successful. No matter why or where that tack would take us, Ed was always there with that gentle support and a few well-placed words of encouragement should any of us go aground.

Ed knew who he was, where he was, and where he was going. He was a kind gentle man, who like his brother and sister, never had an unkind word to say about anyone.

FROM TOM WHIDDEN

Richard: your parents were very special people. Your dad's advice on so many different fronts was really valuable for me. He helped my decision making in business and in my America's Cup career. I valued his opinion always, but I also knew that his approach was always the high road, high integrity, honest and straight-forward way to do things. Not only did I appreciate his advice but he was a role model for me. He was the most principled person I have known in my life. I only hope that I can be somewhere close to the person he was.

The natural and necessary compliment to a great man is a great woman. Obviously Ed had that in Eleanor. I will never forget her enthusiasm for everything your dad did. She was spirited, funny, friendly, and very principled like Ed. Her reason for living was her family but not far behind were her friends. Betsy and I often speak of your parents… there are no greater role models for us.

I will miss Ed's calls and will now have to make some decisions alone that he would have helped me with. I hope that I will live up to his expectations. Your parents were the best…but you know that. I will continue to use what Ed taught me in so many aspects of my life. I am so sorry for your family's loss, Richard. Life goes on but a big presence won't be there.

FROM MARY ANN MORAN

I want to let you know how sorry I am for your loss… and our loss…and everyone's loss. Your mom and dad were one of the first couples I met when I started dating Patrick. I will never forget thinking that they were such a regal looking couple—she reminded me of Katherine Hepburn and he was a dead ringer for Rex Harrison—Ed was actually better looking!

By losing your dad we have truly lost a Sailing Legend and one of the truest gentlemen to ever live. How he handled the death of your mom, sister and aunt all in a six month period with such grace was just amazing to me.

FROM BILL TRIPP

I have just heard this minute of Ed's passing. I feel as though an age has passed. I am certain there is tremendous sadness, but what a full life your father had! At the age of 91, he came to know most of what life could offer, and he certainly knew the love of many.

One of the things I think of when I hear mention of him is the way he helped a certain group of teenagers and young men find their way into sailing circles by getting them rides on boats—me, Johnny Mac, Bill Trenkle, Scott Vogel, Bill Rogers— so many had the intense pleasure of seeing your father's eyes light up as he worked a little of that magic, doing something to help just that little bit.

FROM KIPPY REQUARDT

The importance of Ed du Moulin's life is both obvious and subtle. Reading through his reminiscences provides a peek into life in the United States through some remarkable times, as seen and experienced by a man who was both self-deprecatingly modest and confidently intrepid, once he had all the information he thought necessary, combined with a wry sense of humor to spark things up. He was secure in the principles he and his wife so obviously shared, delighted by his – and others – good fortune; by his – and others – abilities to read the winds, know the boats, choose a course, see paths through mazes others didn't. A competitive sailor indeed.

Ed lived in a time when the goal of being a Good American meant something fine and noble, and was compatible with the accepted idea of success. Ed was a Good American who lived a successful life. He and his wife Eleanor believed in the efficacy of networking, and made and used their considerable circle of friends and acquaintances to further the lives and careers of others with every good hope for others' successes, as well as for their own pleasure.

While I had met Ed at several America's Cup

events through the years, I only got to know him late in his life, through his writing endeavors. In writing this book, he wanted to leave, particularly for his family but also for friends and those he had yet to meet, stories that would be instructional, historical, entertaining, and possibly inspirational. I wish that we had lived next door and not states away.

FROM JOHN ROUSMANIERE

What I think of most are Ed's caring for people and his mission to make connections between them. For a man who was surrounded by peak accomplishments, he was unusually and admirably concerned with humanity itself, not merely its achievements.

Just yesterday I came across a note from him recommending that I get in touch with a friend of his with whom I share an interest. I suppose I have had dozens of such notes over the years. Knowing full well that I was not alone, I would guess his kindnesses and acts of thoughtfulness would fill the world, were they all known, which of course they are not, for his modesty was as big as his generosity.

FROM RICHARD LEATHER

There immediately came to mind the passage from *Genesis* that reads: "There were giants in the earth in those days; mighty men which were of old, men of renown."

I knew no mightier man in wisdom, prudence, and human kindness who walked the earth in my time. Ed's grace, skill and generosity in so many arenas were gifts without price for all of us.

FROM DAVID PEDRICK

I count Ed as one of the most significant mentors of my life, for which I know that I am but one of many whom he inspired. He loved his role as "Dutch uncle" which was especially influential to me in my early years out of college with no immediate family nearby. His kindness, warmth and interest in others will always be a guiding example to all who have had the pleasure and honor of knowing him.

FROM ROGER VAUGHAN

I got to know Ed writing about the America's Cup. I've had experience dealing with many people in his position and none of them came close to the thoughtful and considerate way Ed handled situations. When things got really complicated, he'd scratch his head and draw us into the problem – how do you think I should handle this? He knew, of course, but it was wonderful psychology to engage us, involve us in the complexity.

It was good luck that doing America's Cup business with Ed advanced into a friendship I enjoyed for many years. When he suggested he was thinking about putting pen to paper about his America's Cup years, it was my turn to be encouraging and play a part in the project.

I spoke with Ed a few weeks before he died. Having maintained good health most of his incredible 91 years, escaping hospitalization until the very end, his voice registered anxiety and amazement. It reminded me how he sounded when Alan Bond showed up in Newport with the bendy mast. But beneath the anxiety was the chuckle Ed could get off in the most difficult times, a chuckle that expressed amazement at events, signifying an empathetic appreciation of man's imperfection.

FROM STEVE VAN DYCK

I was very saddened to hear that your wonderful father had passed away. I have admired him since the first time I met him in the 1970s. Steady, straight, bright, loyal, extremely competent, and always a friend. He gave so much to so many, and never asked anything for himself. Simply put, he was a great man.

FROM JOHN BURNHAM

Ed worked with Halsey Herreshoff to found the America's Cup Hall of Fame at the Museum in 1992. Once that was done, Halsey turned to Ed to establish the by-laws and modus operandi. In my role as current Chairman, I was trained by the best. No matter who is the Chair of the Hall of Fame Selection Committee, this Hall of Fame has been marked forever by Ed's dedication and leadership.

A common lesson learned from Ed. It's OK to retire from business and be involved for a couple of decades in the America's Cup. Just remember, when you begin creeping up to the age of 80, you are just getting started.

FROM CHRIS MOREA

I think it is pretty special for a 25 year old guy to have a 91-year-old Grandpa as a best friend. His vision was all about you guys- family first and friends second. He had a genuine interest in others. You just felt better about yourself. It was all about you and never about him.

FROM GRANDSON ED DU MOULIN

I am honored to share my grandfather's name.

FINAL PRAYER

"One thing that bothers many people about a burial at sea is that there is no grave marker, no headstone. How can you possibly remember a person if there is no neatly trimmed monument? The answer is that the sea is a gravestone, the waves are the flowers left on its edge. The wind in the rigging is the music. So the sea is his memorial, and I can remember this man whenever the bow rises to meet a swell or the surf crashes on the shore."

BY CHRIS CASWELL

This book was designed by Metze Publication Design. The text is set in Baskerville MT.
All photographs courtesy of the du Moulin family archive.